Church

Church

Ephraim Radner

CASCADE *Books* • Eugene, Oregon

CHURCH

Copyright © 2017 Ephraim Radner. All rights reserved. Except for brief quotations in critical publications or reviews, no part of this book may be reproduced in any manner without prior written permission from the publisher. Write: Permissions, Wipf and Stock Publishers, 199 W. 8th Ave., Suite 3, Eugene, OR 97401.

Cascade Books
An Imprint of Wipf and Stock Publishers
199 W. 8th Ave., Suite 3
Eugene, OR 97401

www.wipfandstock.com

PAPERBACK ISBN: 978-1-4982-9709-7
HARDCOVER ISBN: 978-1-4982-9711-0
EBOOK ISBN: 978-1-4982-9710-3

Cataloguing-in-Publication data:

Names: Radner, Ephraim, 1956–, author.

Title: Church / Ephraim Radner.

Description: Eugene, OR : Cascade Books, 2017 | Includes bibliographical references and index.

Identifiers: ISBN 978-1-4982-9709-7 (paperback) | ISBN 978-1-4982-9711-0 (hardcover) | ISBN 978-1-4982-9710-3 (ebook)

Subjects: LCSH: Church.

Classification: BV600.5 .R35 2017 (print) | BV600.5 .R35 (ebook)

Manufactured in the U.S.A. 10/26/17

Contents

Introduction: Loving the Church | 1
The Midst of a New Era | 1
Assuming—and Loving—the Church | 4
Contested Collectives | 9

1 "The Wounds I Received in the House of My Friends," Part I: The Complicated Theology of the Church | 13
Defending the Church: The Apologetic Roots of Ecclesiology | 15
Ideologies and Options | 20
Images of the Church | 22
Ecclesiology: Whose Church? | 27

2 "The Wounds I Received in the House of My Friends," Part II: Our Church, Not Yours | 29
Catholic | 30
Protestant | 40
Shaped by Time | 49

3 Talking about the Church: The Possibility of a People | 53
Translating Church | 55
Scriptural Churches | 58
Divine Word, Divine Act | 60
The Church as a Divinely Created People | 65

Contents

4   **Talking about a People: The Possibility of Election | 69**
     God Creates by Kind: The Origin of the Nations | 71
     The Christian "We" | 75
     The Animating Spirit of "We" | 78
     Adam to Adam: The Election of the Church | 81

5   **Arguing about the Church: The Church and the Nations | 90**
     The Church Is Ordered by God for the Sake of All Other Nations | 90
     The Church Is Judged with All Other Nations | 96
     Formation: The Church Is Structured like the Nations, in Its Relation to Past and Present | 98

6   **The Church as Israel: The Repentant Missionary | 115**
     Some Twentieth-Century Developments in Ecclesiology: People of God and Communion | 115
     The Church as Israel: Figural Ecclesiology | 122
     Israel, Jew, and Gentile | 125
     The Missionary Church as Repentant Israel | 132
     The Church and the Nations: Jacob and Esau | 135

7   **The Figure of the Church | 144**
     A People Called | 145
     Animated by God | 148
     Gathering | 157

Conclusion: A Longing People | 168

Bibliography | 175
Subject Index | 183
Author Index | 187
Scripture Index | 189

Introduction

Loving the Church

The Midst of a New Era

THIS BOOK IS ABOUT the Church. In it, I seek to outline some basic elements that inform how we think about the Church, and perhaps how we *should* think about the Church. This involves some history. It also involves, more crucially, theology—that whole realm of discussion in which we seek to speak truly about God and God's work in the created world. Christian theology in turn takes in a range of phenomena, from the reading of the Bible to the writings of important Christian thinkers, from the authoritative and sometimes conflicted claims of this or that group of Christians to the practices and experiences of Christians across time, to the presuppositions that inform these various elements. Just putting it this way leads us back to the Church before we have even sorted the matter out: "authorities," "groups," "claims," "readers of the Bible," "Christian thinking." These realities involve, if not logically then at least practically, notions about the Church and the Church's shape and order, and our place within it. If we want to think and talk about the Church, we will in a basic way always be talking about ourselves, about something we cannot grasp "from the outside," but which we must struggle to know and articulate as a given that already makes and defines us as who we are. Thus we cannot see clearly, because the Church is more intimate to our Christian selves than we can ever identify.

This constitutes a tremendous challenge. We are already a part of that which we are trying to isolate for thought. This was perhaps less obvious in the first days of the Christian Church, when distinctions seemed more stark and the lines between the few believers in Jesus as the Messiah of Israel and the rest of world were solidly drawn. The Church today faces something unprecedented in its history: Christians are now found in over 230 nations in the world, of which almost half are majority Christian. Fully one-third of the world's population is Christian, which represents almost 2.5 billion persons. The distribution of Christians in the world is increasingly even, with relatively similar numbers in the Americas, Africa, and Europe, although the latter are falling, while the numbers in Asia are growing. There are even signs in North Africa and the Middle East, and in Asia too, of chinks in the hard walls of Islam as Muslims are turning Christian also, and regions so long impermeable to Christian growth are opening up. Christians in large numbers have simply become ensconced in the dynamics of global life.

Indeed, the very notion of a "global life" is new, and the rapid expansion of Christian numbers in the world coincides with a revolution in human life. In the 1980s the biologist Eugene Stoermer and later the renowned atmospheric chemist Paul Crutzen began referring to the "Anthropocene" as a new geological era, beginning in the late eighteenth century, distinct in its planetary forms from earlier eras. The features of the Anthropocene Era have generally been defined in environmental and climatic terms. In fact these features themselves coincide with enormous cultural changes that are only now coming into view: national contacts and encounters, radical changes in human life span and health, reorganizing of sexual behavior, forms of labor and leisure as well as nourishment, transportation and knowledge-sharing, educational environments, technologies of killing and warfare, political reinvention and frustration, concentrations of impoverishment, the landscape of human dwelling and crowding, including urbanization, noise, light pollution, and more. Together, these constitute something utterly novel in human history. And this completely revolutionary and ongoing human upheaval coincides with the explosion of Christian numbers outside Europe. In the past century, that explosion tracks tightly with the social changes, bound to certain technological forms, associated with the concept of the Anthropocene.

At least two questions arise here. First, is Christianity itself now so intertwined with a particular set of cultural changes that its distinctiveness from that change is hard to define? Second, is the Church the same as this now explosively expanded Christianity? Most Christians would be appalled to answer the first question affirmatively; and many would be equally

INTRODUCTION

averse, perhaps for similar reasons, to making the second equation. Christianity is not the same as a changing global culture, especially one whose revolutionary forms are frightening in many respects; and the Church cannot simply be the same as the unfolding and often unordered currents of expanding global populations. For myself, I agree that Christianity is and will remain—and, morally, must remain—distinct from the cultural cascades of the Anthropocene. Nonetheless, I believe that these changes in global human culture are ones whose forms are bound to the mission of the gospel, in the sense that the great modern missionary movement was itself an impetus to the globalizing process. Second, just because of this binding of mission and world in a way that is now raised up in a novel profile, the Church and Christianity writ large have become more and more evidently one and the same.

Catholics, Protestants, Pentecostals, Anglicans, Orthodox, Evangelicals . . . each of these groups of Christians, who have defined the Church in very particular and generally exclusivist ways, are today losing the impermeability of their Christian claims in the face of sheer numbers and ecclesial movements to and fro, often pressed by energies that structural forms and leaders cannot direct. This is not to say that the theological insights of these ecclesial self-identities have either been empty or are no longer truth-telling in some way. Rather, their meanings are being evidently taken up by God in new directions and ordered to purposes by which the power of the Christian gospel will do its work distinctively and supremely vis-à-vis the human cultures of this world.

We can take the example here of Catholics and Pentecostals. The Roman Catholic Church constitutes about half of the Christians on the earth. It is, of course, logically conceivable that the half a billion Pentecostals who also dwell upon the face of the earth are not members of the Church. But the sheer dynamics not only of growth but of engagement, energy, cultural influence, changed lives, and love of God that Pentecostalism represents in comparison with this or that part of the Catholic Church, in the midst of this great epochal upheaval, practically undercuts such a conception. This is especially so as Catholic and Pentecostal are often one and the same, in this or that family or even individual. These sorts of reflections could be multiplied across the many groups of Christians who together are caught up in this strange movement of Providence. It seems that the Church is being swept into a new visibility according to a still-emerging form. This book will trace, in part, what this form for the Church might be.

Church

Assuming—and Loving—the Church

Notice that here I am writing the word "Church" with a capital "C." We will have to think about why we may wish to do so or not. For now, I am capitalizing "Church" simply to underline this fundamental way that our Christian life and existence is bound up with this thing we call "church." Theology must question all this, pull things apart and examine aspects of this fundamental reality. In what follows, I will problematize the concept of "church," trying to discover its inner tensions and difficulties within the stream of history. My goal is not only better understanding, but through that, better appreciation and thanksgiving for the reality of Church that God has given us. Nonetheless, the theological study of the Church is a critical task, and it can sometimes seem to be negative in its analytic questioning. So, before launching into this critical work, in the course of which the fundamental positive reality of the Church might be obscured or forgotten, let me emphasize the divine giftedness of the Church from the start, as the base from which all Christians, including myself, do our thinking.

I say "all Christians," for there is no Christian who does not assume the Church as an essential reality bound up both with the shape of the world God has made and with the life God has shared in Christ Jesus. It is true that we all know individuals who can say "I am a Christian, but I don't believe in the organized church." It is true, furthermore, that this kind of attitude can be traced back at least to the sixteenth century. According to scholars like Leszek Kolakowski and Henning Graf Reventlow, the sixteenth century was a period during which the often violent religious and political struggles of vying churches led to the rise of "spiritual religion" among some Christians. In Kolakowski's words, these were individuals who sought to be "Christians without the church."[1] But even for these individual seekers, the Church always hovered as an informing reality. Some, like David Joris or Antoinette Bourignon, became leaders of movements after all; and their followers would meet and engage in common acts of prayer and teaching. This was true of initially non-ecclesial movements that continue to have great influence, like the Salvation Army. The Scriptures they continued to read spoke of congregations and churches, and these entities, even if spiritualized in their minds, were believed in and, finally, cherished. Christians in more recent times may well have followed these first tentative steps toward a more purely "spiritual religion," and they too may have

---

1. Kolakowski, *Chrétiens sans église*, 1.

Introduction

dispensed with doctrinal confessions, bishops, designated meeting houses, and material sacraments. But "the Church"—the *true* Church—is almost always something they have sought to discover and enter.

Given facile contrasts between Catholics and Protestants, constructed over centuries of antagonism and competition, it is important to stress the common love of the Church that both groups hold, imbibed like the air we breathe. Texts like Ephesians 5:21–33 are part of every Christian's Bible, and all Christians therefore have been formed by Paul's image of the Church as the "bride of Christ," whom the Son of God "loves" like a husband who sacrifices his own body for his beloved. Nothing could be more divinely intimate than this claim, such that Catholics and Protestants both have implicitly realized that the Church is closer to the Christian's self than one's own flesh might be. There is a centuries-long history of reading the Song of Songs as a theological poem concerning this reality, and it may surprise some to learn that Protestant and especially Puritan readers of the Song of Songs made the same ecclesial connection between the Bride and the Church as did their Catholic counterparts. In fact, in the early modern era, some of the richest and most elaborate ecclesial readings of the Song of Songs were done by Protestants. We could take as a very typical example the Scottish Presbyterian divine James Durham. Here, just in the discussion of the Church, caricatures of Protestant "literalism" are exploded as Durham embraces an "allegorick" [sic] reading of the biblical text in order to uncover the affection, delectation, and love that infuses the Church's life as it is taken up by Christ:

> The excellency of this Song is expressed in this, that it's a Song of Songs, a most excellent song . . . preferred to all other Songs . . . [It is] purposely intended to treat of the most choice and excellent subjects, to wit, Christ and His Church . . . in their most glorious, lively, and lovely actions, to wit, his care of, and his love unto his Church, and that in its most eminent degree; and also, of her love to him . . . by way of dialogue and sweet colloquies betwixt these two parties, having in it many excellent and various expressions . . . It's set forth in a most lovely, excellent, majestic style and strain, which exceedingly ravishes and captivates the affections, making the love contained in it, sweetly savour and relish through the beautiful garment of borrowed expressions, which is put upon it.[2]

---

2. Durham, *Clavis Cantici*, 33–34.

Part of the often frightening hostility that seems to have motivated Catholic and Protestant conflict in the early modern period stemmed not simply from confessional disagreement, nor from some opposition between corporate and individualist attitudes. Rather, the hostility arose from a commonly held *love of the Church*, which drove all Christians to a desperate but divergently pursued search for the authentic Bride. Song of Songs 1:7 was taken by Catholics and Protestants as a profoundly demanding call, not only for truth, but for true *love* within the Church: "Tell me, O thou whom my soul loveth, where thou feedest, where thou makest [thy flock] to rest at noon: for why should I be as one that turneth aside by the flocks of thy companions?" (Song 1:7 KJV). Catholics accused Protestants of having run off with a "whore" (Luther, Calvin, *sola scriptura*); Protestants were certain that the real Bride was not dressed in papist robes. Both, however, knew that divine beauty was conferred upon a person only as that person was identified somehow with the ecclesial woman embraced by her divine Bridegroom. Both believed that God's glory and love were wrapped up essentially with the Church.

Love for the Church, then, has been universal among Christians; and "love is strong as death," as the Song of Songs also states (8:6 KJV). Thus, when there are disagreements, jealousies, betrayals, the Church that is bound to every Christian's love can, and has, become the object of deep bitterness and conflict, sometimes reaching a deadly pitch.

To keep to the text of the Song of Songs, it was always the case that the Bride in the text was identified not only with the Church, but also with the individual Christian soul. As we shall see in our concluding chapter, the collective and individual aspects of the Bride speak clearly to central aspects of the Church's reality that are properly joined together, although they can also be pulled apart. In fact, as Christians in the modern era became more and more divided over the Church, the individualist side of the Song's reading came to predominate more and more, again among both Catholics and Protestants. There seemed to be too many brides on offer, and the prospect of a kind of spiritual polygamy seemed too real. Hence, the notion that there are "Christians without church" or "without churches" became, in many people's minds, not only a possibility but even, for some, an attraction.

That said, what has been called a "nuptial" view of the Church—the Church as Bride of Christ—has proven not only influential but also central in the history of Christian reflection. It is not just one among many

INTRODUCTION

possible ways that the Church has been described. It is in fact arguably a foundational concept, and we will return to it later. It is also a way of describing the Church that curiously binds Christians together in the most intimate and challenging of ways—a single "body," "members" of a single organism, common affections, shared movements. As one nineteenth-century Christian put it,

> "Jerusalem! Jerusalem! my tears shall fall for thee! When thy children's griefs I view, Their distress becomes my own; All I hear, or see, or do, Makes me tremble, weep, and groan." The people of God, as citizens of Zion, may, on account of the Church's distresses at the hand of God, say likewise to him, "put thou my tears into thy bottle." While Jesus Christ is styled in Scripture "the Head of the Church," the Church, in the spirit of this figure, is called "his body." In like manner, all true believers are spoken of not only as "members of his body, of his flesh, and of his bones," but as "members one of another"; and when "one member suffers, all the members" are said to "suffer with it." Thus it is peculiarly true of them, that "each is always linked to all." For such reasons, even when everything is faring well bodily and spiritually with individual believers, if the Church as a body, or any true branch or member of the Church, is visited with adversity or any kind of distress, every true Christian feels for the Church, or for that branch or member of it, almost as much as if it were his own case.[3]

We can weep for other Christians because we are somehow joined to them as a single person. The notion of marriage is exactly what this involves. How this happens is another matter. In a classic passage, at the end of Dom Gregory Dix's *Shape of the Liturgy*, Dix lyrically extols the extent of eucharistic celebration in the Church:

> Was ever another command so obeyed? For century after century, spreading slowly to every continent and country and among every race on earth, this action has been done, in every conceivable human circumstance, for every conceivable human need from infancy and before it to extreme old age and after it, from the pinnacle of earthly greatness to the refuge of fugitives in the caves and dens of the earth. Men have found no better thing than this to do for kings at their crowning and for criminals going to the scaffold; for armies in triumph or for a bride and bridegroom in a little country church; for the proclamation of a dogma or for a good crop of wheat; for the wisdom of the Parliament of a mighty

---

3. Currie, *God's Bottle for Believers' Tears*, 64–65.

nation or for a sick old woman afraid to die; for a schoolboy sitting an examination or for Columbus setting out to discover America; for the famine of whole provinces or for the soul of a dead lover; in thankfulness because my father did not die of pneumonia; for a village headman much tempted to return to fetich because the yams had failed; because the Turk was at the gates of Vienna; for the repentance of Margaret; for the settlement of a strike; for a son for a barren woman; for Captain so-and-so wounded and prisoner of war; while the lions roared in the nearby amphitheatre; on the beach at Dunkirk; while the hiss of scythes in the thick June grass came faintly through the windows of the church; tremulously, by an old monk on the fiftieth anniversary of his vows; furtively, by an exiled bishop who had hewn timber all day in a prison camp near Murmansk; gorgeously, for the canonisation of S. Joan of Arc—one could fill many pages with the reasons why men have done this, and not tell a hundredth part of them. And best of all, week by week and month by month, on a hundred thousand successive Sundays, faithfully, unfailingly, across all the parishes of Christendom, the pastors have done this just to make the *plebs sancta Dei*—the holy common people of God.[4]

Here there is a doing, an act that goes beyond the agency of a single person and touches millions. Dix's more traditional Eurocentric and rather dated vision—Joan of Arc, yams and fetishes—should be rewritten, a thousand times over, with the images of global Christians weeping with one another in joy and faith. So, for instance, when Japanese Christians in the seventeenth century were driven by horrendous persecution into hiding, some were able to exist for centuries as secret communities, only to be rediscovered in the twentieth century, bound to a Church whose invisible forms had nonetheless survived the worst assaults over time, while yearning, praying, and waiting. Native Kiowa Christians, whose experience with white settlers was hardly exemplary, weathered their sufferings with common hymn singing that expressed the deepest love of the Church in ways few contemporary Christians know how to articulate. Everything about who they are as a people held by Christ is sounded in these gatherings. African farmers, with material resources that count as abject poverty in the West, raise their church buildings together by hand, where they meet for Bible reading and song, understanding that the Church that exists in and behind these places and activities is worth "all the living" that they have (Luke 21:3–4 KJV).

---

4. Dix, *Shape of the Liturgy*, 744.

INTRODUCTION

Contested Collectives

The binding of individual to people and people to Church as a kind of heartbeat of faith is simply a given. In the turmoil of a global faith, the Bride somehow still asserts her personality. But the assertion is also one filled with challenges. The lines between Christian identity and local or popular identities are often unremarked and ignored because they lie so deeply in our consciousness as to be hidden. Cultural and national dynamics can easily hold sway in ways that overwhelm the Church's specific faithfulness to the gospel. These challenges have demanded attention in our era just as the great expansion of Christianity has linked hands with the global revolution, and nationhood and collective identity and belonging have become difficult and contested realities. Ironically, as the Church faces these realities, she has also, for the first time in her history, begun to face the greatest failure of her navigation of collective identity—that is, her relationship to the Jews. Having become a "Church of the Nations," now with an unexpected reach and energy, the Church's own peoplehood as Israel has been called into question by her sins against her forebears and brethren "in the flesh." Jew and Greek, Barbarian and Scythian are now capable of being named as the Church's own in difficult ways that were never imagined in the past. We are in a moment where our ideas of the Church are being changed from the root up.

Thinking about the Church, then, is filled with new tests. Christians' primordial sense of the Church's universality as a vast and embracing object of God's love, and as a subject who loves God in return, is being pressed to engage human struggles on a global scale, and in such a way that local demands become themselves more insistent. Indigenous peoples, minority claims, regional needs, disenfranchised groups, ethnic reconciliations, power-sharing, cooperative treaties, environmental disputes—these kinds of specific aspects of social life cross over into the Church's internal debates and decision-making in ways that have complicated how one thinks about the Church in a basic way. If it is true that all modern notions of the Church fall into two categories—the "ideal" and the "concrete," the universal and the particular, the spiritual and the embodied, the theological and the practical—then this is only because today humankind itself is being forced to sort these aspects of reality out in a very public way.

It is to some of these basic challenges that we now turn. The ordering of this book, however, cannot be comprehensive in this regard. We will not try to answer the question of what is the "true" Church. We will not try to explain in any significant way why Christians order their churches in one fashion or another, or what the differences mean. The goal of this volume is instead to outline the theological shape of the Church, its divine ordering as it has come to exist in this unprecedented era of global encounter and confusion. This will involve a range of approaches—philosophical, sociological, linguistic, but especially scriptural. I will first look at how the theological study of the Church has been pursued, since I think that will suggest certain alternative ways of studying the Church today. I will then spend two chapters trying to tease out what we mean when we use the term "Church" in the first place, recognizing that it is such a hard concept to navigate. My own sense is that "Church" has to do with a collective reality. If this view is true, it will orient our thinking in very specific ways that are both second nature to us and also particularly challenging in the present era. The challenge will lead us back into Scripture, exploring the Church's verbal roots (chapter 3) and the notion of the Church's divine election (chapter 4). This, in turn, will help us specify where we are to seek an understanding of the Church, that is, in a theology of the Nations more broadly (chapter 5), and in a missionary theology of Israel more specifically (chapter 6). The final chapter will try to suggest that we look at some of the specific features we associate with theologies of the Church—her sacraments, ordering, marks—as elements of just this scriptural outline of Israel's elected and missionary life. Our conclusion will return to the question of love, in this case, not only our love *for* the Church, but the Church's love of Christ, as his Bride.

As will become clear, my conclusions have to do with looking at the Church as a specific "people"—Israel herself—with a mission aimed at all distinct peoples or nations. In this sense, I will present the Church with a very missionary focus. But I will also try to describe this mission, not in strategic terms but from the perspective of God's own ordering of humankind. In doing this, I will offer a particular way of talking about the Church that is defined by the person of Jesus Christ as rendered scripturally, something I will call simply a "figural ecclesiology." The point here is that the Church is a kind of historical image of the figure of Jesus, who himself represents and transforms many of the other persons and realities we read about in the Bible. The person of Adam in particular, as created to be taken up by Christ, seems to me central in understanding the Church, and it is at this "Adamic" point that I will aim. It is not as if the strategic issues in terms of mission, church order, ecumenism, or forms of teaching are unimportant. But these must be approached through concrete acts of

Introduction

decision-making among Christians, the contours of which I will suggest, but the work of which needs to be done by real people who grasp their place within the purposes of God for "the children of Adam" taken as a whole. I hope to indicate an answer to the question, "What is God doing with the Church for the sake of humankind?" Having answered that, Christians may be led to make decisions that reflect faith in this creative act of God.

Further Reading

Arias-Maldonado, Manuel. *Environment and Society: Socionatural Relations in the Anthropocene.* Cham, Switzerland: Springer, 2015.

Center for the Study of Global Christianity. *World Christian Database.* http://www.worldchristiandatabase.org/wcd.

Clarke, Elizabeth. *Politics, Religion and the Song of Songs in Seventeenth-Century England.* New York: Palgrave Macmillan, 2011.

Currie, Archibald. *God's Bottle for Believers' Tears.* Edinburgh, 1854.

Dix, Gregory. *The Shape of the Liturgy.* London: Dacre, 1964.

Durham, James. *Clavis Cantici; or, An Exposition of the Song of Solomon.* Edinburgh, 1723.

Iriye, Akira, ed. *Global Interdependence: The World after 1945.* Cambridge: Belknap of Harvard University Press, 2014.

Kessler, Edward. *An Introduction to Jewish-Christian Relations.* Cambridge: Cambridge University Press, 2010.

Kolakowski, Leszek. *Chrétiens sans église: La conscience religieuse et le lien confessionnel au XVIIe siècle.* Paris: Gallimard, 1969.

Lassiter, Luke, et al. *The Jesus Road: Kiowas, Christianity, and Indian Hymns.* Lincoln: University of Nebraska Press, 2002.

Matter, E. Ann. *The Voice of My Beloved: The Song of Songs in Western Medieval Christianity.* Philadelphia: University of Pennsylvania Press, 1990.

Morgan, Timothy. "Why Muslims Are Becoming the Best Evangelists." Interview with Dave Garrison. *Christianity Today*, April 22, 2014. http://www.christianitytoday.com/ct/2014/april-web-only/why-muslims-are-becoming-best-evangelists.html.

Ormerod, Neil. "Recent Ecclesiology: A Survey." *Pacifica* 21 (2008) 57–67.

Pew Research Center. "Global Christianity: A Report on the Size and Distribution of the World's Christian Population." Forum on Religion and Public Life, December 2011. http://www.pewforum.org/2011/12/19/global-christianity-exec.

Reventlow, Henning Graf. *The Authority of the Bible and the Rise of the Modern World.* Philadelphia: Fortress, 1985.

Turnbull, Stephen. *Japan's Hidden Christians, 1549–1999.* 2 vols. Surrey, UK: Japan Library, 2000.

Church

Discussion Questions

1. Do you love the Church? What reasons could you give for loving the Church? *Should* Christians love the Church?

2. Do all Christians "assume" that there is a Church that is fundamentally important, maybe even essential, to them? What reasons might a Christian give for thinking the Church is or is not essential?

3. Do Protestants and Catholics "love the Church" in different ways or in the same way? What might this tell a person about the nature of the Church?

4. Recent global changes are affecting human life in major ways. Do any of these changes affect the way Christians should think about the Church? How and why?

1

"The Wounds I Received in the House of My Friends," Part I

The Complicated Theology of the Church

Histories of the Church's self-understanding abound. The notion that one "breathes" the Church, or at least "assumes" it tacitly, most would agree, seems to apply to discussions from the earliest time of Christianity. When Matthew (16:18) records Jesus as speaking about "my church," no explication of the term is given, as if its meaning is well understood. Paul seems to vary his usage of "church," but he doesn't seem to think this is particularly problematic. Practical as well as conflictual demands provided moments of self-conscious reflection on the Church. Still, most theologians of the Church for the earliest centuries rely on indirect evidence for views of the time: liturgical forms (not very plentiful until the fourth century), polemic, and of course biblical exegesis. By the fourth century, canon law from councils adds to the mix, and the monastic movement's rich practical and spiritual direction provides insights into the breathing set of assumptions. They are never systematized, however; and their import, just as with scriptural exegesis from these centuries more generally, has been debated with respect to its normative significance for Christians more broadly within this or that locale.

Augustine is often credited with providing the most focused set of theological tools or categories for talking about the Church, certainly in the West. Among his most potent contributions is his emphasis on the *totus Christus*, the "whole Christ" who includes "head" and "body" together. This underlines the way that Paul's discussion of the Church as "body of Christ" (e.g., 1 Cor 12:27, or Col 1:18) is to be taken in a literal or ontological sense as pointing to the Church's actual "being." Historically, the *totus Christus* was extended to the eucharistic gifts, and the extended result of this vision was of a vast divine-human network of historical realities that caught up believers, both of the past and present, into the living form of Christ. Later Protestants (and some modern Catholics) have worried that this *totus Christus* notion of the Church overly divinized its structures, and thus accounted for the way that Roman Catholicism imbued its hierarchy and sacraments, indeed the very delimited communion of its members, with an identity of intrinsically indwelt Spirit or grace. Here arises the category of "infallible mystery" as applied to the Church. Protestants therefore tended to use the "body of Christ" language of Paul as a kind of linguistic metaphor, focusing instead on the way that the various aspects of the Church's life and structures act more as "signs" of some other "external" truth regarding God's work in Christ. The visible Church thus lives to "tell us things" about God, not "to be" these very things—something which, given the Church's human fallibility, it could in any case never be. Modern Catholics, in response, have tried for some balance between the two, often to the point of dazing the mind with their elaboration of multiple categories for understanding the Church. As one Catholic critic put it,

> [because the Church] is at once earthly and heavenly, temporal and eternal, present and eschatological, human and divine, active and contemplative, collective and individual, personal and suprapersonal, united in love and ordered by laws, visible and invisible, proper reflection about her requires a system that balances all these aspects.[1]

But Catholic systematization had its challenges, as twentieth-century theologians admitted. Much of this had to do with the "apologetic" orientation that almost all thinking about the Church involved, for almost every Christian group. Defending this or that version of the Church has in fact defined our thinking about the Church almost exhaustively until relatively recently.

---

1. Jáki, *Les tendances nouvelles*, 263.

"The Wounds I Received in the House of My Friends," Part I

Defending the Church: The Apologetic Roots of Ecclesiology

The theological study of the Church is today referred to as "ecclesiology." The use of the term in English dates only to the nineteenth century, although it was taken over as a transliteration from Latin (*ecclesiologia*). Even in Latin, it was not a common term, deriving from the early modern period of the seventeenth century. It seems, in fact, that the notion of a "Church" as a distinctive topic of theological reflection does not itself arise until the twelfth and thirteenth centuries, and here mostly in reaction to growing conflict among Western European Christians.

The great French Dominican scholar Yves Congar laid this out most fully in his many historical studies of the Church's self-understanding. His basic argument points to this crucial medieval period as the time when the Church was radically reenvisioned, at least in conceptual terms. For centuries, Christians had maintained a rather broad view of the Church as the *congregatio fidelium*, the "gathering of the faithful," which embraced simply all those who had a true faith in Christ. Emphases could vary within this definition. Sometimes these fell in the direction of historical breadth—all believers from "Abel" (whose faith in Christ was implicit in his acceptance by God) to the present. Sometimes the focus was on more immediate affiliations—those in communion with certain bishops and councils. Still, it was not until the twelfth century, Congar suggested, that these aspects split into opposing conceptions of the Church. At this time, with reforming movements gaining traction and heretical groups like the Albigenses in southern France growing in numbers, more exclusive clarity was sought as to the Church's true being. Some reformers, concerned with the visible failures and sins of ecclesial leaders and structures, began to identify the Church's integrity only with its (often invisible) predestined faithful. This obviously relativized the visible forms of the Church's life. Reactively, an alternative theology of the Church arose, finally triumphing in Western Catholicism, which identified the Church's nature precisely with its visible forms, structures, and members. By the early seventeenth century, the Jesuit Robert Bellarmine could assert that the Church was "a popular assembly," as "visible and palpable as the people of Rome, the Kingdom of France, or the Republic of Venice."[2]

---

2. Bellarmine, *De conciliis*, 317–18.

Congar's historical argument has been generally accepted. It is true that treatises devoted to the Church—"De Ecclesia"—do not start appearing until the Middle Ages. We see them written on the one hand in conjunction with discussions of "heresy," and on the other hand with reflections (often bitter) on political power and the relation of Church and civil authority. Some of the categories involved—who is in charge, who owns property, how to deal with the sin of church leaders, who determines the truly faithful—become increasingly compelling as the Western European church descends into schism (e.g., battles among Franciscans over faithful poverty, and the division of the papacy into rival popes in the fourteenth century). John Wycliffe wrote an important text, *De ecclesia*, as did his Bohemian disciple John Hus. Tinged with a growing concern over biblical prophecy and apocalyptic worries and hopes, the topic "Of the Church" passes into the sixteenth century. It is now on the one hand ready-made for debate amidst the Reformation divisions, and on the other hand suited to parse and inform the revolutionary encounters of Europeans with non-Christians peoples— "the Nations"—around the globe. Finally, seeing how formal theological reflection on the Church came to be shaped in this context, it is possible to identify related dynamics much earlier. Cyprian's famous third-century essay on "the unity of the Church" was forged within conflict and schism, just as Irenaeus's earlier notion of Catholicism and Augustine's later elaboration of its meaning grew out of hostilities with Gnostics and Donatists, respectively. Jews, Gnostics, Manichaeans, Monophysites, Nestorians, Muslims: they were, from the beginning it seems, the shadow of the Church, and to know the Church was to grapple with its opposite. Hence in the late twelfth century, one of the first formal treatments on the Church by Hugh of Amiens could be called "Against Heresies, or On the Church" (*Contra haereticos sive de Ecclesia*): they amounted to the same thing.

Treatises *De Ecclesia*, "On the Church," continued to be written with greater frequency and fury by both Catholics and Protestants from the sixteenth century on. Their form was driven by the disputes each group held with the other (and with Protestants among themselves). There are countless tracts and volumes of polemic here, often without systematic order, and there is no typical approach to talking about the Church. A massive tome like Juan de Torquemata's *Summa de Ecclesia*, written in the fifteenth century's struggle between Pope and Council, was revived a century later. It provided the basis for many post-Reformation Catholic treatments of the Church, unsurprisingly, given its interests in defending

"The Wounds I Received in the House of My Friends," Part I

Roman supremacy and the pope's role in church councils. De Torquemata's fourth and final book of the treatise is devoted to schismatics and heretics, a focus particularly suited to Protestant defectors. Almost two centuries later, however, little has changed. Honoré Tournely's two-volume *De Ecclesia* (1726) breathes a bit more freely, concerns itself with basic theological definitions, including the marks of the Church (the most important being catholic unity, rooted in the papacy). But even here, the weight falls on Roman apologetics almost immediately (despite Tournely's personal commitment to the relative autonomy of the French Church), so that the marks of membership distinct from Protestant errors predominate, and questions of authoritative decision-making end up enveloping all concerns.

Protestant treatises are not so different, although they obviously press their own distinguishing concerns. Richard Field, one of the calmer early Anglican theologians of the Church, orders his pioneering English work (*Of the Church*, 1606–10) around five themes that are worth enumerating in order to see the focus. First, he explains the nature of the Church mostly in terms of membership issues, but in a way that involves matters of election. Second, and most briefly, he examines the "notes" or marks of the Church. Here he mostly disputes catholic views regarding "succession," "antiquity," "universality," "unity" and "catholicity," and proposes instead common Protestant notes involving Word, sacrament, and discipline or governance. Third, and more diffusely, Field lays out the history of the Church, arguing for Protestant continuity and against various heresies present in Rome. He links all this to a supplemental discussion of Scripture as the basis for Christian teaching, arguing against a host of Catholic doctrines like purgatory and transubstantiation. Fourth is a book dealing with the ordering of the church's authority (Scripture again, vs. the pope and tradition). In the final section of this tightly-printed 750 page book, Field addresses the governing ministries of the Church. This vast discussion covers Old and New Testaments, as well as the two natures of the mediating Son and his salvation as it relates to the Church's ministry. With this in hand, Field can comparatively discuss priests, bishops, ministers, popes, councils, Lutherans, and Calvinists. Despite some considerable constructive insight—and Field's is one of the most engaging of its Protestant kind—it is all very predictable in its antagonistic structure and content. Over the centuries little changes, and despite interest in the Scriptures or in holiness as the shape of the Christian life as a people, or even in forms of worship, sacramental or otherwise, the main concern is authority and jurisdiction: who runs the Church.

"Ecclesiology" as a distinct term or practice seems to refer specifically to the debris that arises from this "debate" over the Church, and the term is colored by the conflictual field of its sowing. One of the first so-called ecclesiologies was by the seventeenth-century German mystic Johann Scheffler, later known as Angelus Silesius. Toward the end of his life, Scheffler, who had become an ardent Catholic and then priest after being raised a Lutheran, turned to apologetics. His last published work, the *Ecclesiologia*, was a two-volume collection of anti-Protestant essays, designed to describe by contrast the true (Roman Catholic) Church. The term *ecclesiologia* in Latin slowly lost some of this hard edge, but never completely until the twentieth century. As the word travelled into English in the nineteenth century, its reference was initially uncertain. One of the earliest appearances (1826) of the word is in a work by an Anglican clergyman, William Vansittart. Vansittart contrasts "theology" with "ecclesiology," the one referring to "God and the truths of his word," the other to "the exterior building of the Church," meaning the external matters of her order. In issues of religious controversy, Vansittart says, theological topics can be treated "with much more moderation, and with less asperity of temper, than ecclesiological." For the latter, having more to do with "an earthly nature," "stir up more of human strife."[3] The sense that arguing about the "earthly" aspects of the church is strife-inducing is deeply imbedded in the theology of the Church as it has evolved.

By 1837 we begin to see some rejigging of the terrain. The term "ecclesiology" (or "ecclesialogy") was proposed as a new "coinage," and its subject matter was a "science" driven by the times in order to treat of these external matters of Christian life demanded by church governance—taxes, establishment, legal relations, missionary structures overseas. "Ecclesiology" continued to be used in this more practical sense for several decades, and thus the study of the Church so indicated moves into the realm of more functional political strategy and debate. By the 1840s, however, the term "ecclesiology" was still trying to find a stable meaning, being used in different ways by writers like Richard Montague and John Mason Neale. On one side, it had shifted gears as to its referent, and now seemed to denote the study of church *architecture* explicitly (and a journal on the topic, *The Ecclesiologist*, was founded). At the same time, however, the debate over the catholicizing Tractarian movement within the Church of England ushered in the claim that "Puseyism" (named after one of the Tractarian leaders)

---

3. Vansittart, *Statement of the Argument*, 67–68.

was a pernicious "ecclesiology," a term that now seemed to apply to the way Catholics puff up the Church's external forms inordinately. So too in America, "ecclesiology" describes the theological vice of "popery," and is linked to the tendency of overvaluing the Church's structures, something called "ecclesiologism."[4]

Ecclesiology, even in its more substantive meaning, is thus a category invented to make sense of the conflicts of the Church, both internally and externally. It is as if simply *thinking* about "the Church" as a particular topic is fraught with unease over the course of Christian communal existence. To the degree that it frees itself from such troubling resonances, the term moves toward the practical, the organizational, and the instrumental. If one looks at how the study of the Church more positively was approached in Protestant seminaries, we see that, through much of the nineteenth century, its more theological features—worship, sacraments—fall under "systematic" theology, while "church governance" has its own course that is devoted to questions of pastoral authority.[5] Only in the early twentieth century, near the end of World War I, do we find for the first time a course at Auburn Seminary entitled "Ecclesiology," which is described as "the study of the theory of the Church, its ministry, creeds, ordinances, sacraments, cultus, terms of membership and relation to the Kingdom."[6] It is an "elective" for middlers. But it is also now a mark of what will, in the subsequent decades, become a new direction of positive reflection on the Church as something that, for Protestants as much as for Catholics, somehow contains the fullness of the Christian life.

We can speculate about how "ecclesiology" made this turn from justifying antagonisms to constructive reconciliation. No doubt it had something to do with the way that Christian world missions, now fully engaging both Protestant and Catholic energies, had reoriented Christian concerns by the twentieth century: now energies focused on the challenges of an evangelism that could be adapted to diverse peoples. Not that institutional

---

4. "Ecclesialogy," *British Critic Quarterly Theological Review* 22 (1837) 218–48; Evans, "Reformation," 4. An anonymous exchange on the etymology of "ecclesiology" occurs in the first volume of the *Ecclesiologist*, 75. See also Clericus Connorensis's *Ecclesiologism Exposed* (1843) and the Ecclesiological Society's *Handbook of English Ecclesiology* (1847).

5. See, for instance, the various iterations of the Princeton Seminary catalogue. In 1832, "Church Government" as a course follows "Polemic Theology." By 1869, "Ecclesiastical" matters continue to be taught separately from Theology, and continue to focus on "government."

6. *Auburn Seminary Record* 12 (1917) 32.

competitiveness had disappeared—far from it. Still, as concerns about translating Scripture and gospel life and how to make sense of the interaction of diverse cultures became inescapable, the center of *what* the Church was seemed to have shifted from previous conflictual worries. The collapse of Christian Europe in 1914, drawing North America as well into a morass of unimaginable mutual slaughter, had furthermore perhaps softened the asperities and relativized the ecclesial oppositions that so controlled thinking about the Church, and it refocused religious concerns on the "children of Adam" more broadly. We see in the twentieth century how "ecclesiology," a term that had poked about in the breakdown of the church, gradually committed itself to finding ways to put the pieces back together.

What this means, though, is that "ecclesiology" is a study of the Church as the Church itself is shaped by historical encounters and challenges. We can say that ecclesiology deals with the "truth" of the Church, but that truth seems to be grasped according to shifting experiential contours. The Church that is part of the breath and abiding love of all Christians moves from tacit to articulate expression, theologically, only in the face of certain pressures. That is what the last two thousand years have shown us. Often these pressures, furthermore, expose struggles and failures, sin even, just as much as they unveil the pristine gifts of God. We live in a time when the fights between divided Christians have died down, certainly in their violent apoplexies. Cooperation is frequent, even if competition and antipathy (or the occasional anathema) are just as present.

Ideologies and Options

This is probably not how individual Christians look at the matter today. For in our own era and society, the Church that is articulated through ecclesiological study is subject in its details more and more to individual choice, not simply historical coercion by forces outside the immediate control of members. Hence, by the twenty-first century, to speak of "different ecclesiologies" no longer reflects the highly conflictual ways that Christians for one reason or another were aligned against others. Today, "differing ecclesiologies," whether Catholic or Orthodox or variously Protestant, may really be about "different choices," and why such choices were made. These will involve choices about authority, sacraments, Scripture, discipline, mission, morals, community, and work, but in ways that are perhaps less systematic than the hostilities structured by former oppositions. Still, formative traditions develop around all of these things, and individuals are brought up into them and discover themselves within them. But these traditions—after the sixteenth century certainly, and before in lesser ways—are increasingly permeable, and their porousness is given on the basis of the choices by individuals and individual groups. One might see this sociologically, or (as I prefer to do) "providentially"; but the dynamics can be described in similar ways at least superficially. Hence, the ecclesiology of Roman Catholicism articulated at the sixteenth-century Council of Trent is defined in ways that are determined quite explicitly by the negative reality of Lutherans, Calvinists, Anglicans and Anabaptists. Trent is a "council" where individuals gathered, reflected, debated, manipulated, and chose. Although one might want to say that the ecclesiology of Trent is consistent with and continuous with the "tradition" of the Church, it is peculiar nonetheless, as even conservative Roman Catholics today (like the late Cardinal Avery Dulles) admit. This is true of every inherited vision of the Church.

This is not to say that any ecclesiology is merely a "justifying" ideology, and that we usually argue for a church that suits our self-interest. But ecclesiology *is* an *expression* of human choices, motives, agents and means. If we do not see this point, our reflection on the Church will move immediately to the question of "who is right?" or "which church or church theologian has the better theology of the Holy Spirit?" and so on. These questions and their immediacy are common in scholarship, but are not helpful in the first instance. They are in fact secondary to the question of God's action among Christians and their life together, questions which point to primary ecclesiology more directly. We need to protect ourselves from jumping in too quickly to the root theological concepts at work in Christian reflection on the Church, because, frankly, experience has told us that this moves us to too-easy and distorted generalizations about actual Christian life. We end up with the common oppositions of East vs. West, Christ vs. Holy Spirit, visible vs. invisible, and common vs. individualist with respect to the Church. These are contrasts which, upon careful examination, appear to reflect ideological positions rather than accurate descriptions of the churches involved.

Images of the Church

It is common in our day to speak of "images of the Church," as if different ways of conceiving the Church constitute possible perspectives, vantage points, even representations on offer. The idea that the Bible is filled with various "images" of important things, like Christ and the Church, is a simple acknowledgment that past systematizations have ended by flattening the scriptural text itself. With respect to the Church, the notion that the Church is given in a range of "images" is a reflection of the very human embrace of specific scriptural forms to the exclusion of others, and hence to the construction of tendentious ecclesiologies. Paul Minear's popular 1960 volume, *Images of the Church in the New Testament*, came out of a period of ecumenical biblical study that sought, in part, to narrow the gap between separated churches by showing a broader scriptural discussion of ecclesiology. Minear came up with 96 distinct images. Some of them entered the common vocabulary of serious ecumenical discussion as the basis for rethinking the Church itself.

Two things about this approach need to be said. First, whatever the motive for an "ecclesiology of images," it has now been taken over by the undisciplined and often consumerist-minded individualized reading of the Bible. "What is your favorite image of Jesus?" one might hear at a Bible study. Shepherd? Vine? Teacher? How would you like to think about the Church? The second thing to be said is that the search for "images" of the Church was itself driven, early on, by a specific apologetic desire. So, for instance, the fervent Ambrose Serle in 1793 published his own discussion of thirty-seven images of the Church. Serle was no great theologian. He had labored on the royalist side in the American Revolution and worked mostly as a political civil servant. But he was an intimate friend of prominent Anglican Evangelical leaders in Britain, and he produced several popular devotional works, mostly aimed at scriptural meditation. *The Church of God* is notable in its topic, if not its approach. Serle considered "the terms of Scripture, the very names of persons and things" to be "God's own language." Thus, the "titles" of the Church found in Scripture "do not stand for abstract speculations" but rather "imply living, interesting, eternal realities" whose linguistic conveyance and true apprehension are required if a person is to be "happy . . . either here or hereafter."[7] This understanding of scriptural terms was common among many Evangelicals at the time (as it

---

7. Serle, *Church of God*, 3–4.

had been for much of the Christian tradition). But by this point Serle, as the title to his book indicates, is working with a developed Protestant notion of the Church as a set of individuals, namely of all those chosen for faith in Christ and hence for salvation. The Church—and this is only a first "title" drawn semantically, if not literally, from *ekklesia*—is a place holder for this set of individuals. The other titles he examines, from Temple and City to Royal Priesthood and Firstborn, are ways of locating this set of persons within Scripture. They are, as it were, scriptural indices. Whatever their Platonic aura as divine "realities," they are on the way to becoming linguistic "images," to be grasped and applied as they are useful by the individual Christian reflecting on his or her salvation.

Talking about the Church in terms of "images" has tended to track with the breakdown of any collective sense of the Church at all, and with a kind of collapse of ecclesiality into personal projection. "Images of the Church" tend to reflect "images of the self," and hence the nadir of apologetic ecclesiology and of self-preference. "Church" ends up being evacuated of non-interiorized content. Certainly, this has not been the intent of those contemporary theologians who have treated the Church in terms of "images." But I stress this point here because, as I will suggest later, describing the Church as "the people of Israel" needs to be distinguished from the whole project of "imaging" or "conceptualizing" the Church, whatever its motives. The most prominent exponent of this project, the late Cardinal Avery Dulles, in his now classic *Models of the Church* (1974), unwittingly played into the project, even though he himself worked hard to avoid its consequences. Yet even in his able hands, readers had a hard time figuring out the referent of "Church" that his proposed set of possible "models" was about. This had the effect of reproducing the apologetic diversity, and ultimately the referential dissolution, that was bound to the journey of "ecclesiodicy," a word that refers to the discipline of justifying a given church over and against the criticisms or oppositions of other churches.

It is worth pausing on Dulles's work, not only because it has been so influential and widely read in our era, but because it can disclose some of the major challenges modern ecclesiology faces.

Dulles begins his work by outlining his method. He tells us that *because* the Church is a "mystery" that is not objectively referenced, other ways of talking about it are necessary. Here he turns to the philosophy of language and cognition, applied especially to religion, drawing on the work of Ian Ramsey. Given the peculiar nature of religious reality, talk about it requires specific forms of language like metaphor, image, symbol, and finally "model" and "paradigm." These are all words and concepts that get at non-visible realities through a kind of analogical linkage: likenesses that imply connection somehow, without identity. These images or symbolic concepts are necessarily *how* we know these realities. It helps for Christians that they come from the Bible, of course. But Dulles is less explicit than the eighteenth-century Serle about why this is the case, and he does not engage the issue of whether a specifically *scriptural* image functions differently than the literary figures used in other (humanly authored) books. Furthermore, he does not grapple with the possibility that images of the Church are not all of the same *kind*, even scripturally. Is "body of Christ" similar in kind to "vine"? Most Christian readers of the Bible in the premodern tradition would have distinguished these two in, as it were, metaphysical reference.

Besides the scriptural criterion (and, as he will later add, the criterion of "tradition"), Dulles offers another essential touchstone for identifying an image or model of the Church. He calls this its "effectiveness," or whether the image actually "works" in its descriptive power for individuals and groups. He explains this in terms of the "connatural" character of an image that joins individual experience with the actual life of the Holy Spirit. When we discern this match, we "know" that the image is "true." Hence, images can change with the times and cultures, as long as the Holy Spirit is at work in the sense of their "fit." How this fit is assessed is unclear. His criteria later will include precisely this notion of "fitting the religious experience of the day." What is unclear is *whose* experience we must count. For from the start we do not know what is the Church whose members provide our benchmark experience. The danger here, borne out by much contemporary usage of this approach, is that diverse traditions and their members simply pick images that reproduce their already self-justifying or constricted self-understandings.

The five models Dulles proposes (he adds a sixth in his later edition) can be summarized as follows.

The first model is one that Dulles (along with most modern Catholics, as we have seen) claims was dominant in Catholicism from the sixteenth century to about 1940, at which point in quick succession new "paradigms" took the field. This he calls the *institutional* model. The Church here is viewed as a *societas perfecta* (a perfected society) like a secular visible society in its structured demands, but in fact "divine" in its absolute givenness. Practices and doctrines and discipline all follow along from this model, which is clearly defined and outside of which there is no remainder, church-wise. The institutional model of the Church is juridical (it focuses on rules and their authoritative executors and interpreters), and, Dulles says, "instrumental," in that it sees the Church's structures as aiming at accomplishing specific tasks. It should be said that the institutional model has not been held only by Catholics; Protestants (and Orthodox) have their own versions.

The second model is one that includes several more distinct images: Body of Christ, Communion, People of God. Following the periodization of someone like Congar, Dulles claims that this model reigned in the West from Augustine to the early Middle Ages, but was then eclipsed by the institutional model. An ecclesial renewal among Catholic thinkers began in the nineteenth century and revived this model. The revived model centered on thinking about sociological "communities" and then communal mysticism (Emile Mersch being an influential exponent). Its formal ascendance as an "official" model came with Pius XII's encyclical *Mystici Corporis Christi* in 1943. Based on Augustine's views, this model engages a view of the Church that is mystical, vertical (more focused on relationships with God than with history), pneumatic, organic, often invisible or ideal, sometimes even sectarian as the markers of actual love are measured. Dulles clearly doesn't like this model, despite it being rather central in the Western tradition (and far more central than he lets on). It is, he thinks, too solipsistic and dependent on "good feelings" and thus not precise enough to locate in the real world (despite the fact that Augustine's concern with the Church as *totus Christus* was to do just this).

The Church as "Sacrament" is third on the list and seems to be Dulles's favorite, until he adds his final model later. Here, following traditional scholastic terminology for sacraments like the Eucharist, the Church is a "sign" (*signum*) of something real that it carries with it (the *res*, or reality to which it refers). This is also a somewhat Augustinian model, but Dulles believes that, by focusing things this way, the model has all the virtues of the two previous ones, without their baggage. Seeing the Church as a sacrament permits specificity and divinity, but without claiming human perfection. As with any sacrament, God is the "author" of the Church's true nature. The theologian Karl Rahner is the influence here.

The fourth model, which Dulles dubs the "Kerygma or Herald" model of the Church, is mostly Protestant. It defines the Church as the place where the Word is given, preached, and received. Bible, sermon, and correct doctrine predominate on this model, as well, perhaps, as certain conversionary responses. Dulles thinks, however, that there is too strong a separation between God and human agency in this approach. Furthermore, this way of looking at the Church provides little basis for explaining the continuity of the Church across both persons and times, or specificity for the Church's actual common life, since it focuses on discrete actions and events in the present.

Fifth, Dulles proposes the "Servant" model, according to which the Church exists as its members (together and individually as linked to one another and Christ), attending to the needs of others, whether the needs are material, emotional, or spiritual. This model is very attractive, Dulles admits, because it reflects the obvious and necessary character of the gospel as Jesus presents it. But taken by itself, it blurs and dissolves specificity, much like the Herald model. It also leads to a kind of measurement by works accomplished, rather than measurement by God's grace, which is tantamount to the heresy known as Pelagianism.

Dulles later adds a sixth model, drawing on the witness of Pope John Paul II. He calls this model "the Church as community of disciples." Drawing on aspects of all the previous models, Dulles argues that seeing the Church this way maximizes the virtues he has come to identify through reflecting on each: visibility, specificity, but openness to other Christians and to the world as well as to the dynamics of self-criticism. Dulles argues that a Church whose members are clearly imperfect is nonetheless upheld by the perfect agency of God—and this relationship is precisely that which a "community of disciples" embodies. Finally, the more dynamic or historical aspect of the Church is also given scope here, because that perfected divine agency will find its will accomplished at the end of the time. Hence, this model includes the "eschatological" character of the Church as a community "on its way" in a fashion the others cannot quite indicate clearly.

Dulles's book, to repeat, has been exceptionally influential and is read by many non-Catholics. But unless one assumes that Dulles is in fact talking about only Catholics, it is not clear what the referent of his "models" actually is. Roman Catholics do not, in fact, consider Protestant churches to *be* "the Church" at all. And many Protestants do not recognize the churches of others, or, in any case, would not attach the capitalized term "Church" to any specific or visibly delimited community. In any case, Dulles's models either apply to a body of Christians whose "being the Church" is already a given; or (as with some congregationalist Protestants), they apply in a vague way to something that stands apart from actual Christian communities, but to which these groups gesture in a more-or-less way. To think of the Church according to images or models in fact presupposes an answer to the question of "what is the Church?"

Ecclesiology: Whose Church?

Images and models of the Church, then, presuppose a referent. But since such a referent is contested, images and models rarely get to the roots of ecclesial reality. They either dissolve into a puddle of individual preference, or are quickly hijacked into existing ecclesiodicies. In fact, to talk about the Church, what "it is," still carries these antagonistic realities with it. They do so because, more than anything, they are born of human antipathy, mixed into Christian living. That is what a discussion about the very term "ecclesiology" demonstrates. Thus every modern ecclesiology, however benign in its contemporary articulation—we are no longer burning heretics—is a kind of palimpsest of past conflictual distinctions among Christians, the marks of stripes perhaps now healed over but still visible. Like the prophets in Zechariah: "And if one asks him, 'What are these wounds on your back?' he will say, 'The wounds I received in the house of my friends'" (Zech 13:6 RSV).

If we want to get at the roots of the Church, we must look first at the "friends" who have left their marks on the Church's back. This will tell us, if not what the Church "is," at least who (some) of its members are, and what they do. To this we turn.

Further Reading

Bellarmine, Robert. *De conciliis*. In *Opera omnia*, 12 vols., edited by J. Fèvre, II:187–507. Paris: Vivès, 1870–74.
Catechism of the Catholic Church. Vatican: Libreria Vaticana, 1993. http://www.vatican.va/archive/ENG0015/_INDEX.HTM.
Clericus Connorensis. *Ecclesiologism Exposed: Being the Letters of "Clericus Connorensis," as Originally Published in the Belfast Commercial Chronicle*. Belfast, 1843.
Dulles, Avery. *Models of the Church*. Expanded ed. New York: Image, 2002.
"Ecclesialogist v. Ecclesiologist." *Ecclesiologist* 1 (1843) 74–75.
Ecclesiological (Cambridge Camden) Society. *Handbook of English Ecclesiology*. London, 1847.
Evans, Hugh Davey. "The Reformation." *American Church Monthly* 2.1 (1857) 4–18.
Jáki, P. Stanislas. *Les tendances nouvelles de l'ecclésiologie*. Rome: Herder, 1957.

Mersch, Emile. *The Whole Christ: The Historical Development of the Doctrine of the Mystical Body in Scripture and Tradition.* Translated by John R. Kelly. 1938. Reprint, Eugene, OR: Wipf and Stock, 2011.

Minear, Paul. *Images of the Church in the New Testament.* Louisville: Westminster John Knox, 2004.

Pius XII. *Mystici corporis Christi. Acta Apostolicae Sedis* 35 (1943) 193–248.

Serle, Ambrose. *The Church of God; or, Essays upon Some Descriptive Names and Titles Given in the Scriptures.* London, 1793.

Vansittart, William. *A Statement of the Argument Respecting Abel's Sacrifice and Faith.* London, 1826.

Discussion Questions

1. Why did it take more than a thousand years for Christian theologians to devote special books to the theology of the Church? Why did such books start being written?

2. "Ecclesiology" is a word that refers to a "theology of the Church": in what ways did ecclesiology, once it became a recognized theological discipline, quickly become a topic defined by "apologetics," or "defending" something? What was being defended in these works?

3. One way to talk about the Church is to describe it in terms of different "images." What are some of the major "images of the Church" that have been used? In what ways are these images useful and in what ways are they not helpful?

2

"The Wounds I Received in the House of My Friends," Part II

Our Church, Not Yours

CLASSIFYING PEOPLE IS ALWAYS dangerous. It is also inevitable. Here I will categorize churches according to both historical origins and also outlooks.[1] The division between Eastern and Western Christianity has been traditional, and it is certainly well-founded and also illuminating. I will make this distinction, but I will also frame it within a broader distinction between "catholic" and "protestant." This broader division is more the result of modern attitudes, fueled by the great Western cultural global advance since the sixteenth century. Since the sixteenth century, "Eastern" Christianity has either been assimilated into Protestant ecclesial dynamics, or it has stood in a position more related to (Western) Catholics. It is a strange world where former antagonists become odd companions on the world-historical stage—not unlike alliances in the past between Jerusalem and Egypt.

In the sketch that follows, I will say less about the explicit theology of Roman Catholics and Protestants than I do about the Orthodox, only because much of this volume takes the Western tradition as its general context and will be speaking at length to Western Christian concerns and traditions.

---

1. The most recent and thorough "comparative" ecclesiology is Roger Haight's *Christian Community in History*.

Church

Catholic

Eastern Orthodox

Orthodoxy is "eastern" in that its origins lie in the eastern Empire, after the split of the single Roman institution in the mid-fourth century. The fact that we can distinguish "eastern" and "western" Christianities is itself something that is theologically significant, as if geography, history, and cultural locale make a difference (something we shall examine later). Theological, political, and cultural differences led, in 1054, to a formal break between the Eastern Church and the Latin (Roman) Catholic Church. The Islamic conquest of much of the Christian East, furthermore, isolated the two sides of European Christianity, and led them to develop in different directions. Whether these directions are substantive or broadly cultural is an unanswered question. I tend to think the latter.

It has been said that the Orthodox "know" the church through experiential affirmation, rather than through formal reflection on the Church as an object. This places Orthodoxy in a kind of premodern place ecclesiologically, and it is why I place them first in order. Recent ecumenical discussion has, to be sure, encouraged more formal orthodox reflection on the Church. Still, in order to describe Orthodox ecclesiology, one needs to describe more particularly how ecclesial practices are tangibly located within a sense of "givenness," from which there is little room to demur.

To get a sense of this aspect of experiential certainty, let us look at the 1965 response by the Russian Metropolitan Philaret to the agreement to lift the mutual "anathemas" that Rome and Constantinople placed on one another in 1054. These "anathemas," it needs to be said, were themselves contested as to their scope—they really originally had only individuals in mind, not whole churches. But they quickly were interpreted as applying to each church, and so, from that point on—known as the Great Schism—a divide between East and West was viewed as resting, in part, on the fact that each church had excommunicated the other in the severest of terms. An "anathematizing" (a kind of cursing) was defined in the pre-Vatican II understanding as follows, according to the late nineteenth-century edition of the *Pontificale Romanum*, the authoritative guide for episcopal liturgical actions:

> We deprive (Name) himself and all his accomplices and all his abettors of the Communion of the Body and Blood of Our Lord, we separate him from the society of all Christians, we exclude him

> from the bosom of our Holy Mother the Church in Heaven and on earth, we declare him excommunicated and anathematized and we judge him condemned to eternal fire with Satan and his angels and all the reprobate, so long as he will not burst the fetters of the demon, do penance and satisfy the Church; we deliver him to Satan to mortify his body, that his soul may be saved on the day of judgment.[2]

Anathemas had been lodged at popes and patriarchs before 1054, but these were hedged and dropped, although gradually adding to immovable suspicions. Even in 1439 when the Turks were ready to overthrow Byzantium (as they did 15 years later), attempts at reconciliation between East and West (as at the Council at Florence) foundered.

In 1965, however, Paul VI and Athenagoras I met together and announced that all these anathemas of the past were over. No, the two churches had not been reunited, but at least the mutual judgments were now things of the past. I will come back to what these two church leaders actually said later. But first, note what the Russian Metropolitan Philaret said in response, rejecting altogether the implications of the pope's and patriarch's rapprochement. First, he pointed out that the two leaders were not in a position to make such decisions on their own:

> We are all guardians of the truth of the Church, which was always protected through the care that nothing of general importance for the Church would be done without the consent of all. Therefore our attitude toward various schisms outside of the local limits of particular autocephalous churches was never determined otherwise than by the common consensus of these churches.[3]

This is a key way of stating the active and integral unity of the church: the Church is an *all*, so much so that it is an "all-or-nothing." Thus:

> We declare firmly and categorically: No union of the Roman Church with us is possible until it renounces its new doctrines, and no communion in prayer can be restored with it without a decision of all churches, which, however, can hardly be possible before the liberation of the Church of Russia which at present has to live in catacombs . . . However, if Rome has much to change in order to return to the "expression of the Faith of the Apostles," the

---

2. Gignac, "Anathema," para. 3.
3. Philaret, "Protest to Patriarch Athenagoras," para. 1–2.

Orthodox Church, which has maintained that Faith impeccable up to now, has nothing to change.[4]

Hence, *if* we say that the Orthodox Church is the "church," it cannot be "partly" right, but must be wholly right; and it will remain so unless "all" are involved in heresy or all change. By definition, if there has been no "all" involved in a decision, nothing has changed at all! Conversely, anyone who wishes to say that they are *not* at one with the Orthodox Church, has by definition excluded themselves from the Church. So, Philaret's conclusion:

> The Tradition of the Church and the example of the Holy Fathers teach us that the Church holds no dialogue with those who have separated themselves from Orthodoxy. Rather than that, the Church addresses to them a monologue inviting them to return to its fold through rejection of any dissenting doctrines.[5]

Philaret's views sound extreme, and were to be questioned by other Eastern Orthodox—and obviously by Athenagoras. But the principles upon which they are based represent ones common to Eastern Orthodoxy: that is, that the Church is an integral entity, established immovably by God, and therefore immune to human manipulation or alteration.[6] We see this common conviction stated in different ways. So for instance, the great Russian theologian Sergei Bulgakov draws on Ephesians 1:4–5 and 1:23 to assert the church as having a divine ontological nature, "one" in its very being from God, established "before the foundation of the world" and constituting the "body" of Christ, indeed the very "fullness of him that filleth all in all."

The world exists for the Church, not the other way around. The world comes to be in order to become the visage of the Church at the end of time. Dimitar Popmarinov Kirov will speak of the way that the Church, through her tradition, reveals to the spirit the true image of the world in her purpose and end. In a metaphysical sense, the Church is "eternal" and defined by her "divine substance" as the very purposive act of God's being in Christ.

It is on the basis of such metaphysically inclusive claims that many Orthodox theologians will say that the church can only be apprehended "by faith," through a kind of spiritual knowledge. On this basis only those already within the Church know the Church and can speak truly about

4. Ibid., para. 6–7 and 10.
5. Ibid., para. 11.
6. An excellent source, with references, for understanding some important modern Orthodox approaches to ecclesiology is found in Kimbrough, *Orthodox and Wesleyan Ecclesiology*.

it. The Church is, technically, a non-empirical reality, unbound by the temporal realities of coming-to-be and weakening. This vision—already an "ecclesiological" claim, and therefore made only within the context of division—goes back to the nineteenth century, as Russian Orthodox thinkers began to mark out their distinction from the West and her Roman and Protestant ecclesial bodies. The sociopolitical aspects of this impulse are obvious, but their ecclesial import remains substantive. Nineteenth-century Russian religious writers like Aleksie Khomiakov and Ivan Kireevsky began the process of laying out "contrasts" in ecclesiology based on deep attitudes and spirits that differed between East and West. So Khomiakov, in various writings to Western church leaders (Catholic and Anglican), laid out the following kinds of contrasts: external authority (Catholic) vs. internal divine truth (Orthodox); rationalist logic (Protestant) vs. pneumatic illumination (Orthodox); partiality (West) vs. wholeness (East). From these, one gets the Western fratricidal competitions between Catholic and Protestant; the heresy-hunting of the West; and the authoritarian and legalistic coerciveness of Western Christianity, incapable of common counsel led by the consensus of the Spirit. For the Eastern Orthodox Church, everything comes down to "life within the whole": Bible reading, decision-making, theological discussion, prayer. Hence, the proper characteristics of the (true Orthodox) Church are integralism, interiority, naturalism, spontaneity, family solidarity, communalism, and organicism. In the Western churches, it is all about compartmentalization—analysis, externalities, abstraction, autocracy, dualism, and lapses into the extreme alternatives of sensualism and despondency. Rome gives us a Church without Christians, Protestantism provides Christians without a Church.

In this vision, the Church "just happens," insofar as God's life is given wholly in love and thus received. The Church is not something constructed; and when the Church *is* constructed, through analysis, strategy, reform, and so on, it is simply wrong, it is not the Church at all. Furthermore, arguing about this kind of vision is hard; and that is part of the point. The Church is not something to be argued at all, but rather to be a part of—although, stated this way, it takes the form of a very particular argument against other churches. Like Dulles's models, the answer to the question of the Church is given in the statement of the vision itself. Here, one simply *describes* elements of the Church; one does not offer arguments for them. Descriptions often include phrases like the following:

- In Christ
- Through the sacraments
- Holy
- Organic
- Always in one mind
- Living the life of the apostolic gifts ("succession")
- The image of the Trinity, unity in multiplicity
- Catholic through love of neighbor
- Transcending time
- At one with her tradition
- Inclusive of and congruent with the Scriptures

The point isn't that you "look" for this or that quality in this or that body. There is only one Church! That Church is indeed the Eastern Orthodox Church, and *therefore* one can say these things about her. There is no "proof" involved here, only experience of the truth by those who know this to be the truth. Circular reasoning? Yes, as reasoning; but it is not meant to be a reason; it is a place, a given reality, as it were.

I want to stress this divinely metaphysical givenness. It is one of the deepest aspects of Orthodox ecclesial self-understanding, and it informs the way all these "elements" are approached—many of them the same as for the West, in terms of their enumeration, but differently approached and measured.

Some Western theologians have argued that this view of the Church, in which it simply manifests itself as God's act in the world, is all too "docetic"; that is, it makes the Church only "apparently," "seemingly" human, historical and temporal. Hence, the issues regarding the Church's sins and divisions are too easily brushed aside. Personally, I believe there is some truth to this criticism. But my point here is that this conviction undergirds the sense of the Church's self-evidence to the faith. To know God is to know what the Church is, and in fact vice versa. Hence, historicizing the Church according to its developmental trajectory doesn't make sense. For the Orthodox, the tradition of the Church is not a body of information that is authoritative. It is the fullness of God's life in Christ, in the Holy Spirit, as given in the Church and lived out through Scripture, holiness, the divine liturgy, icons and their veneration, the saints and their wisdom. It is all one piece, as a living being, and cannot be analyzed and broken down, or picked apart and measured in constitutive terms. Questions that Western Christians have regarding their churches—individually or more broadly—simply don't make sense here. What ought to be the proper emphasis on the Bible? Music? Gifts of the spirit? Lay or priestly leadership? These, for the Orthodox, are questions of human religious contractors, who simply do not live in the Church itself.

This of course makes ecumenical discussion difficult. It also makes self-criticism and reform difficult. It makes decision-making in new times difficult. It makes entry into this world by those not already in it difficult. It makes talking to the Philarets of Moscow difficult. And it raises questions about the reconstruction of Eastern Orthodoxy in the West as a denominational "choice" for those dissatisfied with their previous "churches."

It may also obscure what actually happens in the Church. For it is also the case that Orthodox theologies of the Church *have* changed, and in so doing have also fed into Western Christians' rethinking of their own churches and the Church more broadly. The theologian Bulgakov drew the ire of some of his colleagues by involving himself in intimate ecumenical sharing with Anglicans during the 1930s. His sense of the Church's divine and eternal reality, lodged in the very heart and being of God, could actually lead to an *open* view of the Church, at least in theory, and not a closed one. If the Church is in fact the heavenly image of creation's purpose, Bulgakov argued, then it is possible to see the Church already present and at work in the "world" that is not yet fully the Church. He called this the *ecclesia extra ecclesiam*, in which the Holy Spirit was reaching outside the formal bounds of the Orthodox body, drawing that body itself forward into new places.[7] This allowed him to see his work with Anglicans—doctrinal agreement, common prayer, study of the word, love itself—as actual "revelations" from God that demonstrated the Holy Spirit at work, drawing these individuals into a new place. The promptings should be followed, as gifts assumed.

Other Orthodox theologians—again, not without opposition—pursued especially this pneumatological vision of the Church. As Nicholas Afanasiev insisted, the Church *is* the presence of the Holy Spirit and his gifts; the Church *is* the rule of the Holy Spirit's love, and not a set of laws and structures. If this is so, we do not define love as "merely human" in advance if it does not fit those structures and law; but we do the opposite, at least in our testing. On this basis, Afanasiev actually looked at the

---

7. Bulgakov, *Bride*, 311.

lifting of the anathemas by Paul and Athenagoras very positively and as a divine challenge. It marked, quite concretely, the movement of the Holy Spirit to take persons and churches that were indeed formed by inescapable historical events, and to move them by the power of the gospel to acts of forgiveness and openness. The common statement of the pope and patriarch in fact focused on these matters: the outpouring of the Holy Spirit at Jesus' death and resurrection, the prompting of the Holy Spirit in coming together for pardon and reconciliation, the demands and power of "charity" in this process, the actual alteration of historical acts (casting them into "oblivion"), the call to a future not yet achieved ("communion of faith, fraternal accord"). Whatever the sources of this hope, it represented a new kind of dynamism in the life of the church, now viewed more historically (as more conditioned and more unfinished) or at least more vocationally.

These developments are real. But they stand in an unintegrated fashion beside the deeper identity markers of Orthodoxy that still lie in sharp contrast to Western ecclesial attitudes. When the Orthodox talk about the Church, they tend to identify its life with Tradition, seen as the "time" God has given that permits the "reception" of truth and practices. Theologically, this is described in terms of the Holy Spirit operating within the community of Christians, and the Orthodox tend to have an operative pneumatology that is both more central but also more stable than that of most other Christians, and not as open-ended as Bulgakov and Afanasiev might have indicated. More broadly, the Trinity is viewed as both the content and container or logic of this receptive life over time, and the community is ordered to this. Later Orthodox thinkers criticized Western Christians for their "Christocentrism," in which the Son seemed to gobble up all the aspects of the Church's teaching, life, and force; and this, they have argued, underlies the centralizing features especially of Western Catholicism.

As most observers of Orthodox church life note, including the Orthodox themselves, the interplay of authority and common life is uniquely configured in the Eastern Church. Bishops and synods carry enormous weight in ongoing decision-making. But this authority is "dispersed," in that it is not expressed or taken up in a single bishop or council of bishops, but is exercised mostly individually in relation to local eucharistic communities (congregations). Each of these congregations, with their priests, maintains its own integrity as a primary location of Christian spiritual power. Here the Holy Spirit does its work through the Eucharist and common prayer, and the congregation is upheld by the ascetic goals of the Christian life, goals encouraged for all but generally taken up by the elite (mostly monks).

The serenity of this vision, publicized in the transcendent liturgical forms of chant, icon, and incense, however, masks a turbulent history, one to which the press for a more dynamic sense of the Church's life is perhaps more attuned. From the fourth century on, Greek Christianity spread east, then south, and later north into what became Russia. It did so through massive and often distorting alliances with political rulers; and Orthodox churches established themselves politically at the sometimes bloody expense of alternative and dissenting Christian groups. As Islam took over many of these lands, new forms of adjustment, social as much as anything, were adopted. Orthodox churches became tied to local cultures and languages, resulting in what some Orthodox critics have called "phylatism," or Christian "tribalism." Antipathies swelled against Western Christians, first Catholic and then Protestant, to the point that even today Orthodox ecclesiology is defined as something not just distinct from Western Christian life, but as substantively "other," the true in relation to the false. Much of this is couched in geographical-cultural terms—the deformed Western mind vs. the Eastern (or Slavic) mind. But Eastern Orthodoxy has migrated to the West, and has been taken up by non-Orthodox converts. This has been done by a series of determined *individual choices*, in a way that simply subverts not only the Eastern/Western divide, but much of the history of the "assumed" ecclesiology of Orthodoxy in the past. Orthodox ecclesiology is increasingly a "constructed" vision. Its future is probably more tied to grasping what it has in common with Catholicism, than in holding out for the contrasts.

Roman Catholicism

The differences between the ecclesiologies of Catholicism and Orthodoxy are evident to most people on the level of authority structures and the way communal life is ordered. This may no longer be a useful way to look at things, but it is certainly rooted in past distinctions. The standard story, not without reason, points to an early and increasingly insistent claim by the Bishop of Rome to a certain primacy of leadership within the whole of the Christian world. It was an insistence that was also resisted, with increasing resentment, by churches in the East. To say that "everything comes down to the pope" in the distinction between East and West is a gross simplification.

But it may not be a wholly unwarranted one. One can point to differences in understanding sanctification, the Holy Spirit, or tradition; but as many modern writers have shown, there is enormous overlap on these matters between the Orthodox and the Catholic, even if emphases vary. What grates is how decisions are made.

For Catholics, tradition functionally *explicates* authority and order, rather than standing as their origin and informing context. The Church is the way it is—with its bishops and cardinals and pope—"because" of tradition's injunctions; but tradition is not their living Spirit, in any obvious way. Although playing a key justificatory role, the Catholic contents of tradition—the "legal" grounds for this or that practice—were nonetheless never systematically organized: Bible, sacraments, morals, and other customs were loosely collected and applied as demanded in controversy. What mattered were the appropriate applications of authority in decision-making. Despite shifting struggles, these tended toward the jurisdiction of the Bishop of Rome, where it remains. The organization of canon law into a formal "code" was a modern invention of the Catholic Church (although with a developing history). This fact explains how the Reformers could often seem so inconsistent, not only with one another, but with themselves over time. Decoupling the contents of tradition from the Roman authority structures (which they attacked), Reformers were left with a mass of what they saw to be disjointed "rules," and they rejected or picked up the pieces as they chose, "in accordance with Scripture" (as they thought).

Theologically, Catholicism and Orthodoxy share fundamental features with respect to the Church: sacraments, spiritual charisms, the place of Mary, the communion of saints, doctrines of the Trinity (with, however, some debate over how best to describe the relation of the Spirit to Father and Son). Even basic institutions—deacons, priests, bishops, archbishops—are shared. For several centuries, finally, common "ecumenical councils" were held together, at least in theory. How then could they explain the distinct *churches* and thus ecclesiologies? Is it a matter of "emphasis," as later Orthodox argued, so that "Christocentrism" leads to "institutional centralization" and hierarchical structuralism? No one doubts that the formal power of the pope, as the Bishop of Rome, has always characterized Catholicism as an ideal, if not always one that was fulfilled. But the ideal itself has also driven certain historical actions that continue to appall observers: interdictions, excommunications, imprisonments, warfare, and claims to divine sovereignty even over whole portions of the globe and their peoples (as in the famous "Bulls of Donation," by which, at the end of the fifteenth century, the pope "granted" Christian sovereignty over non-European lands to Spain and Portugal).

Explaining this feature has been at the root of most ecclesiological commentary on Roman Catholicism. Some have focused on the emphases in reading Scripture in a certain way (e.g., the central role given to Peter in the Gospels). Others have noted the character of ancient Roman society, especially in the West, whose legal and patriarchal focus survived more robustly than in the East and spread through Western Europe after the collapse of the empire. Some would argue that Catholicism grew out of a confluence of all these elements, and out of the ordering of the Church that emerged from the experience of early persecution and heretical conflict, more potent in the West than in the East. So, for instance, North African Montanism stirred up troubling mixtures of division, moral rigorism, and martyrdom, which the Church was forced to bring to heel. Then came the Novationist schism and struggles over the purity of church members complicit in betrayal, which gave rise to the centralizing visions of Cyprian and Augustine. No one denies that Roman Catholicism looks and feels different than Eastern Orthodoxy. But in the modern world, it is not clear what this amounts to *theologically*, and how to justify the difference as divinely significant. The fact that Catholicism is the single largest Christian church in the world, and, unlike Orthodoxy, has engaged (for all kinds of unique political reasons) in a global missionary outreach since the sixteenth century, may provide a providential context for the answer. But the answer itself is not obvious.

Oriental Orthodox Churches and the Church of the East

I will not say much here about these groupings of churches. The first refers to those churches—Coptic Orthodox (Egypt), Ethiopian Orthodox, Eritrean Orthodox, Syriac Orthodox, Armenian Apostolic, and Malanakara Orthodox (India)—who did not accept the decrees of the Fourth Ecumenical Council at Chalcedon in 451. At issue was the proper way to describe the divine and human being of Christ incarnate. There were various reasons for the rejection of the Council, but all these churches, related differently, were called "monophysites" ("one-nature-affirming") because of their supposed rejection of the "two natures" definition of Christ as both divine and human. They were labeled as heretics by the other Orthodox and Catholics both. Only in the last few decades have agreements been made between these churches and their antagonists to resolve at least these bitter disputes. But the churches remain separated from both West and East, and have been subject to intense persecution from Muslim powers, horrendously so in the past decades, and to subversive competition from other Christian Churches.

The phrase "Church of the East" refers to those Christians, originally of Syrian origin, who dissented from Chalcedon's decisions and followed the teaching of the monk Nestorius, who was concerned to keep sufficiently distinct the divine and human aspects of Christ. Nestorius was anathematized for splitting Christ into two separate "persons," and his followers, who spread East especially to Persia, were viewed as heretical. The Nestorian churches over the years have suffered numerous splits and diminishments. Today, grouped mostly in the Assyrian Church of the East, they have been decimated by contemporary religious and political persecution in the Middle and Near East. The Assyrian Church, like the Oriental Orthodox, has reached agreements with its antagonists over long-disputed doctrinal differences, even as it remains isolated and separated from the larger churches of East and West.

While each of these traditions has its own collection of saints and spiritual writings, specific liturgical customs and ordering habits, they all share with Eastern Orthodoxy a common fund of theological patrimony and common forms of life and witness. Their lives testify to the way that doctrine often has little to do with ecclesiology, even while politics and location—and personal destiny—count for everything.

Protestant

Luther

Although Lutherans are no longer a large church in the West, they have a global presence. Furthermore, as the church that emerged as the first Protestant alternative to Roman Catholicism, Lutheranism claims a certain ecclesiological priority among modern Christian churches. I have listed Luther and his followers here as a kind of ecclesiological "premise," rather than its own specific ecclesial form, because it sets Protestantism in motion rather than carrying it through in any major way.

"The Wounds I Received in the House of My Friends," Part II

When Martin Luther in the early sixteenth century began to question publicly and passionately various practices of the Catholic Church, he did so out of reforming motives, not schismatic ones. His concerns with the moral abuses of church leaders, including Rome herself, were not new, and had been voiced and prosecuted for centuries. But Luther's acute mind and scriptural passion came to link these criticisms with deeper theological worries. When these worries were both opposed by church authorities and upheld by local colleagues, they set in motion a dynamic of ecclesial dissolution that finally resulted, in the mid-1520s, in a new and distinct church organization, detached from the authority of Rome. Lutherans today, just as Luther's followers in the sixteenth century, argue over the "real Luther," and certainly over the "real church" that should follow the truths of Luther's scriptural vision. This variety is itself related to the basic principles that Luther's reforming vision embraced.

From the perspective of ecclesiology, Luther's own vision was simple: the church is the gathering of the believers in and by the Word, the assembly of the "saints" in this sense.[8] The Church is a "priesthood of all believers." Luther himself obviously had a complex and rich theology concerning the Word and the nature of sin and forgiveness through Christ's "alien" grace, carried by Christian faith. His radical refashioning of the doctrine of "justification by faith" proved decisive to all his theology. The Church for Luther was that which brought the Word's work to bear upon the individual. He could speak of the Church with all the traditional language of his era: the Body of Christ, the Bride of Christ, and more. But the work of the Word—understood as Christ himself addressing us personally—in the believer was the fundamental definer of the Church.

As I mentioned above, the Catholic approach to tradition as a collection of justifications for the shape of the Church came into play here. For moral and then ultimately theological or evangelical reasons, Luther attacked the authoritative institution of the Roman Church, leaving the tradition's contents, including various theological principles, dangling apart from their justifying purposes. For the new church, the chosen principles of organization became faith and gathering, as tied to the Word. Other elements remained as well: the Bible, sacraments, discipline of sorts, community, morals. But Luther's approach to institutional authority and the

---

8. Luther's writing on the Church is extensive, if not always clearly focused. See the chapter by David P. Daniel, "Luther on the Church," in *The Oxford Handbook of Martin Luther's Theology*.

traditions to which it was attached left these categories basically optional and pragmatic. The fact that Luther himself changed his mind on some of these matters in the course of his life was consistent with this optional pragmatism. It explains as well the variety of Lutheran churches that developed (e.g., some with bishops, some without), and the variety of practices governing the Eucharist (some more central and dependent on the transformative presence of Christ in the elements, some less so). The same variety appears in other Protestant groups, springing in part from the logic of pragmatic optionalism left behind by Luther's central concerns: Christ the Word promises and saves those with faith.

It is important to stress how practically variegated ecclesiologies could result from this. There was a larger theological framework that could actually explain this possible variation: the Church as the invisible collection of all the elect. Luther inherited this view from later medieval discussions, and at times (although not consistently) he drew out the full logic of "double predestination" that went with it. But any invisible Church of the elect will leave open a range of visible possibilities, without imbuing them with eternal significance. When elements of authoritative tradition are retained now, it is according to values ancillary to the main ones of Word and Faith (e.g., righteousness, peace, love or service). These may even come to exert a formative power over how a church is organized in certain circumstances, as we can see in Luther's own case, when rebellions and turmoil spurred by Christian "enthusiasts" like Karlstadt and Muentzer led him to reassert "external" formal authority, lodged in the state, over the individual interior conscience he prioritized theologically. But there is no logic—and hence ecclesiology—that says it *must* go in this direction. Karlstadt and Muentzer, and later "free church" congregationalism, are consistent with Lutheran ecclesiology in the main. The "alien" character of God's grace "frees" the inner person for a range of *possible* "outer" forms. I believe, therefore, that Roman Catholic arguments about general Protestantism deriving from Luther are correct. The "structural" or "catholic" component of Lutheranism (defined in connectional terms, through state churches) is a social epiphenomenon of sixteenth-century Germany and its political needs. They developed in a certain direction, but they did not have to, and when Lutherans came to America, these different directions asserted themselves.

There is certainly a theology at work here. But the *ecclesiological* theology is secondary to Luther's "discovery" of the work of God in the individual over and against the claims made by the Roman Catholic institution and its supporting traditions. The theological claims deriving from this "priesthood of all believers" are the ground for *many* ecclesiological possibilities.

Reformed

John Calvin was a generation younger than Luther, and grew up in France, not Germany. His most lasting work took place on the borders of France, in Strasbourg and then most importantly in Geneva. He was different in temperament from Luther, just as he was distinct in his background and education. But most readers of Luther and Calvin agree that they shared a basic commitment to the simplified gospel of "grace in Christ, the Word, through faith." This meant that they shared what have become known (in the modern period) as the "Three Reformation Solas": *sola gratia* (by grace alone), *sola fide* (through faith alone), and *sola Scriptura* (on the basis of Scripture alone). But Lutherans and Calvinists did not get along, and indeed were engaged in fierce controversy and even mutual violence, especially in Germany. Work at unifying the two traditions has seen some success in Germany, but not elsewhere. More recent commentators on Calvin's ecclesiology have stressed how his concern with order moved toward imposed ecclesial institutions in a non-optional and positive manner. Calvin, as it were, reasserted the fundamental connection between visible and invisible realities with respect to the Church. He worked this out on the basis of the theocratic character of the human community that exists through the grand sovereignty and authority of God. God *wills* a human community that lives according to divine Law, which means the Law of Christ; and God actively orders this community through the Church's exercise of public discipline and formative obedience. Yet Calvin did not, and logically could not, divinize the state; and because he didn't, the Church came to bear the weight of obediential embodiment. Where church and civil authorities could order their lives in faithful tandem—as often in Geneva—that was fine; but if not, then the Church's common life took priority. Even though Calvin made more explicit the two-poled predestinarian vision that Luther played with, his press for embodied communal obedience tended to put weight on the visible Church. Most of us are aware, if only vaguely, of the psychological pressures and contorted spiritual calculus this encouraged among Christians who sought "assurance" for their election.

Again, modern commentators note how Calvin also underlined more fully than Luther did the logically necessary work of the Holy Spirit in ordering visible obedience, through authoritative discernment. Without the ballast of justifying tradition, visible structures of communal life required another source of authority, and the Spirit's work was appropriately unmediated, at least in theory, in directing truth-telling and decision-making, particularly on the basis of reading Scripture. Indeed, for Calvin the Spirit begins to do a range of things that the articulations of the tradition used to explain in more conceptual terms. In addition to guiding the reading of Scripture, the Spirit unites believers with the ascended body of Christ during the Eucharist; the Spirit also, through specific protocols, chooses and equips ministers. But in theory, the Spirit's central role in ordering the Church could take a variety of forms, ones that Calvin himself could not claim were essential. Thus, pneumatological centering *can* lead to formalized authority as the means of the Holy Spirit's effective work; and this might even include, as it did for many Anglican Calvinists, the institution of the episcopacy. *Or* it could lead to a certain quietism, where individuals wait to be "moved" by the Spirit, something that also happened on the margins of Reformed and Anabaptist tradition both. The pneumatic and institutional sides of Calvin's ecclesiology were in practice hard to hold together, once the network of tradition and canon law unraveled.

Various Calvinist churches—often called Reformed churches—emerged. The Church of England, and hence much of the Anglican Communion, derives from Calvinist orientations, although the history of the Church in Britain from the seventeenth century on was so peculiar as to alter that Calvinism significantly. Presbyterianism and Puritan congregationalism arose in England as distinct churches, and they flourished in North America. Certain brands of Evangelicalism—Anglican and later Baptist—renewed their Calvinist roots. Calvinism also flourished in Holland, and it remained the main Protestant church in France and Switzerland as well as parts of Germany, Hungary and elsewhere.

Anabaptism

I would in fact put Anabaptism as a subset, ecclesiologically, of reformed Calvinism. The sixteenth-century origins of the Anabaptists are complex, and only in some cases relate to Calvin directly. From diverse although sometimes networked groups and movements springing up in Germany, Switzerland, and Holland, they came to cluster in a few larger groups, the most numerous of which are the Mennonites. Mercilessly persecuted by other Christians, both Catholic and Protestant, they were pushed further and further east, ending up in what is now Russia, and then, following the Revolution, moving to North America in large numbers. Some, however, remained in Europe, in Holland especially. But in terms of ecclesiological structure (rather than historical origins), Anabaptism is Calvinism that takes the "sectarian" route, quite consciously (eventually) apart from the larger civil institutions that might otherwise uphold the community of the elect. In this case, gathered faith is upheld through visible discipline and holiness, just as in Calvinism, but its communal "glue" is provided by individual commitment rather than communal demand. Part of the distinction between Calvin's retaining of infant baptism and the Anabaptist rejection of it, the latter in favor of "believer's" baptism, derives from this issue of what holds a people together.

It is true that among Anabaptists there is a new (but really only evolving) focus on the "commands of Christ," which in most groups ends up being concentrated on the Sermon on the Mount. But this development is not logically necessary either. As it turns out, Anabaptist churches, like the early Church, are pressed by persecution to invent new forms of discipline, which aim at maintaining individual faith, or at least the integrity of communities of individual believers. Anabaptists draw from Calvin the stress on visible communities and obediential holiness, with its necessary guards; and from Luther a general valuation of the individual believer and his or her direct connection to Christ. The mix can be seen as subverting this or that element of Calvin and Luther both, but not in any essential way, simply because the essence of the Church Calvin and Luther has, in any case, been located outside the realm of human manipulations: the true church is "invisible."

Congregationalism

Similarly, Congregationalism as it emerged in seventeenth-century England, or today's "Free Church" Evangelicalism, follows a parallel development whether it derives from Puritan sources or Baptist ones. Free Church ecclesiology is one direct outcome of the Lutheran decoupling of the container of tradition (institutions) from their contents (traditions). One is left with however small a containing unit as one wishes to have or is pressured to accept: a conventicle, congregation, small conglomerate of congregations, or even free-floating individuals of faith. The Congregationalist ecclesiological "principle" can be scripturally moored, but not in one single fashion.

Its main basis is the believing individual in relationship with God, and the relationship can happen variously via faith, obedience, service, good will, testimony, religious experience. In practice, contemporary Protestantism has become more and more Congregationalist in its self-understanding and practice, whatever the denomination: Anglican, Methodist (which derived from Anglicanism), Presbyterian. This, of course, has a lot to do with political, cultural, and economic factors—individualist association as a value—rather than theological ones. But the actual variety of Free Churches is in fact an indication of a deep common set of ecclesiological principles.

Liberal Protestantism

Liberal Protestantism is not only a broad term, but it is applied to quite different historical and geographical referents. In this case, I am referring to a general movement dating from the eighteenth century, mostly of British and then American origin, that sought finally to unify Protestantism in a common witness. Sometimes this had a political set of hopes in mind, later on a more missionary one, and finally what we would call a specifically ecumenical horizon, informed by the first two hopes. It was deeply committed to the value of God's "universal" claim on human life in Christ, and thus it parallels, if in a very different way, Catholic sensibilities about the global reach of the gospel. The assumption of a common "brotherhood" of mankind, calling forth the gospel's proclamation and ordering its receipt, was a powerful motive in liberal Protestantism. It was fueled, on the one hand, by hopes of overcoming Christian division and its socially destructive effects, as well as by a growing sense that Anglo-American forms of constitutional democracy melded perfectly with the purposes of the gospel. Doctrinal and scriptural outlooks that were later identified as "liberal" may or may not have characterized the liberal protestant ecclesiology as I am using the term, and that is important to note. In someone like the twentieth-century reformed church historian John T. McNeill, it was a highly disciplined and intellectually rigorous orientation. It did mean reading the past, however, in a certain way that may or may not have been accurate.

Writers like McNeill still played into the Catholic-Protestant contrast (though in a manner not quite like the contrast made by the Orthodox). Catholics value the virtue of "obedience," while Protestants prefer that of "communion." It is an odd way of reading history, but it plays off the notion of coercion (and hence tyranny) versus engaged consensus (deliberative counsel). The Protestant Reformers, in this view, were not individualists in their faith, but understood faith as something whose origin and nurture depended on common relationships of encounter. Far from retreating into some privatized realm of piety, Protestants assumed the necessity of a "visible" Church. But because it was one in which all manner of Christians were to be found, its fallibility demanded serious ecclesial accounting of a quite political kind. According to this story, Luther and especially Calvin dealt with this problem by reaffirming the authority of the visible Church, not rejecting it because of sins. The visible Church, although fallible and not wholly congruent with the full collection of the predestined elect, should be viewed as *connected* to the invisible church of the elect through a historical and gradual unveiling. By the nineteenth century, this idea had taken on somewhat Hegelian overtones: history was itself the act of God's own divine manifestation in time, in a progressive fashion.

What Liberal Protestant ecclesiology harkened back to in Luther was his emphasis on "love" working out from faith, and finding its focus among neighbors in service—free from all, servant of all. The "priesthood of all believers" is not about individualism but a turning to others. For Calvin, the issue is solidified in the marks of the Church. Word and sacrament (as Luther put it), clearly visible elements, now had the added mark of "discipline," the ordering of the church's life for the sake of consistent moral purpose and obedience. What is specific to Liberal Protestantism is how this well-known move is described in terms of *sociality*, rather than of moral or obediential purity and faithfulness. With "sociality" or "community" at the center of Protestant life, there comes a new sense of personal vocation tied to the larger commonwealth: work, service, business, use of excess money for reinvestment, and the search for an ever more inclusively networked community among humankind.

If this doesn't sound very much like a theology of the Church, that would be to misunderstand it. This is *precisely* the theological basis of much twentieth-century mainline Protestant ecclesial life. The Christian Church exists in order to infuse and uphold the larger social life of Christian individuals together—in local communities, in larger ones, and finally in international ones. This is the early Christian notion of the Church as the "soul of the world" in a particular form,[9] and it underlies many contemporary liberal *and* conservative evangelical views of the Church.

---

9. Mathetes, *Epistle to Diognetus*, ch. 6.

Church

Pentecostals

Pentecostalism is almost wholly a twentieth-century movement, now widely established as such around the world in the twenty-first century, making up almost 15 percent of global Christianity. On a basic level, it is a movement rather than an ecclesial reality, founded on the experience of a specific act of God in time, ordering new life by the Holy Spirit through a determined historical outpouring of divine life. But as with all Christian forms of life, the Church lurks below and orders human experience conclusively. On an ecclesial level, furthermore, there is no reason to place Pentecostals outside of Congregationalist / Free Church ecclesiology. But the peculiar growth of Pentecostalism suggests that one should at least try to identify certain distinctives in order to see if they have ecclesiological significance.

There are three historical elements or dynamics from which flow various Pentecostal theologies. If nothing else, these color the general Protestant trajectories across the board in the twentieth and twenty-first centuries, at least on a broader global front. The first element, the press for democratic political structures, was already at work in aspects of the sixteenth-century Reformation, and can be associated with several early Protestant leaders like Nikolaus Storch and Melchior Hoffman. In nineteenth-century America, however, "democracy" was a culturally-influenced value, both demanded and responsively embraced in religious spheres as much as anywhere. Christian churches, especially in the area of authenticating (and hence authoritative) religious experience, had begun to democratize themselves through new revival and holiness movements, which first sprang up within existing denominations and then led out of them. Pentecostalism, founded on the specific experiences of the Holy Spirit at work in a believer though visible signs, is predicated on this democratic thrust not only sociologically but theologically, as the early racially-integrated and gender-recalibrated Pentecostal congregations stressed in their self-understandings.

Second, the search to embody an individually liberative power has characterized the spread of Christianity since at least the late nineteenth century. Mission and the alleviation of poverty through individual transformation have been linked, and those churches where this link has been stressed have grown rapidly, as every demographic study shows. The transformative work of the Spirit has had its explicit fruit in the elimination of alcohol abuse, reengaged employment and labor, reordered familial existence, and a general material uplift. The so-called "prosperity gospel" of later twentieth-century Pentecostalism is directly related to this.

Third, cultural pluralism and then globalization have been embraced by Pentecostal openness to synthetic and even syncretistic approaches to common life as one sometimes sees in some of the African Independent Churches like the Aladura Pentecostals out of Nigeria. This is especially true in Pentecostal churches outside the West, in the growing areas of the Global South.

Culturally, these three elements are definitive of Pentecostal character—which is one reason that Charismatic Christians within existing structured denominations should not be numbered among Pentecostals. Ecclesiologically, however, these three key historical elements are merely adaptive ingredients within a general Protestant Congregationalist ecclesial outlook. They tell us nothing about "the Church" beyond the principles of general Protestantism. There are large Pentecostal denominations—e.g., the Assemblies of God—that are organized in almost every way like other Protestant groups, just as there are many individual and unaffiliated Pentecostal congregations led by leaders or pastors who have emerged according to particular histories. As a movement, furthermore, Pentecostalism derives from and has spread through the missionary work of Free Church Protestantism. The forms of its worship and the consequences of its activities are specific but highly variable. It would be a mistake to make the "experiential" aspects of Pentecostalism central to its ecclesiology, as some have tried to do, raising a special interest with "the presence of God" or the "Holy Spirit" to a theological claim. After all, *all* religious life is experiential in a fundamental way, and "the presence of God"—as Holy Spirit or otherwise—cannot be denied simply by defining it in this or that specific fashion. All Christian ecclesiologies are in a basic fashion "pneumatic." Rather, what is key to Pentecostalism is the *framework* of experience that is in place: it is self-legitimating. Since only the individual can ultimately determine the Spirit's work, however much the community may observe, the individual's experience can then lead to a range of affective realities in play within the Church. But this framework was always available to Protestant thinking.

Shaped by Time

All this may be interesting. Laid out briefly as above, it is probably mostly confusing. After all, for many today, all we see is the Church *without* a history at all. The twentieth century, at any rate, has muted the negative aspects of the accumulated ecclesial features in the eyes of many. But while various Catholic and Protestant aspects of the Church seem no longer off-putting, it is unclear how to integrate them. Individuals join churches for a variety of reasons today, but they are all reasons each has more or less sorted through on his or her own, without the benefit of some common standard for evaluating the Church. "The Church" is simply a group of individuals who freely gather together as Christ-believers. It is no more than that. The various ecclesiological configurations associated with each of these traditions outlined above are today really diverse chosen orderings of these gatherings. They are not on the face of it organically-derived expressions of some deeper "thing."

Then is the Church loved? And if she is loved, is she not the one whom "they smote and wounded" as she wandered through the city (Song 5:7 KJV)? Thus, we cannot escape the Church's history. Ecclesiologies today—as in any day—"bear the marks" of the Church's or churches' various historical experiences of self-distinguishing against enemies: antagonisms, assertions, exclusions, flights, rebellions, specific renewals. Christians have recognized the difficulty in which this puts them with respect to "finding the truth" about the Church, especially when dispute about that truth is rampant. The "primitivist" instinct that has led many over the years—Catholic and Protestant both—to "go back to the Apostles" to find the true shape of the Church has been nurtured by this recognition of marred ecclesiologies. Medieval monks sought to reform their monasteries by living "the apostolic life" anew, and people like St. Francis caught something of this vision. Puritans, most famously, wanted to get "back to the New Testament church," and studiously examined the details of their contemporary churches for elements that needed to be discarded. The modern Charismatic movement looked for the renewal of the Holy Spirit's original gifts to the apostles. Does the oldest get us to the truest? Catholicism (including Orthodoxy and Roman Catholicism) is historically earlier than Protestantism; but it is not without its deep and formative scars, some of which (as I will argue later) constrict its movement and, in any case, formed Protestantism in its mirror image. We cannot get to a Church *before* her subjection to history!

Christians who recite the Nicene Creed (though many do not!), will point to the "one, holy, catholic, and apostolic church" the Creed confesses as at least some ground for ecclesial understanding. These words at least must be explicators somehow of this gathering of believers. But they will be so only to the degree that their ecclesiological import can be grasped in terms of a dynamics and historical reality that today's church members often shy away from. "And if one asks him, 'What are these wounds on your back?' he will say, 'The wounds I received in the house of my friends'" (Zech 13:6 RSV). The Church is something that exists in time, subject to time's contours, and ordered by the roles that individuals and their cohorts in time have played. People have come together in certain ways, for certain reasons, and have explained themselves according to certain reasonings; and these in turn have developed and/or dissolved similarly. The question is, "What is going on in all of this that we can and *must* call 'Church'?"

Further Reading

Afanasiev, Nicholas. *The Church of the Holy Spirit*. Translated by Vitaly Permiakov. Notre Dame: University of Notre Dame Press, 2007.

Bulgakov, Sergius. *The Bride of the Lamb*. Translated by Boris Jakim. Grand Rapids: Eerdmans, 2002.

Calvin, John. *Institutes of the Christian Religion*. Edited by John T. McNeill. Louisville: Westminster John Knox, 1960.

Daniel, David P. "Luther on the Church." In *The Oxford Handbook of Martin Luther's Theology*, edited by Robert Kolb et al., 333–49. Oxford: Oxford University Press, 2014.

Dorrien, Gary J. *The Making of American Liberal Theology: Imagining Progressive Religion, 1805–1900*. Louisville: Westminster John Knox, 2001.

Gignac, J. "Anathema." In *The Catholic Encyclopedia*. New York: Robert Appleton. http://www.newadvent.org/cathen/01455e.htm.

Haight, Roger. *Christian Community in History*. 3 vols. New York: Continuum, 2004–8.

Jakim, Boris, and Robert Bird, eds. *On Spiritual Unity: A Slavophile Reader*. Hudson, NY: Lindisfarne, 1998.

"Joint Catholic-Orthodox Declaration of His Holiness Pope Paul VI and the Ecumenical Patriarch Athenagoras I, December 7, 1965." 1965. http://w2.vatican.va/content/paul-vi/en/speeches/1965/documents/hf_p-vi_spe_19651207_common-declaration.html.

Kärkkäinen, Veli-Matti. *An Introduction to Ecclesiology: Ecumenical, Historical & Global Perspectives*. Downers Grove: InterVarsity, 2009.

Kimbrough, S. T., Jr., ed. *Orthodox and Wesleyan Ecclesiology*. Crestwood, NY: St. Vladimir's Seminary Press, 2007.

Mathetes. *Epistle to Diognetus*. Translated by Alexander Roberts and James Donaldson in *Ante-Nicene Fathers*, vol. 1, edited by Alexander Roberts et al. Buffalo, NY, 1885.

McNeill, John T. *Unitive Protestantism: The Ecumenical Spirit and its Persistent Expression*. 2nd ed. Richmond: John Knox, 1964.

Philaret. "A Protest to Patriarch Athenagoras on the Lifting of the Anathemas of 1054." http://orthodoxinfo.com/ecumenism/philaret_lifting.aspx.

Church

Discussion Questions

1. What does it say about the Church that there are various traditions—Orthodox, Catholic, Protestant (and various kinds of Protestant)—that describe the Church differently?

2. What does it mean that, for Eastern Orthodox, the Church is "given" rather than "argued for"?

3. If Catholicism acts out its life in a way that is very similar to Orthodoxy, in what way is the Catholic understanding of the Church nonetheless distinctive?

4. Protestantism comes in many forms: is there anything that holds together various Protestant views of the Church? What elements distinguish these views one from another?

3

Talking about the Church

The Possibility of a People

To know what is going on when so many churches refer to themselves as Church, we must know what we are talking about when the word "Church" is used. I have already indicated one area where talking about the Church raises some difficulties. Is the Church a single "thing"? If it is, how is it that individuals can be said to be a "part" of the Church? Is the Church a "people," that is, a group of individual persons? How then can it be described as a single person, such as a bride to whom Christ Jesus is betrothed? Finally, if it is a single person of some kind, how is it that we can speak of there being "many churches" in the plural, some of which are themselves made up of numerous smaller groups of "local churches," who may in fact have hurt one another?

We are used to navigating these varying ways of using the word "church" without thinking too much about it. But there are times when such an unthinking use of the word in so many different ways becomes difficult, even hard to square logically. So, for instance, Mormons call themselves "The Church of Jesus Christ of Latter-Day Saints." But in many places, local councils of Christian Churches—say in a given city—refuse to consider the Mormon Church "really" a church at all. (I am now going to move to using "church" in the lowercase, in order simply to indicate that in practice people *do* disagree as to what the word "church" refers to. As long as our discussion is about such disagreement, I will continue to use the lowercase.) What does "really" mean in such a context? Some would say that "really" being a church has to do with the way baptism is done. If baptism is done "in the name of the Father, the Son, and the Holy Spirit," then the group into which persons are thus baptized can be called a true "church."

Roman Catholics, however, do not officially consider Protestant churches "real churches," and when they are speaking technically, they prefer to call Protestant groups "ecclesial [church-related?] communities." This is a way of saying that Protestants may organize themselves into church-*like* groups or communities, and they may even have certain characteristics that the true church may have (like baptism), but this does not amount to *being* the church. Catholics (like Mormons in this case) reserve the capitalized "Church" for themselves. Still, if they address Protestant churches, Catholics will usually include the word "church" in that title, as when addressing or referring to, say, "the Methodist Church." Many Protestants, on the other hand, are happy to use the term "church" as applying to this or that group—whether Mormons or Episcopalians—but they may claim that the teaching and practice of such groups is not really Christian, and hence "church" itself is not a significant descriptor for their character, one way or the other. Finally, some will be forthright in saying that there is such a thing as the one true "Church," and that all these other groupings variously called "church" or "churches" are either a part of that bigger Church, or are, each in their own way and to different degrees, reflective of that Church, if only vaguely.

When one faces the very complex use of the term "church," one begins to realize that the meaning of the word is perhaps more arcane, perhaps even more confused, than our everyday speech might lead us to imagine. Given the struggles among Christians over "the Church," this is perhaps not surprising. Beliefs, practices, and attitudes can all be used to distinguish the meaning of "church," but these elements are often applied differently and in a different manner among Christians, and not always in a consistent fashion. When I was first ordained a deacon and then priest in the American Episcopal Church, I went to work for several years in the Episcopal (and then, as they changed their name, Anglican) Church of Burundi in Africa. Was it the "same" church? In what way? According to what criteria? While in Burundi, I initially studied and then often worked side by side with Roman Catholic priests and nuns. Some of them said we were "different churches," but most said that we were really part of "one Church," and I was often invited to share in their eucharistic services. Thirty years later, this is no longer said or done by most Roman Catholics in relation to Anglicans like myself. What has changed? Can we make sense of Ephesians

5 in such contexts, such that it is possible to confuse who is the "bride" at different moments of our lives?

At this point, I want to work through some simple questions about what the word "church" can mean in a common-sense way. My interest here is not really theological. But simple usage, as I have tried to point out, raises many theological issues, at least implicitly. Common contemporary discussions of the church, from "Communion Ecclesiology" to "The Missional Church," often move to their theology without making explicit their fundamental assumptions about the word itself; and sometimes these assumptions are held in inconsistent ways. Even if we end up accepting such inconsistencies as necessary to the task of thinking about the Church, we should at least try to be aware of where some of them lie.

Translating Church

The origins of the English word "church" are contested. The *Oxford English Dictionary*'s etymological discussion points to different possibilities, but asserts that the most likely root was an actual Greek word from the fourth century, *kyriakon*—something "of the Lord"—which applied at first to church buildings.[1] The term entered northern European usage, e.g., Gothic, through transliteration and wended its way into becoming the Germanic *kirche* and finally the English "church." In shifting from material referents like buildings, "church" quickly took up the more theologically expansive semantic elements of the term *ekklesia*, which many Romantic languages like French (*église*) had adopted as their main term from the Latin.

Not everyone accepts the consensus decreed by the *Oxford English Dictionary*. Perhaps "church" derives from a Latin term related to the *circus* or circled assembly, which was applied to pagan worship. Since the sixteenth century, much theological freight has been invested in distinguishing the word "church" from its original New Testament Greek referent, *ekklesia*; and the debate still rages, especially in Evangelical and Messianic Jewish groups. *Ekklesia* in the New Testament, we are told by some of the dissenters from the *OED*, refers to a gathered people, not an institution, not to a building or a worship format—something that "church" may etymologically and misleadingly imply if the *kyriakon* origins are dismissed. The "people" vs. "institution" argument remains lively![2]

---

1. *Oxford English Dictionary*, 2nd ed., s.v. "Church, n.1 and adj" (3:199–203).
2. See, for instance, the Yahweh's Assembly article "Why We Are an Assembly Not

But etymology is not always the most useful approach to understanding a word's meaning, and it is certainly not very illuminating when dealing with a word whose own semantic range has been enlarged and made dizzyingly complex through centuries of variegated usage and then debate. Does trying to translate a biblical word into a foreign language shackle that word to the meanings of the new language's adapted contexts? Missionary communication and formational conversion have faced this question frequently, and the matter of how to translate "church" is revealing on this score.

In general, translations of the word used in scriptural or liturgical mission—let us say, from the New Testament Greek *ekklesia* or the Latin *ecclesia* or the English *church*—fall into one of two categories. In many cases, the term is simply transliterated—as, according to the theory, "church" itself was transliterated from *kyriakon*, or the Latin *ecclesia* from the Greek *ekkelsia*. Thus, the Latin *ecclesia* became, as we said, *église* in French; or *eliza* in Basque; or even the Farsi *kilysa* or Bengali *girja*. Transliteration like this means that one doesn't really have to explain the *meaning* of the term by finding a new term for it in the local language. One only need associate it with the practices of, in this case, the Christian missionaries and their witness to their faith. The decision (or lack of decision) to do this parallels cases where, as in Japan, Catholic missionaries decided after some initial missteps not to use a vernacular word for God, but simply to use the transliterated word from the Latin, *Deus*. (Today, similarly, some use the transliterated *Goddo*.) Words like the Hausa *coci* (from the English "church") are transliterated loanwords, which can be filled in as required. Of course, one often "fills in" an otherwise incomprehensible word according to a range of influences that are no less culturally impregnated than are the vernacular translations.

Besides transliteration, then, there are vernacular *translations* of "church" into evangelized linguistic cultures. These translations cluster around describing what "happens" from a local perspective with respect to Christians and their churches. This usually relates to a generalized analogy with practices already understood in the local culture. Thus, most vernacular translations of "church" point to the "prayers" or "worship" that takes place in or through the church: Hawaiian *pule*, for instance,

---

a Church," http://www.yaim.org/web/index.php/literatureside/things-not-in-scripture/110-why-we-are-an-assembly-not-a-church. Karl Barth engaged in this debate himself; see *Dogmatics in Outline*, 141.

or Tagalog *simbahan*. Obviously, this raises theological questions. Is the prayer of the Christian of the same general category as prayer to local spirits? Or of those used by Muslim believers in their mosques? Some translations, e.g., the Farsi *sijda* used for both Muslim and Christian places of worship, or the Nahuatl *teopantli* (a traditional temple), could at least give this impression. Sometimes the description of Christian practices associated with "church" is oddly given in the vernacular version. The Navajo *eeneishoodi bikin* is a phrase for church that describes people dragging around heavy robes or vestments. Many East Asian translations—Japanese *kyoukai*, Mandarin *Jiao*, Vietnamese *giao*—use a word for church that refers to "teaching." But which is more central: prayer or pedagogy? Finally, there are those vernacular translations that simply describe the "assembling" function of the *ekklesia*, e.g., in the Kirundi term *ishengero*, or the Arabic *kanisa*. Yet even this kind of simple descriptive translation, which some would approve of as getting close to the original Greek meaning of *ekklesia*, could have its problems initially, since a term could be associated, e.g., in Burundi, not with just any gathering but with particular political exercises like those at the royal court.

There are no translations, therefore, or even transliterations, that are semantically innocent in the end. Still, such terms are also not destinies. What is important is how the terms are in fact applied and used over time. Every English-speaking Christian has a set of unconscious associations with the term "church." Among Catholics and Evangelicals today, the use of "church" has followed sometimes divergent trajectories of meaning that carry with them whole histories of application and unconscious association. Catholics can still speak of "mother Church," which doubtless conveys a range of theological, pastoral, and affective meanings. Evangelicals can speak of the "believer's church," connoting not just the church as a container of diverse kinds of faith, but the existence and ever-present danger of counterfeit and "unbelieving" churches. Where Protestants do not use the Nicene Creed regularly, let alone authoritatively, then phrases like "I believe in the one, holy, catholic, and apostolic church" will resonate only faintly, if at all, with their reading of the scriptural term, or in its deployment in prayer or witness.

Thus, whatever the etymology or original inventions of "church," the word has *come to mean* a number of often divergent things. And even if Catholics and Protestants—and Orthodox, we should note—have taken quite different paths at times in their understanding of the word, the word itself has also acquired a reach and depth of meaning that no one group can actually control. Thus, in English "church" actually came to mean the same as religion itself, indeed *any* religion. As early as the ninth century, "church" in its younger Teutonic articulation could be used for any religion's building, and consistently later on "the church" could refer to mosques, synagogues and pagan places of prayer. By the late sixteenth century, one translation of Livy's *Histories* applies the term to the religion of the ancient Romans (their "religion and church matters"). Finally, in the nineteenth century, "Church" could apply to *any* religion that had some kind of organizational claim. Today we still speak of people who are "de-churched," as referring to their fall from religious faith altogether.

Scriptural Churches

If this seems a bit confusing, it is meant to be. Furthermore, simply going back to the Bible to sort it all out isn't as easy as one might suppose. There have been numerous studies of how the Scriptures define the church, but it is not self-evident that we even know what we are to look for in the Bible to pursue such a study. Do we look for specific words themselves that have been either transliterated or translated into our English word "church"? As I have indicated, words gain their meaning from context and usage, not just from the form of their vocalization. Or do we engage clusters of words and their associations? If that is so, where do we find these associations? In narratives or in didactic claims?

As it turns out, the lexical place of "church" in the New Testament is central, but it is not overwhelming. *Ekklesia* appears about 118 times, although only twice in the Gospels. By contrast, "kingdom" (as in "kingdom of God") or *basileia* occurs more than 150 times, mostly (but not exclusively) in the Gospels. The notorious judgment of the modernist Catholic critic Alfred Loisy is, in part, based on this simple statistical reversal: "Jésus annonçait le Royaume, et c'est l'Église qui est venue"—"Jesus came preaching the kingdom, and what arrived was the church."[3] For Loisy, this was the mark of a certain religious degradation that followed Jesus. But it also assumes some kind of tension if not opposition between the church and the kingdom of God. In fact, the relation between the two concepts continues to be the subject of much careful discussion. Still, it is hardly clear whether

---

3. Loisy, *L'Évangile et l'église*, 110–12.

lexical frequency and focused location in this or that part of the biblical text (Gospel vs. Epistles) should carry theological weight, and if so, what kind.

There are, in any case, other New Testament terms that at first glance ought to exert certain semantic pressures on the meaning of "church," and in fact have done so both tacitly and explicitly over the centuries. Thus, *laos* or "people" occurs around 150 times. Many of these uses are not seemingly references to the followers of Christ, but some of them clearly are, especially when they translate Old Testament references to God's own chosen. Hence, in Romans 15:10, Paul takes up the Greek translation of Deuteronomy 32:43, "Rejoice, oh nations, with his people!" "Nations" or "Gentiles" (*ethne* in the Greek, *goyim* in the Hebrew) is coordinated with "people" (*laos* in Greek, *am* in Hebrew). How important is the notion of "God's people" for understanding the church? Not only, as worship leaders like to tell us, is the word "liturgy" derived from *laos*—the "work of the people"—but the notion of a "people" is clearly linked to a key biblical semantic context for the church, albeit a knotted one, that is "Israel." Israel itself is used about 70 times in the New Testament, although rarely in places where the church is being referred to. Still, the two concepts are linked here and there (as in Revelation 7:4 and 21:12, and perhaps in Galatians 6:6). Furthermore, Israel seems to lurk as the unmentioned reference in so many New Testament quotations of the Hebrew Scriptures, now used as fulfillment texts for the present (e.g., Rom 9:25–26, where prophecies applied to Israel are now given meaning in the present context of Christian believers). Speaking of "believers," what are we to make of the fact that the term "disciple" (*mathetes*) appears almost 270 times (that is to say, more than twice as frequently as the word *ekklesia*), yet exclusively in the Gospels and Acts?

This direction of discussion, of course, leads us straight into the Old Testament. Many commentators have dwelt on the fact that *ekklesia* in Greek translates the Hebrew *qahal* or *edah*—the gathering or congregation of Israel—which together occur almost 275 times. The Greek *synagoge* was, in any case, used even more frequently than *ekklesia* in these contexts, although the nuances distinguishing the choice are less clear. The English word "nation" translates an extremely common Hebrew word—*goy*—that is used almost 560 times in the Old Testament, almost always for non-Jewish peoples, yet occasionally for Israel herself, one "nation" among many, though chosen by God as a "holy" nation (e.g., Exod 19:6), and joined to the "nations" at large in sharing Abraham's blessing (Gen 12:2 and 17:4–6). The English word "nation" here is sometimes used as a synonym for "tribe" or "family," which also have distinct Hebrew and Greek words. As for Israel herself, the stand-alone word is used over 2,500 times, and the phrase "children of Israel" (*ben Israel*) around 600 times. One could add patronymics (a name taken from an ancestor) like the national term "Jacob," or even (in the New Testament) "Christian." (And of course "Christ" appears about 570 times in the New Testament, though "Spirit" occurs frequently too, as does the "law" and the "commandment.")

It is true that, in the shadow of these multiple and agglomerated usages, the church as a distinct term seems to fade a bit; or perhaps it simply gains depth, texture, and takes on a profile that moves in many directions. For looming large, if almost always contextually placed, are larger semantic clusters and narratives, so that we must ask if it is even *possible* to speak of the church apart from the persons and stories of Jacob or Moses, of the rise and fall of Jerusalem, of the Law's form and reach, of promises and warnings from God, of Assyria and Babylon, or of Rome and Athens, weeping women and yearning brides; or apart from the lively images often used of Israel and Jesus' followers: vineyards, whores, wives, warriors, sheep, children, branches, a body of Christ, temples, and the like.

Divine Word, Divine Act

I am trying to indicate how difficult it is even to identify what kind of word "church" really is, just in biblical terms. Thus, one reason why there has been such a struggle over the "church" is that we are uncertain or at least inconsistent as to whether we are referring to a "thing" at all. Even if we are referring to something specific, we are unsure whether it is something that can only be grasped in the context of, say, the scriptural narrative in its richness, or whether it is not so much abstract as non-contextually ordered, something that can be picked out of a narrative and identified apart from it.

If, for instance, we assert that the church is "the redeemed people of God, elected of God, the Bride of Christ," what kind of "thing" are we referring to, in relation to other things that we can indicate with our words? There is, on this topic, a common distinction that theorists have made between "concrete" and "abstract" nouns or objects. This is a very modern (not ancient) method for approaching nouns, often associated with the German logician and mathematician Gottlob Frege. Frege worked out his distinction between "concrete" and "abstract" by centering on the status of arithmetical numbers. He argued that such numbers were not simply mental ideas (say, articulating to oneself a feeling of being hungry), nor were they material objects (like cats, rocks, or automobiles). Rather, these numbers were constitutive realities bound up in the very nature of all things—hence the possibility of a mathematical science that was universal. Frege wanted to call arithmetical numbers real "objects," but "abstract" ones. The actual notion of "abstract" is that there is, as it were, a *third* "kind" of object other than physical or mental.[4]

Perhaps this is rather hard to get a handle on. Popular degradations of the distinction have confused matters by simply contrasting concrete as physical with "abstract" as mental or conceptual. The twofold distinction may be simple, but it doesn't do nearly as much work as it should. One popular online writing guide, for instance, gives as an example of a "concrete noun" the nation of Turkey.[5] But nations, even if they take in specific geographical areas, are in many ways quite abstract. Turkey itself is an odd notion historically, having come into existence as a nation only recently, and having done so in ways that are contested by some of its own "concrete" citizens. Hence, people have different "ideas" as to what Turkey actually is in a geographical sense—they blow people up on the basis of these different ideas—let alone a historical or cultural sense.

Another way to approach the special character of the term "church" is simply to call it a "proper noun," which is a name of something that could be concrete (my friend "Sam"), or is a specific mental concept that refers to a real or imaginative place, person, or object that has a specific role in a narrative. "Turkey," in this case, works better as a "proper noun" than it does as a concrete or abstract object. Still, part of the role of a proper noun in a narrative would be to take on one or the other of these kinds of objectivity, and here we are still stymied in trying to describe the church. Certainly, saying that the church is a "proper noun"—a name in a narrative—does help bring to the fore the way the church is bound up with a scriptural reality or a history of Christian believers. But it does not clarify whether, in that story, the church is a concrete object or a mental idea.

In fact, the church does not fit into these now standard ways of talking about words that relate to objects. The church is neither like a pile of rocks nor an idea a person might have in their mind. What actually constitutes the church—unlike, say, numbers—are concrete individuals, *their* own ideas,

---

4. On all this, see Lewis, *On the Plurality of Worlds*.

5. "Concrete versus Abstract Nouns," http://www.write.com/writing-guides/general-writing/mechanics/concrete-versus-abstract-nouns.

and whole sets of events bound up with the Christian Scriptures, which refer to a real people as well as to images and ideas. Finally, the church is tied to a reality that includes all of the above, but in the fashion of a divine being, that is, Jesus Christ. The church is a proper noun or proper name, but it is a name whose referent takes in other proper names. The meanings of those names move in all kinds of directions of reference, including in a direction that finally transcends the very character of human language, thought, and objectivity itself, that is, in the direction of God. This one fact indicates that the word "church" is unique: God is the foundation of the proper names that constitute the church.

When in the early sixteenth century William Tyndale came out with his English translation of the New Testament, he riled readers such as Thomas More with his use of the word "congregation" for the Greek *ekklesia*. In explaining himself, Tyndale noted (as we have done) several uses of the word "church." There is first, he says, the meaning of a church *building*, where prayers to God are said and the truth of Christ taught. Tyndale's reformist worry is that, where church buildings are places of popularly incomprehensible (i.e., Latin) speech, no one really knows what is going on, and they become the locales of wooden obligation (that is, "works"):

> Where now we hear but voices without significations, and buzzing, howling, and crying, as it were the hallooing of foxes, or baitings of bears . . . by reason whereof we be fallen into such ignorance, that we know of the mercy and promises, which are in Christ nothing at all."[6]

Second, Tyndale explains that the word "church" can be used more institutionally, to refer to its bureaucratic officials—popes, bishops, clergy, chancellors, monks. The problem here is that the word "church" has become associated with the "thousand names of blasphemy and of hypocrisies, and as many sundry fashions of disguisings."[7] If we think of church in this way, and with these associations, it begins to smell foul. Finally, Tyndale lays out the third meaning of "church" in his time: "a congregation: a multitude or a company gathered together in one, of all degrees of people."[8] For Tyndale, the highest or most theologically rich meaning of church is this one, as it

---

6. Tyndale, *Answer to Sir Thomas More's Dialogue*, 11.
7. Ibid., 12.
8. Ibid.

applies to "the whole multitude of all them that receive the name of Christ to believe in him."[9]

Tyndale grants that the word "congregation," like "church," can refer to gatherings of unbelievers, of Turks and hypocrites and evil-doers. But its value as an English translation of *ekklesia* is that it focuses precisely on the *multitude* first, on what binds them together (e.g., a comprehensible language), and on their common purposes or faith (whether it be for good or ill). Tyndale is well aware that this congregational understanding of church can and often does go beyond a local gathering, and reaches to the very "elect . . . in whose hearts God hath written his law with his holy Spirit" with "faith of the mercy that is in Christ Jesu [*sic*] our Lord."[10] But even here, the term "congregation" is helpful, he argues: it underscores the clear relationship of peoplehood and God, or of persons and their common bonds with the divine Person who has created them as such. That relationship, furthermore, is given in the rich details of divine history described in Scripture. Everything Tyndale wrote was connected with this conviction.

Despite the outcry over Tyndale's translation—and by and large the Authorized Version of the King James translation preferred to return to the use of "church" for *ekklesia*—his underlying intuitions were in accord with the great Christian tradition that preceded him. All the great contestations over the character of the church at the time of the Reformation mirrored, after all, earlier disputes about the church: Montanism in the second and third century (is the church determined by a moment in time which is specially graced by revelation?), Augustine and the Donatists in the fourth century (is the church determined by the moral purity of its leaders and members?), and, paradigmatically even, Christians and Judaism (that is, Jewish Israel) from the second century on. Theologians sometimes interpret these disputes in terms of diverse "ecclesiologies" (or "theologies of the church"), which is true to a point. But such evaluations can obscure the fact that each party to these disputes tended to have a common understanding of the actual dynamics that constituted the church, ones in fact shared with Tyndale's Congregationalist framework. For all, the issue at stake was not "what is the meaning of the word 'church'? and is the church this kind of thing or that?" Rather, the question was "who are the people of the church, and how has God ordered or gathered their lives in accordance with the Scripture?"

9. Ibid.
10. Ibid., 13.

How is it possible not to know the difference? Today we may choose to write "church" in the lower case, as a simple code that we are referring to this or that concrete group rather than to some transcendent reality. In theory, we would not capitalize the term for such a concrete group (e.g., this congregation *is* "the Church"!) unless we could be sure that this group's gathering, in its persons, motives, and being, is in fact concretely "true" over and against all other claims. To be sure, we capitalize proper names for churches—"the Methodist Church," "the Lutheran Church." But this is a matter of address, no more. For all other matters, when we are making broader judgments, we leave ecclesial reality in the lower case, perhaps because we are uncertain or we don't want to give offense by choosing one capitalized Church among all the others. But what if we *were* certain? Could we ever claim that our own (personal) church is also *the* true church, so that we could use "Church," capitalized, as truly referring to *us*?

The only way we could make this claim is on the basis of rightly perceiving the action of God when it comes to an actual "divine gathering," so as to create and sustain a divinely ordered people. The difference between a "true" and a "false" church is located in the action of God. When we can say that God has done such and such with this body of people, and that such and such is according to the purposes of God so that this people might be *God's* people, then we can call that "the Church," and not simply a "church" among contested and even perhaps self-evidently wicked churches. God's choice, action, and purpose make the difference. This was Tyndale's point, for it means that talking about the Church can only take place within the broader discussion of God's concrete purposes in time. That is why all Christian traditions in the past have asserted, finally, that these purposes are laid out in Scripture's complex textual narrative and discourse. It is also why departures from such traditions—including Montanism or Gnosticism—have been labeled heresies by virtually all other Christians. These groups claimed that God's action in constituting the church was discernible through means other than the common gift of the Scriptures.

Obviously, this common orientation has not quelled disputes, in this case over the Scriptures themselves and their meaning. Nonetheless, one basic element that holds all Christian ecclesial attitudes together is the claim that there is no Church to be known apart from the fullness of the scriptural witness in its whole, as it describes the people whom God has formed and led, promised and fulfilled. God gathers a people; they are God's people; and Scripture tells us what that means. The church is a congregation; the congregation is Church. But Church is Israel, People, Vine, Obedient, Redeemed, Body, Bride.

The Church as a Divinely Created People

We can draw from this discussion about words a few directive hints upon which to build a more theological picture of the Church.

First, the clearest way to engage the Church is through the human reality of peoplehood. From the perspective of theology, this means that we must make critical use of the category of "corporateness," where the notion of a given people is encountered as an objective entity. Tyndale was surely right in his intuitions here, even if the word he chose to apply has now itself lost its semantic dynamism. But in his context, the English word "congregation" got at this aspect of corporate peoplehood in a way that was quite specific, concrete, and thus objective, avoiding approaches to the Church that were initially founded on abstractive concepts.

The problem with "congregation" today is simply that it has become too constricted, too domesticated and geographically and socially limited. People today use "parish" and "congregation" as synonyms, for instance. But as sociologists have shown, nineteenth-century understandings of the Church, just in those places where congregational life was quite vibrant (as in the young United States), shifted into frameworks that took in wide spaces, openness of engagement, and finally rapidly malleable organization. The Church, in this context that is still with us both in America and now elsewhere around the globe, is bound more to a "movement" of people, that is, to people "on the move," than to local gatherings. The rise of missionary societies and their work, conversionary networks, and portable formational frameworks like the Alpha series and larger renewal conferences have not obscured the reality of the Church as a people, but have rather characterized that people in ways that are less geographically specific. "Congregation" is a helpful word. But "Church" is better.

Second, the Church's corporate character should not be understood in terms of purely human objectivity, but must somehow manifest the unique way in which God's life is logically prior to a people's life. As we will see, the word "nation," while it will figure prominently in our discussion of the Church, cannot be understood in purely political terms. If it were, it would subject the meaning of the Church to some of the strange semantic uncertainties we have already indicated (e.g., the nation of Turkey), even as it would blur the lines between political ends and their often immoral character and the purposes of God (as has often been the sad case with various versions of "manifest destiny," including those in the United States). It is simply not the case that sociological study could exhaust or even properly expose from the start the Church's actual life. Peoplehood itself is not an uncontested category! Just the opposite. But in the Church's case, the arguments over what constitutes a people are peculiar. They are based on the historical form of God's doing something to multiple persons—a "multitude"—and then on the apprehension of a person's or persons' relationship to that divine doing.

Here is where the contextual character of "church" in the New Testament becomes so significant. It is not possible to understand "church" except as it is located within the larger scriptural set of forms—narrative and non-narrative, Old and New Testaments both—that mark out the canonical "purpose" of God as given in God's actions. Peoplehood in this case is personally coordinated, something that has been frequently identified within non-Christian understandings of social polities, as when a "kingdom" is dependent on a founder or ruler, who is its "king." Take away the monarch, and there is no more monarchy. With respect to the Church, this kind of popular constitution that is bound up with a person is given exclusively through the reality of God: God creates and leads a people, and that people is called God's Church. Deny God, and one has denied the Church.

If one were to ask then, "What is God doing?" the answer will always (if not exhaustively) be "Church" in some fashion. That means that the preaching of John the Baptist, for instance, or the Fall of Jerusalem, or the Temple of Solomon, or the killing of the Amalekites, are all "about the Church," because they are scriptural determinants of the meaning of how we speak of God's actions with respect to his people. They are "Church-forming," insofar as the purposes of God frame these persons, within the peoples of the earth, according to some particular form, in relation to which the "Church" is articulated as a people.

Finally, that articulation is always "emergent" within the context of the doings of God. The Church is not obviously a stable object, whose aspects and facets can be definitively described in an absolute fashion. This is key to understanding the character of ecclesial contestation, onto which this first chapter has sought to open a small window. If one asks "What is the Church?" and if the answer one gets is "What God is doing in having a people that is God's," then there is never a *single* object that one can identify as fully describing "Church" itself, because one could never identify the *one* thing that God is doing. The best one can do in that direction of definition is to discern and point to transtemporal realities, the describable "sets" of concrete persons and their complex locations within space and time with respect to the Church, in a way that is somehow ordered to God. Here is where, perhaps, it makes sense in talking about the Church to speak of singular forms such as Scripture provides in its variegated imagery. Since God is, in theological terms, the creator and sustainer, the sovereign and director of the Church, then the transtemporal forms that describe various sets of popular ordering will somehow reflect the very personal character of God's own self. In this way, the emergent reality of the Church, from a human point of view—and this is the Church's contestable aspect—must always be ordered to a personality (bride, spouse, Israel, flock, vine), as each relates to its being formed by a single Person (God).

In the next chapter, we will begin a more theologically focused discussion of the basis of these conclusions. The Church is a people formed by God according to Scripture, and we now need to explore what "peoplehood" might mean in such a context.

Further Reading

Barth, Karl. *Dogmatics in Outline*. Translated by G. T. Thomson. London: SCM, 1949.

"Concrete versus Abstract Nouns." http://www.write.com/writing-guides/general-writing/mechanics/concrete-versus-abstract-nouns.

Congregation for the Doctrine of the Faith. *Dominus Iesus*. Rome, 2000. http://www.vatican.va/roman_curia/congregations/cfaith/documents/rc_con_cfaith_doc_20000806_dominus-iesus_en.html.

Lewis, David. *On the Plurality of Worlds*. Oxford: Blackwell, 1986.

Loisy, Alfred. *L'Évangile et l'église*. Paris: Picard, 1902.

Nelson, Samuel, and Philip Gorski. "Conditions of Religious Belonging: Confessionalization, De-Parochialization, and the Euro-American Divergence." *International Sociology* 29.1 (2014) 3–21.

Tyndale, William. *An Answer to Sir Thomas More's Dialogue*. Cambridge: Cambridge University Press, 1850.

Yahweh's Assembly. "Why We Are an Assembly Not a Church." http://www.yaim.org/web/index.php/literatureside/things-not-in-scripture/110-why-we-are-an-assembly-not-a-church.

Church

Discussion Questions

1. What do you think is best the approach to translating the English word "church" into another language that does not already have such a concept? What criteria would you use to evaluate such translations?

2. What words in the Old and New Testaments have been most centrally linked to our English word "church"? Have these links been helpful or illuminating of the truth? What is more important in a scriptural understanding of the "church": individual Hebrew or Greek words, or related clusters of words, narratives, and ideas?

3. Why did William Tyndale prefer the English word "congregation" as the main translation for the biblical word *ekklesia*? What is gained and what is lost in this choice?

4. How does the role of God with respect to the Church distinguish the term from other words that refer to a "people"?

4

Talking about a People

The Possibility of Election

WE HAVE SPENT SOME time uncovering some of the challenges in just using the word "church," despite the fact that the Church is something that Christians love and feel is among the most intimately given elements of their being. "O LORD, I love the habitation of thy house, and the place where thy glory dwells" (Ps 26:8 RSV). As I have emphasized, Catholics and Protestants both have freely declared their love for the Church, even if they have articulated the object differently. The "habitation of thy house" could easily shift for readers of this psalm from a building where prayers are said, analogous to the Jerusalem Temple, to the ordering of the Church's life in its panoply of ministry, to the gathering of those who worship God in truth, and finally even to the body of Christ, the place of divine incarnate tabernacling. All of these were "the Church," and all ranged across and even beyond Tyndale's threefold set of references. Yet all were spoken without guile, and out of profound affection, from Augustine to Charles Spurgeon.

It is curious how the Church, in Christian speech, can move from being a gathered people, to standing as an artful pile of rocks (a building) where a people gather, to being a single person, a body of its own. One could see this as the natural development of linguistic metaphor. But even Protestants wanted to avoid a purely literary explanation for this spectrum of references. After all, Jesus himself compares his own body to the Jerusalem Temple (John 2:21; cf. 1:14) and Paul speaks of individuals being part of a single body of Christ (Rom 12:5; 1 Cor 12:27; Col 1:18). Something different was going on, such that many bodies—let us say Israelites or Christian believers—were literally, if perhaps spiritually, "joined" into a single being. The key element, all agreed, is the work of God—divine agency as itself ordering these forms of the Church. Or, put differently, the Church *is* truly a people who can be a place and a person at the same time, because God makes it so. More fundamentally, the Church is truly a people, only because God makes peoples, and that divine making is what underlines everything a people is.

Peoplehood is thus an aspect of a divine act. This is no longer a modern presupposition, which is precisely why it is hard for contemporary thinkers to grasp the Church as a people of God, and to see how such a people can be accurately described in ways that also go beyond the basic forms of collective character, e.g., as Body of Christ and Bride. Even serious theological attempts at speaking about peoplehood in this way have faced cultural-conceptual difficulties, as I will note in a later chapter with respect to the modern Roman Catholic embrace of the terminology of "people of God" for the Church at Vatican II.

Yet the reality of being a people is embedded in the scriptural narrative in a basic way. It informs the very nature of being a creature made by God. In the 1930s H. Wheeler Robinson, a well-known scholar of the Old Testament, published two papers that later became the influential book *Corporate Personality in Ancient Israel*. In talking about Israel, Robinson made use of a range of anthropological and political reflections from his era, some of which now seem dated. But Robinson also ordered these debatable data according to his sense that at the center of Old Testament theology was the reality of divine covenant. Covenant in Israel, he argued, is embodied in the relationship of a personal plurality, bringing individuals *together* into a new single relationship: two are made to act like one. Most basically, God's relational stance toward human beings makes all covenants possible; and Israel is constituted by this divine covenantal outreach. This means, for Robinson, that individual persons in a covenantal relationship stand for plural persons (even peoples), and peoples stand for persons. To speak of "Israel" as a person—as having a corporate personality, as Robinson put it—is to say that God has brought them together in a single relationship with himself.

Talking about a People

God Creates by Kind:
The Origin of the Nations

Robinson's treatment of a divine covenant as central to the way that God draws persons together is important, especially in the way it emphasizes the priority of God's action in gathering. But we should probably go further. In fact, I believe we *must* go further and see the gathering or incorporating dynamic of God as something that defines creation itself, in the forms of all its creatures. From the perspective of the human creature, individuals are at best contingent moments within a more fundamental movement, scripturally described in terms of family and peoples. The creation of Adam is almost immediately unfolded in terms of male-female union and procreation (Gen 1:26–28). From this beginning, the genealogies of Genesis immediately spin out in terms of filiated lines of relation, families, and finally nations and languages. A "people"—the English is derived from the Latin *populus*—refers at root to the idea of multiplication, of "the many"; while a "nation" is simply the product of "natality," of birth from a line of procreative connectivity. Peoples and nations, then, become the main building blocks of human history, among whom Israel is given a special place, not only in relation to God but as reflected in relation to the other peoples of the world. Obviously, the New Testament and Christian reflection focus upon this set of developing national relations as something central to the gospel itself. Jerusalem is defined in terms of progeny, and progeny in terms of peoples (Ps 45:16; Isa 54:1–5; Rev 21). All these are drawn together in Christ.

This historical movement from Adam through the multiplied nations into Christ is essential for understanding the Church, and we will come back to it. Here, what is important to emphasize in the light of this movement is how being created is itself to be ordered toward multiplication and species. The earth "brings forth" fruit-bearing vegetation, each plant "after its kind"; the waters bring forth creatures "abundantly," as do the birds of the air in their forms, and then the land animals, each in their "kind." The swarming and teeming creatures appear, like light, darkness, and water itself, to "cover the earth" (Gen 1). Both the form of the *genus* (as the Greek translates the Hebrew *miyn* for "kind" or "species") as a category that joins individual creatures into common purposes and life, and the proliferation of these collective forms across the globe, are given in words of divine command over the shape of creation. Each aspect—kind and multiplication—establishes the temporal outworking of the world that God has made according to God's purpose.

Human kinds or peoples are thus the divinely given form of experienced history. They are the way in which God's gift-giving, or creative making of things, takes shape. This seems to be a basic feature of what it means to be created at all, and within this shape the Church's corporate being not only makes sense but is simply inevitable.

But is this a reasonable way of looking at the Church? One perspective on various modern views of the Church is to categorize them in one of two ways, realistic and idealistic. One growing tendency—or set of currents—in contemporary ecclesiology is to press for studies of the Church that are based on churches' "concrete" life, their actual practices and members. This "realist" view is contrasted with what is seen as the old way ecclesiology was done, "idealist," "abstract" and "ahistorical" (the terms are borrowed from, among many critics, Roger Haight). In the past, so the argument goes, Christian theologians focused on ideas, like doctrine, in order to describe the church, but to the detriment of the embodied life of Christians in this or that concrete situation.

Talking about the church as a people can indeed seem idealist. In the eighteenth century, the study of "peoples" became popular, as we can see in the bestselling and encyclopedic reflections of Montesquieu in the *Spirit of the Laws* (1748) and even Adam Smith's *An Inquiry into the Nature and Causes of the Wealth of Nations* (1776). Montesquieu has been called the founder of modern sociology because of his interest in the particularities of culture and geography, and the way popular outlooks are shaped by the contours of local history and experience. But modern readers of his work find its theories of climate, customs, and politics fanciful and more reflective of the ideas generated in the library of elite European gentry than in actual engagement with real people. Montesquieu's younger contemporary, the great eighteenth-century Lutheran philosopher (and minister) Johann Gottfried Herder, was one of the first to take up the notion of national or ethnic identity and try to theologize it by locating each within the movement of the greater Spirit of God in history. Herder too has been accused of being an idealist (and unfortunate in his influence on German nationalist ideology): in what sense can a historical people be shaped by a divine spirit? Peoples may perhaps be studied according to the tools of sociological analysis, contemporary critics might say. But to imbue national existence and character with the expressions of a divine causality seems for many today to be an exercise in fantasy or perhaps even a dangerous will to power.

The worry here, then, would also apply to a view of the Church as a divinely shaped people. More recently, scholars have focused a great deal of attention on the "invention" of a national political order and consciousness ("ethnogenesis") in terms of the interests and pressures of various social groups. These groups may deploy a range of traditional materials or construct material from scratch (histories, songs, images, educational curricula) to bolster the idea of a special national character or destiny. The nineteenth century in particular (e.g., Mazzini's quest for something he called "Italy," or Snellman's Finnish movement) was mirrored by the later twentieth-century concern for national integrity in the face of post-colonial struggles for survival and social justice (as in the complex cases of Kwame Nkrumah in Ghana or Nyerere in Tanzania). While the motives for nation-building in these contexts may still be affirmed, contemporary scholars of nationalism tend to question the very morality of national identities. Their studies are often aimed in a larger way at undermining the notion of nations altogether, arguing that, as products of human imagination, nation-building or nation-maintenance often serve as avenues for conscious or unconscious manipulations of power.

Some of this debunking of nationalism began with studies after World War I—e.g., George E. Partridge's *The Psychology of Nations*. (Partridge was the first to conceive of the category of "sociopathy" and he applied it to collectives.) More recently, however, the deconstruction of nationhood has been applied across the board, not only to the ideologies of American or French patriotism, but to religious groups, like Judaism and Mormonism. Again, the worry is that when people start thinking that they are part of a group—hence, "group-think"—bad things happen. Furthermore, the history of human interaction seems to be littered with the broken leftovers of such corporate mythologies.

John Breuilly, a prominent scholar of nationalism, sums up the way peoplehood, civil or religious, has achieved a position of contemporary denigration:

> Nationalism today is a word with negative connotations. Those who stress the values of the nation and a proud grasp of national history, look for other names, such as patriotism or homeland. Oppositional movements are now inclined to focus on human rights and democratic institutions instead of ethnic or national

difference, recognising a shift in what language is most congenial to the international community.[1]

Breuilly goes on to point out that groups may well continue to appeal to the reality of nation and ethnicity in order to *claim* rights that have been denied them, but in doing so they are engaging, it seems, more of a political rhetoric than something they actually assert as being a governing reality. "Internationalism" or more broadly the "human community" is something not only more valued today, but something viewed as more fundamental than locally-determined group identity. To the degree that many political critics are willing to grant rights to groups, they prefer that these groups be "associative" in nature (individuals themselves choose to join them) rather than "ascriptive" (they are somehow "given" by history or political or social fiat). Still, there remain huge moral burdens that indigenous peoples have placed on the scruples of larger polities, often with adjustive responses in the direction of regional autonomies based on national identities. The tension between peoplehood and the dangers of violent Balkanization have not been resolved.

So are peoples "real" or are they figments of the mind, however influential these figments may end up being for decision-making or strategy? The general Christian tradition of reading Scripture says that peoples are real indeed, and in some sense are even prior to individual reality. When Paul writes that we are all "in Adam" (1 Cor 15:22), he is talking about a specific kind of corporate identity that determines our very thinking and desiring, as well as the outcome of our existence. He also speaks of the destiny of nations—"the Gentiles"—whose formation from Adam, in conjunction with the particular nation Israel, reflects in a way quite precisely the purposes of God (Rom 9–11). If "nations" are often the products of limited human projects of self-interest, and therefore tools of unrighteousness, they seem nonetheless to bear some real connection with "peoples," a term whose status in God's eyes is historically central and certainly designates something "real" in a historically absolute sense.[2]

---

1. Breuilly, "Nationalism," 20.

2. On more positive though realistic approaches to nationalism today, see Craig Calhoun, *Nations Matter*.

Talking about a People

The Christian "We"

Interestingly, new lines of philosophical reflection agree with the Christian scriptural tradition, or at least show how some of the assumptions of this tradition are plausible. One recent set of philosophical interests has been labeled "social epistemology." Well-known representatives of this school are Margaret Gilbert and Alvin Goldman. Goldman has been interested in a more process-oriented question of how individuals get their particular beliefs and gain their particular knowledge through interaction with others. This kind of research underscores at least the way in which it makes sense to say that "there is no such thing as an individual knower," but that all knowledge in an individual seems to derive from that individual's being a part of a socially-networked community. This kind of discussion converges closely with recent research in human cognition and learning, and it is deeply significant for understanding how knowledge is itself a social action, not basically an individual quest. But Gilbert has gone further, and she seeks to understand what it means to talk about a "we," especially as the subject of a verb: "we have decided," "we want," "we thought it through," and so on. Her volume *On Social Facts* (1989) reinvigorated an approach to thinking about what is "real" in the world that stands as an alternative to the individualism of so much postmodern thought. She has gone on to work through a range of questions surrounding what she calls "plural subject theory," which touch on daily activities from friendships to school boards to business and political reflection.

It is possible that ecclesiologies can be divided between those who believe in the "we" as the fundamental unit of the church, and those who believe instead in the "I," and finally, those who believe in a necessary interaction among "I's" so that the true "I" or the true "we" can find its realization. Perhaps we could even map these distinctions onto the differences between High and Low Ecclesiologies (which often refer to ways decisions are made) or between Catholics and Protestants. Some have tried to do just that. But Gilbert's point is that all of us actually assume the reality of a "we," whatever our church identity or political persuasions. The trick is to understand what this assumption amounts to.

One obvious case where the "we" is assumed is in the legal sphere. The term "corporation" or "corporate personality" is today mostly attached to business firms, not to nations, let alone churches. Businesses are taxed, they can make contracts of sorts, they can be sued (although often in a way that leads to the persons of its individual board members). But by and large, this legal context is probably among the weaker forms of the "we" that we assume. The thirteenth-century Pope Innocent IV, himself a scholar of canon law, is often seen as a pioneer in this line of thinking. He wrote about the *persona ficta*, or "figured" personality, that one might attach to a university or monastery, in a phrase that became much cited: *cum collegium in causa universitatis fingatur una persona* ("the college in corporate matters is figured as a person").[3] He noted, however, that this was only a useful fiction, because in reality corporations were not beings and thus could not be excommunicated, having themselves no "souls." The "we" of the firm is purely functional and limited; it requires no subsuming of individual intentionalities and does not really make decisions at all.

Whether or not the development of the legal version of the corporate personality contributed to other forms of "we"-speak, Gilbert insists that we do indeed live today—and always have—with a robust sense of corporate subjectivity. One thing Gilbert emphasizes is the way that corporate "belief" is a real belief and not a fiction at all, and that individuals who are a part of a corporate entity will quite readily and sincerely speak of a "common belief" in a way that describes an almost "coercive" power that shapes their own wills into a genuine agreement. At a certain point, often quite early in a discernment process, there has been a real shift in identifying agency. No longer is it "this is what I think, in relation to what this or that other person may think," but rather and through whatever means, "this is what we believe." For me to say "we believe" may or may not involve changing my personal beliefs. In a way, my "personal" beliefs become irrelevant. "We believe" is about a different kind of belief, no longer of the "I" but of the "we." Gilbert quite deliberately makes use here of the image of a "body" with its parts: to be a "we" is to have become members of a single body. That is exactly what we mean. When it comes to joint belief, she writes:

> How are people to act so as to emulate, as far as possible, a body that believes that p? As I understand it, they are not required personally to believe that p, nor to try personally to believe that p. Nor are they required to act as if they personally believed that p, whether or not they do. Rather, they are to act as would any one of several mouthpieces of the body in question, thus

---

3. See the discussion in Dewey, "Historic Background," 655–73, and Koessler, "Person in Imagination," 435–49. The translation is Koessler's, though there is debate about the phrase's exact meaning. See also Michaud-Quantin, *Universitas*, 201–8.

uttering its beliefs, as opposed to the beliefs of any of its members, including the utterer.[4]

But is the "we" truly existent, as an agent? Other philosophers continue to argue about this. Some insist that the "we" nonetheless, when it comes right down to it, is a "collective entity," in the sense of referring to a set of individual persons. From a metaphysical point of view, this would mean that what "really exists" within the social sphere are "individual ontologies" that manage to work together in various ways. If this is so, then when one speaks of the "we" as an agent who does something, one is really talking about an intentionality ("we want") that is projected onto the group, as a kind of metaphor: the "we" only as an "extrinsic," not an "intrinsic intentionality." It is a common assumption in our historically-minded culture to say for instance that institutions like the ordered organization of a church or the shape of familial relationships simply express norms and patterns in place over time that have come to be through the plural cooperations (or impositions) of individuals. In this case their reality is truly a "figment," and their agency is only extrinsically granted by willing or coerced individuals. Gilbert and others, by contrast, insist from a purely philosophical perspective that institutions are indeed constitutive of reality, whatever their historical genesis: they make decisions, they order individual desires and wants, individuals in fact identify their own reality as given within these institutions, and their actions have consequences. Furthermore, we understand this to be the case in everyday life, and talk as if it is.

From a theological point of view, the issue is crucial: for if institutions are constitutive of reality in general, then at least some of them are constitutive of reality in a prescriptive sense, in that they may be "created" by God. So, to use a currently contentious example, the marriage of husband and wife, just like the Church, has traditionally been seen by Christians as just such an institution that is constitutive of reality. More recently, just as notions of corporate realities have been weakened, so too has marriage been seen less as constitutive and more as descriptive of some pattern of relationship that people have come to put together on their own steam over time. And if so, at some other time individuals may decide, singly or together, to refashion these patterns of relationship, calling it whatever they choose, whether marriage or something else. Given the traditional Bride-Bridegroom understanding of the Church, the example is hardly arbitrary, and it shows how much is at stake in how

---

4. Gilbert, *Joint Commitment*, 140.

we talk about the intentional reality of the "we," and more broadly, of peoples. Is the Church also constitutive of reality as a divinely ordered agent? Or is it a name given to a social organization that has come to be through cooperative give-and-take by individuals over time?

The Animating Spirit of "We"

Philosophers like Gilbert, as I have said, have made a case for the plausibility of the corporate agent as a real entity. But the exercise of embracing that conceptual plausibility and attaching it to the traditional "we"-agency of the Church does not neatly fall into either side of the argument over extrinsically or intrinsically ascribed subjectivity. For the "we" of the Church is attributed not to the way people express themselves singly or even as many, but to some external/internal reality altogether distinct from the human persons involved: God, the Holy Spirit, the Spirit of Christ. In the words of James, as he explains the decision made by the apostles at the so-called Council of Jerusalem, "it seemed good to the Holy Spirit and to us" (Acts 15:28 KJV). The *way* this *populus* or corporate body speaks may indeed follow Gilbert's outlines, but it does not explain what specifically the *Church* is. For the Church is a "we" in which the Spirit of God dwells. In this way, somehow, the multiplying creature is actually ordered by its creator, precisely in its multiplied membership.

Augustine was one of the first theologians to explicitly call the Holy Spirit "the soul of the church," likening it to the soul in a human body, although in this case he meant the body of Christ.[5] The image was frequently taken up in the Middle Ages, and later ensconced in official papal encyclicals by Leo XIII and Pius XII. But Protestants also understood something similar. In the distinctive social-biological language of the early twentieth century, the great Scottish theologian P. T. Forsyth attempted to describe how social organizations like discrete congregations and denominations could have a single realistic subjectivity and agency. Such "churches," he wrote, constitute

> a federation of corporations each catholic in genius but none catholic in compass, varying in origin and circumstance, but still knit in a spiritual unity as positive as the moral personality of a super-individual Christ. This is what is meant by the unity of the Spirit. It is more than a sympathetic unity or a contractual, more

---

5. Augustine, "Sermon 267," part 4.

mystic and wonderful; it is the unity of a corporate personality indwelling and creative; a unity whose bond is not provided by organization but by an organizing life, by the only kind of life that organizes persons as such, by the distinctively Christian principle of the interpenetration of persons and their cohesion in a supreme personality—the principle of the Christian Triune God. The Church is more than an organization; it is an organism. But it is a moral organism (lest we be victims of biological metaphors), it is a group-person.[6]

Dietrich Bonhoeffer, the great Lutheran theologian whose witness for Christ against national socialism in Germany cost him his life, was perhaps the first to grapple with the concrete-abstract tension that we have noted in all this. In his early treatise on the Church, *Sanctorum Communio*, Bonhoeffer struggled in great detail to find a way to relate the "empirical" church, capable of being described sociologically, with the actual Christian understanding and claims regarding the Church's singular reality. He focused especially on the question of "will," and in ways that show a great sensitivity to the kinds of problems contemporary philosophers are today engaging. In the end, Bonhoeffer emphasized the traditional Christian affirmation that, in the community of the Church, the Holy Spirit realizes God's "will" of love within the ordered lives of its members: God's will becomes their will.[7]

Bonhoeffer's discussion is really quite complex. He labored mightily to hold together the "objective" reality of individuals ("multiple spirits"), with all their limited forms and desires and even sins, within their individual congregations, along with the true and "essential" Church of the "one" Holy Spirit. In the end, he seems to have decided that this complex relationship is one of "becoming" and is located in a historical process in which the Spirit "actualizes" God's single relating love within persons only over time. Yet Bonhoeffer also wanted to be clear that this movement in time was not from something that was *less* than the true Church to something that becomes more and more true. That way of putting things wasn't quite right either. Rather, what the Spirit actualizes in time, Christ has already "realized" in fullness. In this case, Bonhoeffer turns to the scriptural claim that Christ is the "new Adam," in whom bodily (ontologically) all human beings are now located, healing and perfecting what had been disordered through

---

6. Forsyth, *Theology in Church and State*, 184–85.
7. Bonhoeffer, *Sanctorum Communio*, 118–55.

the fall (cf. 1 Cor 15:22, 45). Interestingly, Bonhoeffer sees this complete realization not as excluding the temporal, but as describing fully what the temporal life of the Christian actually is: being taken up in the full range and direction of the new Adam's own existence, which itself follows a temporal path, such that Christ is not only the Son of God but also the "pioneer" who goes before us along a certain trajectory of life. In this way, Bonhoeffer is able to show how "actualization" over time coincides with "realization" in being: each is fully inscribed in the scriptural revelation of Jesus.[8] Applied to the Church, Bonhoeffer wanted to show how the Church's "becoming" is also an aspect of its fully realized being as the Body of Christ.

This is all quite difficult to sort out, and Bonhoeffer's attempt is admittedly often opaque. As he himself would come to experience personally, through his confrontation with Nazism and complicit Christian churches, one can spin in circles trying to affirm a "we" governed by the Spirit of God when this "we" willfully acts in ways that deny its divine "soul." Yet I think that Bonhoeffer's attempt is significant, with all of its dense and detailed attentiveness to how social groups move through time, how social groups come to have a "collective" identity, and thus how the Church must also be understood as a peculiar social personality or even person. His conviction, rightly, was that the Church's specific way of being such a social person, a "we," was intimately bound up with its incorporation into the person of God in Christ, and thus to *that* Person's passage through history, wholly God's time, but wholly given over to the Church's human membership.

If we were to locate the Church in a fundamental way, it would be in the creative act of God in "filling" his work through the particular forms of "fruitfulness" and "multiplication" (Gen 1:22, 28; 8:17; 9:7; 16:10; 17:2; etc.). The act of "filling" (*male*) in its Hebrew connotation invokes the theological concept of "fulfillment" or "perfection" as it is given in Christ, who fulfills the "times," the "law," and finally all of creation. That this happens through "fruitful multiplication" establishes peoplehood in its temporally dynamic form of natality—the birthing that stands behind "nations"—as the key creaturely vehicle for God's purposes. It is true that the Church is particular in its historical movement. The Church, like any given people, has a form and a culture and a set of experiences. But arising out of the very act of creation, the Church is also properly understood to be universal, just in its identity as that through which God's purposes as creator are "filled up," brought to completion, and perfected. The Church is born in Adam

---

8. Ibid., 104–15.

and is fulfilled because it is realized in the new Adam, Christ. In doing so, one nation becomes all nations.

Adam to Adam: The Election of the Church

If we trace the peoplehood of the Church in Scripture, then the right places to turn will be those that describe, in Old and New Testaments, just this movement from Adam to Adam, via the grand genealogical trees that grow and blossom across time. In a culture that seeks summaries and outlines, there could be no better framework for understanding the scriptural truths of the Church than to follow out and reflect upon the tendrils associated with Luke 3:23–38 and Matthew 1:1–17. These, among other locations, stand as ecclesial creeds in their own right, alongside the more theologically compact sections of the Apostles' and Nicene creeds. For here we are led along the socially embodied channels of *ben Adam, am Israel, ben Israel, laos tou Theou*, to their consummation in the "last Adam" (1 Cor 15:45), the "second man" (1 Cor 15:47), the "One New Man" (Eph 2:15), the *hes kainos anthropos*, "of whom the whole family [*patria* or lineage] in heaven and earth is named" (Eph 3:15 KJV).

There is a traditional figural parallel that Christians have drawn between Eve being created from the side of Adam, and the Church from the open wound in the side of the crucified Jesus. This parallel, sometimes displayed pictorially within medieval illustrated Bibles, was asserted by theologians from as early as Hilary of Poitiers to the sixteenth-century (among them, the English theologian Richard Hooker). A central element in the picture, including its common associations with the eucharistic blood also drawn from the side of Christ, is the propagating breadth of human creation formed through the peoples of the earth. This breadth finds its fullest actualization in the Church's communal gathering, its "we," which is wrapped up in the self-giving body of Jesus. The Church, then, is a nation among nations, and its meaning is a kind of nationalism-on-the-way, from Adam to Adam, being "actualized" by God through the Spirit. The Church wends its way through time, among the peoples of the earth, particular in one fashion, yet particularly aiming at the inclusion of all nations into the one source of natality itself, the Christ "by whom and for whom all things are made" (Col 1:16).

The way that this particularity and universality ascribed to the Church is integrated scripturally is in the figure of the "firstfruits" (Jas 1:18; cf. Rom 8:23). It is a rich figure that leads back to Genesis 4 and through the practices of the sacrificial life of Israel. That the Church is itself an enacted offering, a "firstfruit" among the nations, here provides a kind of temporal explanation of why or how one group can exist in a divinely willed fashion (fully "realized" in Bonhoeffer's sense) that is not historically congruent with the complete meaning of the term (that is, not yet fully "actualized"). There has always been, as we have seen, a conceptual problem in having a real entity that is historically concrete (a particular people) also embody something that is—"ideally"—inclusive of all time and space, humanly speaking (e.g., humanity, the communion of saints). This tension between the concrete and the ideal is resolved by the simple claim that the Church's temporality, its becoming, is in fact the temporality of Jesus Christ's own incarnate existence. For *before* the Church as firstfruits of the nations, in terms of the reality and ground of the Church, there is Christ Jesus, the firstfruits of the dead now alive in God (1 Cor 15:20). He is the "firstborn" among the children of men (Rom 8:29), "among many brethren." As his life moves through human history, the Church follows along as his first disciples, his first witnesses, his first brothers and sisters (cf. Heb 2:10, 13), turning nations into the one variegated *patria* of the new Adam (cf. John 10:16; 11:52), who is, in any case, the First and the Last (Rev 1:17).

It is in this context, finally, that we can make sense of the particularity that is the Church's in its most formally dogmatic articulation: election. This concept of election is a very Western one, at least as applied to the Church in particular. The English word has often been associated with, sometimes even used as a synonym for, "predestination," but certainly they are not the same in their biblical roots. In the Old Testament, the election of Israel (later coordinated by many Christian writers with the election of the Church) is bound up with root words that connote choice and especially a choice made out of affectionate motives. The most famous place this is expressed is in Deuteronomy:

> For thou [art] an holy people unto the LORD thy God: the LORD thy God hath chosen thee to be a special people unto himself, above all people that [are] upon the face of the earth. The LORD did not set his love upon you, nor choose you, because ye were more in number than any people; for ye [were] the fewest of all people: But because the LORD loved you, and because he would keep the oath which he had sworn unto your fathers, hath the

Talking about a People

LORD brought you out with a mighty hand, and redeemed you out of the house of bondmen, from the hand of Pharaoh king of Egypt. (Deut 7:6–8 KJV)

In Deuteronomy itself, this kind of "choice" describes God's selection of Jerusalem and the temple for his dwelling, and thus the "election" of Israel is bound to a whole range of divine engagements and orderings of time and space and multiple persons and events. In the New Testament, Paul surely has something like this in mind when he uses (though rarely) *ekloge*, which is traditionally translated as "election" (as Tyndale does, based on the earlier Latin word), as in the "purpose of God's election" (Rom 9:11), and Israel as still "beloved" by God according to their "election" (Rom 11:28), despite being "enemies of the Gospel." The term is also linked, in this case for Christians, with their divine "calling" (2 Pet 1:10). In any case, while election certainly connotes fixed ends, the concept is more holistic, and practically speaking takes in the breadth of history and its contoured range.

The alternate notion of divine election as a kind of predetermined divine playbook of creaturely moves and outcomes, while perhaps logically if vaguely related to the notion of election above, has little purchase in the scriptural texts from which the term arises. The alternate conception is linked more naturally to the word "predestination," whose connotation is more future-oriented (as its Latin root, involving "aiming" and setting goals, seems to indicate). Again, it is mostly Paul who furnishes the Latin and English translations with their root word:

> For whom he did foreknow, he also did predestinate [to be] conformed to the image of his Son, that he might be the firstborn among many brethren. Moreover whom he did predestinate, them he also called: and whom he called, them he also justified: and whom he justified, them he also glorified. (Rom 8:29–30 KJV)

In this case, the original Greek translated in terms of predestination (*proorizein*) has more of the "blueprint" sense to it, pointing to the way that a thing's form and boundaries might be laid out ahead of time. Still, even as Paul uses the term, it takes in a range of divine actions: knowing, calling, justifying, glorifying, for the larger purposes of "conforming" to the "firstborn." (Elsewhere in 8:27 Paul also speaks of the need for suffering in this set of divinely formative actions.) These elements, then, form a whole in which "predestination" is at best a way of describing one aspect of the divine work that shapes the whole into what is described as the life of "the elect" (Rom 8:33).

When the concept of predestination is applied to the Church, as it is somewhat indirectly in Ephesians 1 (see 1:5, 11, 22), it is in the context of election, literally (1:4), and within a range of divine purposes that are as broad and narratively rich as anything in the Old Testament: the concrete spaces of Ephesus, the body of Jesus in life, death and resurrection, forms of holiness and love embodied within human relations, a place within the comprehensive scope of divine creation in heaven and heart both, and the expansive shape of creation's historical movement into the "fullness" of Christ's rule. The Church here is finally equated with that divine "body," "the fullness of him that filleth all in all" (1:23 KJV). Election, as Paul writes, is election to "conformity" with Christ, something we will return to in our concluding chapter. The "we" becomes "like" Christ, to the point of being joined in union *to* Christ, as Christ's "own" self in ways informed by utter grace.

There is nothing about election here that stands in tension with what has been said above regarding the firstfruits of the nations in the fundamental creative work of God. A tension, however, *did* arise, starting arguably with Augustine in the early fifth century, and turning into a full-blown definition of the true Church in someone like John Wycliffe by the fourteenth century. The Church was now described simply in terms of the "number of the elect." Wycliffe's definition was to become a commonplace in some Protestant circles. But as Bonhoeffer himself noted, the equation of election with individual predestination—that is, the Church is properly defined as the full number of those whom God has predestined to salvation—is first of all a tautology. Because the salvation of human creatures is part of the fundamental ground of God's relationship with his creatures, equating the Church with that work in respect to those creatures being saved tells us nothing new about the Church's nature and meaning in itself. It is like defining a "vegetable field" as a "field in which vegetables are grown." Furthermore, approaching election in terms of "individual" numbers, which are in any case unknown to us in their particulars (as every Christian theologian since Augustine has emphasized), obscures the real content of election. Election is constituted by the life of Christ—his passage through the world—as the "firstborn" of "many brethren." Election is defined by Christ Jesus, by *his* form and content, as Karl Barth famously insisted so relentlessly and profoundly, not by the quantified bottom line of individual creatures left standing at the end of time, even if the fact that there *are* individuals who will be so numbered is itself a given.

Talking about a People

The "we-ness" of the Church arises among those whose individual lives are now confessed as being part of Christ as he orders the created world from Adam to and through his own incarnation as the new Adam. The Church is given a place among the peoples—she is elected—so as to participate in the creative rise of the multiplying abundance of the world through her nations, in their integration into the fullness of God's life in Christ. The possibility and shape of becoming such a single people, willingly following just this movement through time, is what divine election describes. To this degree, the election of the Church discloses the divine destiny of the world, and it is of the *world* in all her peopled fullness that the Church functions as the firstfruits, not of something else.

The remarkable African American priest Alexander Crummell encapsulates many of the challenging aspects of this ecclesial reality. Crummell, who died in 1898, grew up in the North as the child of a former slave. His intellectual capacities and energies led him against many odds to pursue the education necessary to become an Episcopal priest. But entrenched racism in the church drove him to England, where he became the first black person to receive a degree from Cambridge University. Crummell's career, informed by his own intensive social and theological concerns, let him to Pan-African outlooks. He stayed in Liberia for a long time as a missionary, shifted his thinking in favor of Christian "civilization" for indigenous Liberians, and finally returned to the United States, where he led a black congregation in Washington, DC, over several decades. Over his lifetime, he saw himself as both a member and a critic of several nations—American Black, African, American, Christian. His understanding of how these various peoples related in God's providence, and his own identity and calling within this interplay of peoples, developed in ways that evidence many of the dynamics that critics of nationalism in our own day have pointedly identified.

Yet Crummell deeply understood, on the basis of the scriptural character of peoplehood, how election properly unfolds. In an 1875 sermon on Thanksgiving Day, "The Social Principle among a People; and Its Bearing on Their Progress and Development," Crummell begins by arguing that peoplehood is divinely built into human creation:

> What I mean by the social principle, is the disposition which leads men to associate and join together for specific purposes; the principle which makes families and societies, and which binds men in unity and brotherhood, in races and churches and nations.

> For man, you will observe, is a social being. In his mental and moral constitution God has planted certain sympathies and affections, from which spring the desire for companionship. It is with reference to these principles that God declared of the single and solitary Adam, "It is not good for the man to live alone." It was no newly-discovered affinity of the Maker, no afterthought of the Almighty. He had formed His creature with a fitness and proclivity for association. He had made him with a nature that demanded society. And from this principle flows, as from a fountain, the loves, friendships, families, and combinations which tie men together, in union and concord. A wider and more imposing result of this principle is the welding of men in races and nationalities. All the fruit and flower of these organisms come from the coalescence of divers faculties and powers, tending to specific ends.[9]

As he says elsewhere, "the nation is a creation and manifestation of God."[10] While he insists that the purposes of God aim at a universal "rule" by Christ over all peoples, ordering them in a common universal "brotherhood," Crummell nonetheless argues that this evangelical purpose works itself out only through the providential ordering and "development" of peoples in relation to another. His interest, then, is in the integrity of individual peoples—in this case, his own black compatriots. It is an odd national set-up here: we are a "peculiar people," he says of his race in America, a "nation set apart" within the nation of the United States, a people within another people.[11] This peculiarity has been molded by the terrible injustices of slavery and of now deep-seated prejudice and exclusion. Everything depends, therefore, on overcoming the evil dynamics of misplaced nationalism. Yet, for Crummell, only another kind of nationalism will do. It is in the interest of the United States as a whole that its black citizens shape their own national integrity, "dwelling among their own people" according to the strictest moral and spiritual demands. American Blacks, he carefully argues, must grasp hold of a special social identity governed by the deepest forms of mutual accountability, a "we-ness" given only by the force of God's calling and gospel. Through this witness of this peculiar people, evil will be overcome and the shape of future peoplehood will be transformed.

One could argue about the political strategies involved in Crummell's approach, just as one could question the deep moralism that shapes his

---

9. Crummell, *Greatness of Christ*, 288–89.
10. Ibid., 323.
11. Ibid., 302.

view of ethnic betterment. But the entire sermon nonetheless exhibits the fundamental strains of popular election that inform a scriptural vision of the Church. One cannot, furthermore, escape the parallels between Crummell's political vision of Afro-American witness and Jewish experience within diaspora oppression, including an underlying sense of election. In Crummell's hands, these elements jar precisely in their concreteness, as well as in their open description of historical change through particularity. That is why his sermon is useful for ecclesiology. However jarring, though, it is no more so than Psalm 147:

> Praise ye the LORD: for [it is] good to sing praises unto our God; for [it is] pleasant; [and] praise is comely...
>
> Great [is] our Lord, and of great power: his understanding [is] infinite.
>
> The LORD lifteth up the meek: he casteth the wicked down to the ground...
>
> He giveth to the beast his food, [and] to the young ravens which cry...
>
> He maketh peace [in] thy borders, [and] filleth thee with the finest of the wheat...
>
> He sendeth out his word, and melteth them: he causeth his wind to blow, [and] the waters flow.
>
> He sheweth his word unto Jacob, his statutes and his judgments unto Israel.
>
> He hath not dealt so with any nation: and [as for his] judgments, they have not known them. Praise ye the LORD. (Ps 147:1, 5–6, 9, 14, 18–20 KJV)

Here, the particularities of (specific) Jewish history "manifest" exhaustive realities of God. Laws manifest the "Word," and Israel manifests the "nations" (Adam). The psalm also reflects the Church. The Church manifests the relationship of Jacob to the Gentiles in its historical outplay, and this is what Jesus *assumes* upon himself in his divine coming. As his genealogy shows, Jacob is included in this historical outplay and its reach to all nations.

Church

Further Reading

Augustine. "Sermon 267." Translated by Edmund Hill. In *Sermons III/7 (230-272B) on Liturgical Seasons*, edited by John E. Rotelle, 271–74. Hyde Park, NY: New City, 1993.

Bonhoeffer, Dietrich. *Sanctorum Communio: A Dogmatic Inquiry into the Sociology of the Church*. Translated by Ronald Gregor Smith. London: Collins, 1963.

Breuilly, John. "Nationalism and the Making of National Pasts." In *Nations and Their Histories: Constructions and Representations*, edited by Susana Carvalho and François Gemenne, 7–28. Houndmills, Hampshire: Palgrave Macmillan, 2009.

———., ed. *The Oxford Handbook of the History of Nationalism*. Oxford: Oxford University Press, 2013.

Calhoun, Craig. *Nations Matter: Culture, History, and the Cosmopolitan Dream*. London: Routledge, 2007.

Carvalho, Susana, and François Gemenne, eds. *Nations and Their Histories: Constructions and Representations*. Houndmills, Hampshire: Palgrave Macmillan, 2009.

Crummell, Alexander. *The Greatness of Christ and Other Sermons*. New York, 1882.

Dewey, John. "The Historic Background of Corporate Legal Personality." *Yale Law Journal* 35 (1926) 655–73.

Forsyth, P. T. *Theology in Church and State*. London: Hodder and Stoughton, 1915.

Gilbert, Margaret. *Joint Commitment: How We Make the Social World*. Oxford University Press, 2014.

———. *On Social Facts*. London: Routledge, 1989.

———. *Sociality and Responsibility: New Essays in Plural Subject Theory*. Lanham, MD: Rowman and Littlefield, 2000.

Goldman, Alvin I. *Knowledge in a Social World*. Oxford: Clarendon, 1999.

Healy, Nicholas M. *Church, World, and the Christian Life: Practical-Prophetic Ecclesiology*. New York: Cambridge University Press, 2000.

Koessler, Maximilian. "The Person in Imagination or Persona Ficta of the Corporation." *Louisiana Law Review* 9.4 (1949) 435–49.

Michaud-Quantin, Pierre. *Universitas. Expressions du mouvement communautaire dans le Moyen Âge latin*. L'Église et l'État au Moyen Âge 13. Paris: Vrin, 1970.

Partridge, George E. *The Psychology of Nations: A Contribution to the Philosophy of History*. New York: Macmillan, 1919.

Robinson, H. Wheeler. *Corporate Personality in Ancient Israel*. Edinburgh: T. & T. Clark, 1981.

Talking about a People

Discussion Questions

1. Does God create "collectives" or "peoples," or only individuals? What is at stake in the different answers one might give to this question?

2. Some modern philosophers are interested in what we mean when we speak in terms of the plural "we," especially as the subject of a verb. In what way is the Church a "we"-subject? Does the Church have a "corporate personality" and whose is it?

3. What does it mean to say that Israel and the Church are the "elect" among the nations? Is this the same thing as the doctrine of predestination?

5

Arguing about the Church

The Church and the Nations

The Church Is Ordered by God for the Sake of All Other Nations

A PROPER UNDERSTANDING OF THE Church is bound to a proper theology of the nations, among whom Israel is chosen. God forms nations with a purpose, and the Church is a nation for the nations, bound to the one purpose of Christ.

We have not yet defined what a nation is, let alone how the Church should be considered a nation in its own right. But I have suggested that, whatever exactly they are, nations arise out of the creative work of God in forming Adam as a multiplying creature, framed by natality (and mortality, we might add) and its forms: families, lineages, tribes. How these are all shaped in time is something we will discuss, because it leads as well to the actual shape and order of the Church. The Christian gospel, in any case, asserts a fundamental connection between this creative work of God that gives rise to human creaturely existence, and Christ Jesus, the Son of God who lives a human life in time. Christians have spoken about this connection both in terms of God's work being in fact Christ's own, and of human creation aiming at some kind of embrace *by* Christ, encompassing human life as it is in fact lived. Finally, Christians have insisted that the description of this embrace is given in the actually lived contours of Christ's being-in-the-world as a human creature, the Adam who subsumes the children of Adam. Put another way, the nations are born out of the work of Christ as their created history, and they are finally reborn into Christ as their destiny, in a sequence of birth and new birth. In the midst of this history of birth and rebirth live Israel and the Church.

In a broad way, this vision of a human history in which the nations move into Christ somehow is firmly associated with Paul. Called by the risen Jesus himself to be his witness among the nations (or "Gentiles" in its Latinate form), he set out on one of the most remarkable human projects in history, deliberately addressing non-Jews in his preaching and journeying at least as far as Rome and perhaps even to Spain in the process (Acts 9:15; 22:21; 26:17). Paul himself speaks of God "revealing his Son to me so that I might preach his Gospel to the nations" (Gal 1:16, my paraphrase). In Ephesians, this is described as a "revelation" by the Spirit of a divine "mystery," not only to Paul but to other prophets and apostles, that "the Gentiles should be fellow heirs, and of the same body, and partakers of his promise in Christ by the gospel" (Eph 3:6 KJV). This divine purpose, furthermore, stands at the root of creation itself, for it is a "mystery, which from the beginning of the world hath been hid in God, who created all things by Jesus Christ" (Eph 3:9 KJV).

God, Christ, creation, nations, gospel, Christ: Paul's whole Christian life is caught up in both following out and announcing this movement. His most substantive letter, to the Romans, is grounded in this reality:

> Paul, a servant of Jesus Christ, called [to be] an apostle, separated unto the gospel of God, (which he had promised afore by his prophets in the holy scriptures,) concerning his Son Jesus Christ our Lord, which was made of the seed of David according to the flesh; and declared [to be] the Son of God with power, according to the spirit of holiness, by the resurrection from the dead: by whom we have received grace and apostleship, for obedience to the faith among all nations, for his name . . . Now I would not have you ignorant, brethren, that oftentimes I purposed to come unto you, (but was let hitherto,) that I might have some fruit among you also, even as among other Gentiles. I am debtor both to the Greeks, and to the Barbarians; both to the wise, and to the unwise. So, as much as in me is, I am ready to preach the gospel to you that are at Rome also. (Rom 1:1–5, 13–15 KJV)

Finally, Paul ends his letter with a paean of prophetic announcements from the Scriptures that declare the character and shape of this unfolding act:

> Now I say that Jesus Christ was a minister of the circumcision for the truth of God, to confirm the promises [made] unto the fathers:

and that the Gentiles might glorify God for [his] mercy; as it is written, For this cause I will confess to thee among the Gentiles, and sing unto thy name. And again he saith, Rejoice, ye Gentiles, with his people. And again, Praise the Lord, all ye Gentiles; and laud him, all ye people. And again, Esaias saith, There shall be a root of Jesse, and he that shall rise to reign over the Gentiles; in him shall the Gentiles trust. (Rom 15:8–12 KJV)

Much of this is familiar to most readers of the New Testament. But many forget its specifically historical meaning, its description of how time unfolds in God's plan as it relates to actual peoples. Contemporary readers can come upon verses like "There is neither Jew nor Greek, there is neither bond nor free, there is neither male nor female: for ye are all one in Christ Jesus (Gal 3:28 KJV), or "There is neither Greek nor Jew, circumcision nor uncircumcision, Barbarian, Scythian, bond [nor] free: but Christ [is] all, and in all" (Col 3:11 KJV). These seem like statements of a given (or perhaps hoped-for) social order, justified by Christian teaching. But in fact their vital reference is to the events of peoplehood as creaturely existence moves to its end. Cicero had divided the world amongst Italians, Greeks, and Barbarians; Paul speaks of Jews, Greeks, and Barbarians; but all are "nations" of one type or another. (Paul calls the Jews a *genos* or "kind"; but the broader term "ethnos" is also applied to Israel.) Each has a place in the creative movement of Christ's own Adamic life, which Paul equalizes with preaching the gospel, literally "evangelizing."

It is crucial to see how Paul's understanding of the Church, and his use of the term *ekklesia*, is a part of this larger picture of the gospel's proclamation. Israel, for instance, "gathered" at Horeb for the giving of the Law and their own historical mission. In the Greek translation of Deuteronomy 4:10, this is emphasized by speaking of the "day of the *ekklesia*," and here the Hebrew and Greek translation is critical, for the "congregating" aspect of the people is exactly what Paul is suggesting, in a scripturally prophetic fashion. Paul's *ekklesia* "in Christ" is just this peopled gathering into which the breadth of the nations—Greeks and Barbarians—can now be drawn alongside Jews, into the presence of the living God, indeed into the midst of God's glory, given in the Spirit of Jesus.[1] The Church is a people into which the nations are drawn, but it is also an act of being drawn together, a people in the process of being peopled and peopling in the life of Christ.

---

1. For some challenging if sometimes theologically tendentious reflections on this, see Eyl, "Semantic Voids," 315–39.

One can get a sense of this historicizing or temporally extended way of looking at the Church in the Gospels. After all, it is not just Paul who invented this claim, for it was given, as we saw, "to prophets and apostles" as a whole.

It is clear, from Matthew for instance, that nations in fact are *not* static things, insofar as they are both touched, taught, and transformed, in this case through the apostolic work of Jesus' disciples:

> Then the eleven disciples went away into Galilee, into a mountain where Jesus had appointed them. And when they saw him, they worshipped him: but some doubted. And Jesus came and spake unto them, saying, All power is given unto me in heaven and in earth. Go ye therefore, and teach all nations, baptizing them in the name of the Father, and of the Son, and of the Holy Ghost: Teaching them to observe all things whatsoever I have commanded you: and, lo, I am with you always, [even] unto the end of the world. Amen. (Matt 28:16–20 KJV)

The nations are locatable geographically, so as to be reached by the movement of the apostles, literally those "sent out." They are also teachable, being about to learn the commandments of Christ and to do them. There is, finally, the reality of Christ's "power" and presence at work in this encounter, which not only enables but also inhabits it. In some fashion, all this is tied to the baptism of the nations in the name of the triune God. In Luke's account, the movement and teaching (here specified in terms of repentance and forgiveness) is linked specifically to the "name" of Jesus and to the gift of the Holy Spirit (Luke 24:46–49). It is also equated with the act of apostolic "witness" that extends through John the Baptist somehow toward the "restoration" of Israel:

> And, being assembled together with [them], [He] commanded them that they should not depart from Jerusalem, but wait for the promise of the Father, which, [saith he], ye have heard of me. For John truly baptized with water; but ye shall be baptized with the Holy Ghost not many days hence. When they therefore were come together, they asked of him, saying, Lord, wilt thou at this time restore again the kingdom to Israel? And he said unto them, It is not for you to know the times or the seasons, which the Father hath put in his own power. But ye shall receive power, after that the Holy Ghost is come upon you: and ye shall be witnesses unto me both in Jerusalem, and in all Judaea, and in Samaria, and unto the uttermost part of the earth. (Acts 1:4–8 KJV)

Scholars have disagreed as to whether Paul and the Gospels are articulating a new kind of interest in the nations, in comparison with the outlook given in the Old Testament Scriptures. A special interest in Jewish attitudes toward non-Jews, and hence toward "Gentiles," arose within the eighteenth- and nineteenth-century European movements of Jewish assimilation. Moses Mendelssohn, the great philosophical proponent of such assimilation, was eager to find a basis in Judaism itself for a more universalist or cosmopolitan understanding of human relations, and hence sought for a "tradition" of humanistic Hebraism. Within the stream especially of Reformed Judaism, theologians sought to overturn the stereotype of Jews as being arrogantly exclusivist in their views of Gentile integrity and even potential salvation. Texts from Torah, Talmud, and Liturgy were combed for indications of a Jewish affirmation of "the brotherhood of all mankind."[2] More recently, some Jewish scholars have been more ambivalent in their conclusions. Robert Eisen, for instance, has suggested that the Scriptures themselves are mixed on this score, and that in any case, these scriptural texts were taken up in Judaism in a complex way, hardly clarified by the history of antagonism that developed between Jews and Christians. It is true that there are prayers, like the *Alenu* that concludes most daily worship services, that bid God to bring all the nations to a true worship of and obedience to their Creator. "May all the isles acclaim [thy righteousness]; and the peoples may go seeking, who knew thee not before, and may the ends of the earth praise Thee," as another seventh-century hymn announces.[3]

These are not random occurrences, and it was proper that this orientation in later Jewish attitudes be singled out. They were, after all, linked to specifically biblical texts, like those from Isaiah, where Israel becomes the bearer of truth and "light" to the nations. These and like verses are well known and have been seized upon especially and consistently by Christians.

> And it shall come to pass in the last days, [that] the mountain of the LORD'S house shall be established in the top of the mountains, and shall be exalted above the hills; and all nations shall flow unto it. And many people shall go and say, Come ye, and let us go up to the mountain of the LORD, to the house of the God of Jacob; and he will teach us of his ways, and we will walk in his paths: for out of Zion shall go forth the law, and the word of the LORD from Jerusalem. (Isa 2:2–3 KJV)

2. See especially the discussion in Katz, *Exclusivism and Tolerance*, and Raisin, *Gentile Reactions*.

3. Raisin, *Gentile Reactions*, 60.

> And he said, It is a light thing that thou shouldest be my servant to raise up the tribes of Jacob, and to restore the preserved of Israel: I will also give thee for a light to the Gentiles, that thou mayest be my salvation unto the end of the earth. (Isa 49:6 KJV)

The Jewish commitment to the "land" of Israel, based on a specific promise from God, has made it difficult to clarify this mission, historically. Subjugation, exile, and diaspora both placed Israel "among" the nations literally, but also heightened an attention to her geographic specificity, as Jews longed for a return to the land, and also associated that return with the very historical end-purposes of God (Ps 130). "If I forget thee, O Jerusalem, let my right hand forget [her cunning]. If I do not remember thee, let my tongue cleave to the roof of my mouth; if I prefer not Jerusalem above my chief joy" (Ps 137:5–6 KJV). Nineteenth- and twentieth-century Zionism and the establishment of the modern state of Israel have concretized but also complicated this religious vision, stirring up debates among Jews themselves, not to mention others, as to the proper place that a limited plot of land should hold in God's design.

It is, however, too easy for Gentile Christians to use this knotted set of traditions and hopes to evaluate Jewish Israel's embodied universal mission, as if valuing a divinely given geographical place is antithetical to an Adamic reach of concern. It may, in fact, be logically necessary to it. One of the more pernicious myths that Christians eventually propagated was that Jews, in addition to their rejection of the Messiah, Jesus, had failed to take this mission to the nations seriously, and thus the Church had been formed to carry it on in Israel's place. Even Jesus himself, however, noted the zealousness of Jews in his time to "traverse sea and land to make a single proselyte" (Matt 23:15), and the work of apostles like Paul was built upon the networks of converted Gentile proselytes. In reality, the Christian Church's mission was continuous with Israel's, not taking its place. Having forgotten and suppressed this continuity, the Church also failed to grasp her own national vulnerabilities. This is a key issue in modern ecclesiology, which we need to examine first in terms of the Church's nationhood more generally, and in the next chapter, in terms of the Church's nationhood as identical with Israel's.

Church

The Church Is Judged with All Other Nations

Most of these scriptural texts and later liturgical petitions are coupled with promises and requests that God utterly will destroy the idols and forms of life the heathen enjoy. The confluence of hope and violence is, as Eisen remarks, somewhat ambiguous. Eisen, for example, points out that however undeveloped a "theology of the nations" may be in the Old Testament (and among Old Testament theologians themselves), the key texts that stand out in the Scripture are ones that, responsibly taken up in a specifically Christian understanding of the nations, should continue to inform what that understanding should be, and in a way more challenging than in the past. Texts like Amos's that relate Israel to the nations as one nation among many, liable to the same judgments from God, were less integrated into a theological self-construal. While Christians might well have used these against Jews, the dynamic of national accountability, especially for the Church as a people among peoples, is deeply unsettling (much like Rom 11:21):

> Thus saith the LORD; For three transgressions of Moab, and for four, I will not turn away [the punishment] thereof; because he burned the bones of the king of Edom into lime: But I will send a fire upon Moab, and it shall devour the palaces of Kerioth: and Moab shall die with tumult, with shouting, [and] with the sound of the trumpet: And I will cut off the judge from the midst thereof, and will slay all the princes thereof with him, saith the LORD. Thus saith the LORD; For three transgressions of Judah, and for four, I will not turn away [the punishment] thereof; because they have despised the law of the LORD, and have not kept his commandments, and their lies caused them to err, after the which their fathers have walked: But I will send a fire upon Judah, and it shall devour the palaces of Jerusalem. (Amos 2:1–5 KJV)

> [Are] ye not as children of the Ethiopians unto me, O children of Israel? saith the LORD. Have not I brought up Israel out of the land of Egypt? and the Philistines from Caphtor, and the Syrians from Kir? Behold, the eyes of the Lord GOD [are] upon the sinful kingdom, and I will destroy it from off the face of the earth; saving that I will not utterly destroy the house of Jacob, saith the LORD. For, lo, I will command, and I will sift the house of Israel among all nations, like as [corn] is sifted in a sieve, yet shall not the least grain fall upon the earth. All the sinners of my people shall die by

the sword, which say, The evil shall not overtake nor prevent us. (Amos 9:7–10 KJV)

The Church's accountability and thus also vulnerability before God is given through its national character, which is something that bears emphasizing. If that character is obscured or degraded, not only is that process itself a form of sin, but its consequences render the sinner—the Church in this case—blind to its own condition. The great "universal histories" that became popular among Christian thinkers (like Bossuet) in the early modern period, influenced by Augustine's much earlier *City of God*, were structured around God's relation to the nations he had created. National righteousness or unrighteousness, in these accounts, colored the fate of peoples across time in a manner fairly consistent with biblical ways of thinking. It was rare, however, that the Church herself came under the same glare of moral scrutiny in these writings, largely because the Church had long ceased to be numbered among the nations. She had transcended them all in kind, and hence in judgment too.

Modern thinkers, by contrast—both theologians and critics of Christianity—have slowly narrowed the gap between Church and nation. That has come through at least two developments. First, there has been a gradual realization that the Church's life has in fact been driven by local national interests too narrowly, often with dire consequences for other nations. The difficult realities of Christian colonialism, in which churches have played destructive rather than healing roles, are perhaps the most obvious example. What was called the gospel turned out to be a masquerade of Spanish, British, or French national interests and culture, embodied in nationalistic churches who claimed nation-transcendent status as the one True Church. This is a case of the Church simply becoming, in most respects, "like the Nations" around her, and descending into the same realm of criminality before God. This fulfilled possibility, now recognized by many and the source of much contemporary rejection of the Church, however, should never have been a surprise, if in fact the Church had been consistently viewed in its national character.

More positively, that character has been more recently recognized once again through the complex way in which the Church's relationship with Israel has been reidentified in terms of continuity rather than replacement. This reidentification has been spurred, of course, by the inevitable fall-out in self-consciousness that has followed rethinking Jewish-Christian relations in the wake of the Holocaust and the work of accounting for centuries of Christian hatred and destruction of the Jews. It is an accounting that is still in progress. In addition, developments in biblical studies from the seventeenth century to the present have contributed to bringing Israel and the Church together in greater conceptual connection. Some of these developments were focused upon historical studies; they lie behind what we call "historical criticism" and can be traced to the questions raised by philosophers like Spinoza. Ancient Israel was now the subject of inquiry—historical, linguistic, archaeological, anthropological—in a way that paralleled the study of other ancient nations, and by the nineteenth century this discipline of inquiry began to include the early church as well. Everyone, Jew and Christian both, was drawn to the same level of historical deconstruction as the Edomites, Moabites, and Assyrians. But along with historical criticism, the seventeenth century also saw the resurgence of a traditional figural approach to the Bible among both Catholics and Protestants. By the mid to late twentieth century, this movement, which was associated with a renewed study and appreciation of patristic exegesis, could exegetically claim an identity between Israel and the Church; and given other developments, that identity was now less jarring than it had been for centuries. When theologians like George Lindbeck began to suggest a theology of the Church in terms of an "Israelology," they were speaking out of a confluence of reoriented perspectives that could permit the Church's peoplehood, with respect to both divine judgment and mercy, to be asserted in biblical terms in the concrete forms of its historical execution.

Formation: The Church Is Structured like the Nations, in Its Relation to Past and Present

The intimate connection in both salvation and perdition between Israel and the Nations, and by extension the Church and the Nations, is obvious; and both Jesus and Paul are consistent in asserting it. It is, in fact, the very meaning of these kinds of texts that make the extension of Israel to the Church obvious. As Israel relates to the Nations, so does the Church, insofar as it is continuous with Israel's popular vocation. We shall examine later how this insight may or may not be related to what has been called the sin of supercessionism—thinking that the Christian Church *supplants* Jewish Israel. For now we can simply say that the continuity is a divinely ordered one, embodied in a single historical movement.

Israel is a nation "for the nations," and the Church is how Israel is just that. The way this happens tells us something about "nations" more broadly. In recent years, as I have noted earlier, there has been debate over how nations come into existence. Nations don't "just happen," nor are they simply (usually) the clear result of human intentions. They are a mixture of all this and more. Ernest Renan, the nineteenth-century French philosopher whose racialist views remain controversial, recognized that nations are often products of not-so-virtuous forces: "forgetfulness, and I would add historical error, form an essential factor in creating a nation. This is why progress in historical studies often poses a danger to nationalism. Historical investigation, in fact, brings to light all the past violence that lies at the origin of polities, even those whose have done great good. Unity is always achieved brutally."[4] All the same, historical studies cannot quite uncover the national "how" either. The "ethnogenesis" debate, for instance, has pitted those who want the Goths to be Roman constructions against others who claim that the theory of national construction is itself a form of ideological suppression. Judaism and its biblical national root in "Israel" have been subject to similar debates. Israel, in the phrase of the modern critic of nationalism Benedict Anderson, is an "imagined community," insofar as its claims regarding origins are mythic and thus obscure actual history.[5]

But as Renan himself notes at the end of his essay, the issue of nations is not just how they begin—something that in the end may not be that important at all—but how they are formed in an ongoing way. "A nation is a soul, a spiritual principle. Two things—really two aspects of a single thing—constitute this soul, this spiritual principle. One is in the past, the other in the present. One is the common possession of a rich legacy of memories; the other is actual agreement, the desire to live together, the will to maintain, indivisible, the heritage one has received."[6] Less an idealized abstraction, a national soul is the "we" that has been shaped by past traditions, and the "we" that makes choices as to how this shape will continue. Earlier Christian discussions, from the early Middle Ages even, of the "soul" of the body of the Church focused on the "faith" that held individuals together—faith in rulers, faith in neighbors, faith of course in God. The point, though, was that faith is a binding of persons in "unseen" realities that are passed on and enacted socially. This is what Renan in part intuits.

---

4. Renan, *Qu'est-ce qu'une nation?*, 41.
5. Benedict Anderson, *Imagined Communities*.
6. Renan, *Qu'est-ce qu'une nation?*, 54.

The scriptural outline of the nations sees the question of historical origins as subsumed in the movement of Adam to Adam, and thus this movement itself (rather than its origins) is the true focus for a "theology of the nations." Nations, therefore, are less about beginnings, and more about how multiplicity survives by "kind." The kinds are given in creation somehow; and their divine significance is disclosed in how they prove to be the form of human propagation. Nations *do* imply families and the responsibilities of such common filiated existence. They therefore imply as well, in any historical reflection, the examination of tutelage and the reality of sin's perversion of such a formative nurture. In one way or another, the nations, Israel, and the Church are all caught up in the dynamics of this movement. They are also subject to an accountability for the past (the "memories" passed on) and a judgment on the present (the integrity of maintaining heritage).

In fact, Scripture speaks of the nations only loosely before such a judgment is first given. Genesis describes peoples from the beginning as geographically dispersed and bound to various lineages. Little is said about them, except to assert their existence and their descent into violence, bringing with it the divine cleansing of the flood (Genesis 6). New nations arise after the flood, in the same way as before, from the single stock of one couple's progeny, in this case that of Noah and his wife. These are noted explicitly as multiplying "after their families" and "in their countries, and in their nations" (Gen 10:20; cf. 10:5). The continuity between the original ordering of the nations from Adam and from the children Noah until today is here underlined. But somewhere into this stream, just as with the flood, the turmoil of Babel intrudes as a divine judgment on human pride and establishes the life of the nations in the particular form we know it today. Originally the nations were "one" (11:6), and however diverse in their make-up, they had "one language" (though, in the ambiguous wording of Genesis, they may well have spoken in diverse ways). Thus, whatever nations *were* in this early period, shrouded in a mystery, they are *now* divided, and the mark of their division lies explicitly in their languages (11:8–9). Language becomes both the trace of national distinction, and the instrument of conflict.

Any theology of nations, and hence of the Church, must deal with this strange mixture of national realities: original distinctiveness yet unity, then subsequent disunity through a certain *form* of distinction, language. If Adam moves to Adam through the peculiar people of Israel and the Church assumed in Christ Jesus, then this movement is one in which "gathering" is ordered *by* the distinctiveness that the nations hold at their core; and we might say it happens through the reconciliation of its divisive edges. Hence, in the early Church, Babel was often one of the key moments in the biblical narrative where the purposes of God were revealed, often in correlation with the cross as Babel's resolution. The twin aspects of past and present, heritage and voluntary formative commitments to that heritage, come into play just here: they determine how the Church will shape its life such that the variety of the nations, provided as the gift of creation, will be taken up in Christ in a way that can reconcile the violent oppositions of verbal division.[7]

The unity-diversity tension has been intractable in modern politics (and before). The tension, often erupting into cascading violence, is one reason why nationalism is feared today, and why also it cannot be overcome. Constant adjustments in both categories and political discourse and decision-making testify to this core problem in human life: ethnic groups, minorities, cultural subgroups, linguistic cultures, autonomous and semi-autonomous territories, seccessions, federations, unifications, rebellions. What are the consequences of determining that Quebec is a national group, while the Inuit are an indigenous "sub-group"? What should we do with the Roma of Europe? How should we gauge the moral threat of peoples like the Uyghurs to the economic survival of millions of other Chinese, dependent on an integrated political system? How many languages must children learn and for what reason?

The unity-diversity question has been central to the life of the Church as well. This is so, not because the Church is simply a political institution that follows the same social map as any other political institution. It is so because the Church's life is given in the form of the people who lead "any other" people. At the same time, the unity-diversity challenge in the Church is, just as with any other people, the source of tremendous creativity and conflict both. Within this challenge is wrapped up the mission, order, and form of the Church. Taken together these constitute the "soul" of the Church as it is caught up by its divine *assumptor*, Christ Jesus in his Spirit. That soul, as the "we" of the Church, is challenged precisely by the fact that diverse kinds, without annulling this divine diversity, must learn to live as the proper kind of "we" that is Christ's together. We will look at these elements in the next chapters within the context of developing ecclesiology. But here we can broadly lay each one out.

---

7. Nothing in English compares to Arno Borst's four-volume work in German on the interpretation of Babel, *Der Turmbau von Babel*.

Mission

The Church's way of bringing unity to the nations even as they maintain their created distinctions is what governs her entire missionary nature. The Church is that nation which *gathers* other nations within the being and rule of God in Christ. Much of this is embodied in the great proclamation of Jesus' ascension, which depicts the sovereign, crucified, and risen Lord as ordering all the world's peoples. "Jesus shall reign where'er the sun / Doth his successive journeys run," as Isaac Watts's hymn puts the case. The relationship of this ascended Christ to the nations' reception of God's truth emerges directly from the prophetic promises associated especially with Daniel. The Church is the missionary arm of the ascended Christ, as Luke's account in Acts 1 makes clear: enlivened by the Spirit of Jesus, the Church moves out to the nations as his witness.

This witness, however, is a fundamentally communicative act, specifically as it engages Israel and the nations together. As Paul writes:

> For whosoever shall call upon the name of the Lord shall be saved. How then shall they call on him in whom they have not believed? and how shall they believe in him of whom they have not heard? and how shall they hear without a preacher? And how shall they preach, except they be sent? as it is written, How beautiful are the feet of them that preach the gospel of peace, and bring glad tidings of good things! (Rom 10:13–15 KJV)

As Matthew's, Luke's, and Paul's discussions make clear, the one witness to Christ involves teaching and preaching with the Scriptures themselves, in Law, Prophet, and Psalm as the core of this articulation (cf. Luke 24:25, 27, 32, 44–48), in a manner that distinct nations can understand. To gather the nations is to communicate the whole Scriptures of Christ to the nations.

Yet the Scriptures are not given in a revealed *language*, but in the act of being spoken and heard in their single truth by specific peoples themselves. It is true, as Paul writes, that "there is no difference between the Jew and the Greek: for the same Lord over all is rich unto all that call upon him" (Rom 10:12). But when Paul speaks of "no difference," he is referring to the standing each has before God, as commonly bound to the Lordship and redemption of Christ, not to some erasure of "kind." Precisely in the preaching of this good news, there must be comprehensible "distinctions" in the language used. Otherwise this one gospel cannot be grasped in the distinction of the nations: "And even things without life giving sound, whether pipe or harp, except they give a distinction in the sounds, how shall it be known what is piped or harped?" (1 Cor 14:7 KJV). The radical scene of Pentecost in Acts 2 lays out how the "wonderful" works of God are given in each language, but spoken by the same apostolic voice.

> Now when this was noised abroad, the multitude came together, and were confounded, because that every man heard them speak in his own language. And they were all amazed and marvelled, saying one to another, Behold, are not all these which speak Galilaeans? And how hear we every man in our own tongue, wherein we were born? Parthians, and Medes, and Elamites, and the dwellers in Mesopotamia, and in Judaea, and Cappadocia, in Pontus, and Asia, Phrygia, and Pamphylia, in Egypt, and in the parts of Libya about Cyrene, and strangers of Rome, Jews and proselytes, Cretes and Arabians, we do hear them speak in our tongues the wonderful works of God. (Acts 2:6–11 KJV)

What the Bible calls "the gift of tongues" became quite explicitly the gift of learning languages and translating the Scriptures into the mother tongues of peoples around the world. This was the judgment of sixteenth-century Jesuit missionaries, who not only lamented the fact that the miracle of Acts 2 was not to be theirs, but also wondered at how marvelously God provided the wisdom and endurance to learn, over years of labor, the strange tongues of those for whom the gospel was a strange truth. Translation of the Scriptures was the great work of the Church's national tutelage: Latin, Syriac, Gothic, Ethiopian, Armenian, and then a host of languages, in Europe, but later across the globe.

More than anyone, Lamin Sanneh has articulated the powerful character of this reality. The vernacularization of the Scriptures was central to the Church's growth. But it handed over the power of the gospel to local peoples, first linguistically and then conceptually, formatively, and culturally. This contributed to national renewal, often unwittingly from the perspective of missionaries and colonial authorities. Sanneh, whose expertise is global although originally centered in the Sahel and sub-Saharan Africa, has demonstrated this phenomenon of national renewal in detail in nineteenth- and twentieth-century colonial and post-colonial contexts. Scriptural vernacularization invigorated cultural resilience among particular peoples, as if a new power of vision had been injected into them. It also engendered adaptability in the face of challenges and change in a way that, over time, could be embodied in deepened moral sensitivities, shaped by the richness and depth of the scriptural texts whose meanings required multiple hearers to articulate. It is easy to romanticize the process of scriptural vernacularization as humanistically and politically liberating; but the process has also proven too easy to forget, with pernicious consequences for the continuity of Christian teaching and life. Pauline "pluralism," in Sanneh's terms, derived from the power of scriptural translatability—the past and present of Renan's conception of the nation finding its vital nexus—and that pluralism allowed, or better manifested, the actual life of the Church as it flourished in time.

Certainly, the markers of the history of Christian mission are indicated by the role of the vernacular in Christian formation. The Reformation made this a central element, in Germany and England especially. But Catholics, with whatever resistance, also understood. Translation was at the center of their missionary witness from China to the Americas, even if the Scriptures themselves were often shielded from the effort. In practice, catechesis and available Protestant Bibles meant that there was more convergence between Catholic and Reformed than one sometimes imagines.

Translation was filled with challenges. We have hinted at just a few when it came to the single word "church." As with "church," decisions were made to withhold translation in favor of transliteration—as with the word "God" or "Christ," or the non-biblical but central term "Trinity"—in order to avoid confusions. But just as often this had the effect of maintaining control on the part of missionaries over understanding and even the wielding of religious power. Maintaining Latin terms (among Catholics) or other European terms (among Protestants) could eventually imbue terms with strange ideas and atavistic resonances. Original translations, especially among Protestants, became "classic" texts, sometimes lodged in earlier and pre-colonial semantics, thereby losing their cultural adaptability in a way similar to limitations on sixteenth-century English translations of the Bible. It was not, nor is it today, always easy to control the dynamics of semantic possession, dictating in advance how the meanings of words will be taken up and deployed. The line between vernacularization and deforming enculturation or outright religious syncretism is often hard to distinguish at first. It has become the source of much debate and conflict, from the realities of African Independent Churches to alternative religions like Haiti's Voodoo to the unregulated movement of single individuals among diverse churches and religious groups within which they may have simultaneous membership. Hence, the project of vernacularization has led to perverted adaptations of the gospel from the side of missionaries and host cultures both.

Some of the positive and negative challenges can be seen in this reflection of an English visitor to an Inuit church in Greenland in the late nineteenth century. The church had two hundred members present, the service was in the vernacular, the singing lusty and beautiful, according to the account:

> I could not but be impressed, as we read that evening in the Psalter for the twelfth day, with the force of the words: "Thou that art the hope of all the ends of the earth and of them that remain in the broad sea"; and again, "They that dwell in the uttermost parts of the earth shall be afraid at Thy tokens." And then it seemed sad to think how utterly lost must be the meaning of those words that follow in the same beautiful Psalm: "Thou waterest her furrows, Thou sendest rain into the little valleys thereof, Thou makest it soft with the drops of rain and blessest the increase of it. Thou crownest the year with Thy goodness and Thy clouds drop fatness. They shall drop upon the dwellings of the wilderness and the little hills shall rejoice on every side. The folds shall be full of sheep, the valleys also shall stand so thick with corn that they shall laugh and sing." They have no idea of furrows. They have never seen sheep, nor sheep folds, nor corn. The beauty of course is lost to them, and they are not aware of the existence of so many of our most familiar things. Fortunately in no way is this knowledge necessary for their practical welfare or happiness. Christian influence has brought about many changes, and they are wisely instructed in religion in a natural native way, without the unnecessary accompaniments of a foreign civilization being thrust upon them—their means of living not admitting of these advantages. Far better for them to know and feel the real truth of religion according to their own standard of civilization, however crude that may seem; to be taught their duty in that state of life in which God has placed them; than to introduce a civilization which would breed a spirit of discontent and lead to the extermination of the race.[8]

For all its challenges, the very effort of translation at the source of the Church's life is bound up with its corrigibility. In the process of revision itself, the project of translation has been both ecclesially expressive and formative. At root has been the synergy between the missionary communication

---

8. Carpenter, "Sunday in an Eskimo Village," 485.

and the enlivening of transformed peoplehood, which, as Sanneh has argued, has consistently defined the spiritual energy of the Church from her beginning. This synergy is properly viewed as divine, although only insofar as these acts of communication and popular transformation could be critically—accountably—seen as all part of the one Church of many languages, itself the place of movement into God's fullness. The Church here is not a religiously institutionalized "United Nations," but the place of national translation literally "into Christ."

Order

The ordering of the Church is bound to this fundamental communicative act of scriptural translation in its broadest sense. Ordering the Church is the expression of the way that the translated "memories" remain intact as received and deployed in the present by diverse peoples. In this sense, it is the way the Church as a nation assures that "we," in our diversity, all hear the same things of God, *God's* wonderful acts, in a way that is understood *together* in a variety of tongues.

There has always been a certain functionalism in talking about church order, at least in a modern context, answering the question of "what the most efficient" means of achieving a given mission might be. In the sixteenth century, reformers from Luther to Richard Hooker could be read approaching the ministry in this way. In fact, though, if the Church is just this movement of a people translating peoples into Christ, then the shape of that movement's consistency and integrity will be inextricably linked to God's own purposes. Holding the past's bequest together with the present's accountability to that past in the dynamic act of translation must subject function to the consistent demands of faithfulness. Even the most radically free-church Christian commitments, devoid of institutional ties to larger networks of congregations, depend on some means of discerning faithful stewarding of the gospel, whether it is by congregational voting, representative boards, cooperative clergy approval processes, or simply individual decisions as to membership. These forms of ordering the congregations, or larger groups of them, reflect quite specific claims regarding the divine directives of the Scriptures and the animating will of the Spirit within the Church—no less so than more catholic versions of episcopal governance and broader authoritative teaching offices. In every case, the ordering of the Church is viewed as the expression of the Church's missionary accountability in moving through time among the nations.

The functions and visible shape of ministry in governance, teaching, and liturgy have no doubt varied historically, even within single Christian traditions. Only the most adamant and ahistorical traditionalists would deny this. But the very claim of the Church to be the nation for the nations means that such variance must, at the least, be subject to profound continuities of purpose and consequence. Some of this continuity, rather than divergence in historical Christian debate and division, has returned to focus in more recent ecumenical discussion, the most prominent being the 1982 agreement among representatives of the World Council of Churches now known as "Baptism, Eucharist, Ministry" (BEM). The section of BEM on the ministry was not so much an attempt to define common denominators among Christian groups, but to locate their fundamental scriptural and providential aims, which might involve the call to reform. One way to get at this fundamental aim is to look at the progress of argument in Paul's discussion of the Church's ordering in 1 Corinthians.

Simply following the sequence of several of the central chapters indicates the fundamental ordering movement of the Church here in the terms we have laid out. The Corinthian church is riven by factions, as the first part of the letter makes clear. The divisions of Babel are embodied in claims to diverse leaders in the church—Paul, Apollos, Cephas, and others; and Paul contrasts this with the single personhood of Christ Jesus. But Paul does not describe this contrast in terms of a single divine authority over and against a multiplicity of vying human authorities, including the divisions of Jew and Greek, although that description is not simply contradicted either. For the single authority of the Last Adam—"the power and wisdom of God"—is given in terms of "folly" and "scandal," that is, in terms of the weakness of the cross (chapter 1), and the cross in its single form does not abolish the multiplicities of human power exercised. There are still various teachers and a range of ministers and laborers; each will necessarily do his or her own work in a way that is distinct and distinctly judged by God (3:10-15). Yet it is this personally and temporally variegated work and judgment that is finally made into the single "temple" that is the household of God's Spirit (3:16-23).

When Paul then goes on to outline the form of ministry within the church, he does so in a way that describes how this variegated and variously judged work must in fact exhibit the integrating life of Christ crucified. It is *this* Adam and his fate who moves the Church forward in a way that maintains rather than subverts the faithful engagement of past truth and present accountability. Paul locates the ordering ministries of the Church—from apostles "first" to prophets, teachers, healers, administrators and so on—in a single "body," as individual "members" of it (12:27–30). The single body is without division ("schism"), and each part "cares for" the other. If there are functions for each ministry, they are ones whose actual engagement is governed by this location and meaning.

Paul explains this in chapter 13 in terms of "love," and he articulates this in a way that is explicitly determined by the form of those who follow Christ, characterized by the elements that his crucifixion draws behind him as he moves through the world:

> Charity suffereth long, [and] is kind; charity envieth not; charity vaunteth not itself, is not puffed up, Doth not behave itself unseemly, seeketh not her own, is not easily provoked, thinketh no evil; Rejoiceth not in iniquity, but rejoiceth in the truth; Beareth all things, believeth all things, hopeth all things, endureth all things. (1 Cor 13:4–7 KJV)

In some ways, this vision of ecclesial order seems somewhat at odds with the kind of apostolic authority Paul often tries to wield in the midst of being questioned or contradicted by his converts. He has already castigated them openly and demanded that they follow his directives (e.g., chapter 5). But even in these contexts, Paul will step back and admit that the "judgment" he may exercise personally is, in the end, itself subject to God's own judgment. In 2 Corinthians, his authority is explicitly wrapped up in the weakness of the cross, which he realizes must relativize the coercive power of his demands (e.g., 2 Cor 11:23–30). His admission, pressed to the point of insistence, coincides directly with Jesus' own description of apostolic authority:

> But it shall not be so among you; but whoever would be great among you must be your servant, and whoever would be first among you must be slave of all. For the Son of man also came not to be served but to serve, and to give his life as a ransom for many. (Mark 10:43–45 RSV)

> For whether [is] greater, he that sitteth at meat, or he that serveth? [is] not he that sitteth at meat? but I am among you as he that serveth. (Luke 22:27 KJV)

For Paul, however, this particular "slavery" given in Christ is linked to the knowledge of God, whose form takes hold of us, in its initiative, before we are able to articulate it fully (1 Cor 13:9–12). Paul the apostle, along with the other apostles, is only so because he has been taken up into the life the first Apostle—the Son, "sent into the world" (John 3:17). What became the three "theological virtues" within the tradition of the Church—faith, hope, and love—now stand as the ordering practice and posture for knowledge-on-the-way.

None of this tells us what disputants might wish to know about bishops or women clergy. But Paul's discussion is given precisely in the context of experienced conflict within the church. It therefore *does* indicate an approach to decision-making that is directed toward holding together the tradition of the Scriptures and apostolic witness, on the one hand, and its communication into the multiplying registers of the nations on the other, in a consistent and non-divisive manner. Church order is about oneness. Furthermore, in Paul's ordering this oneness is very specifically oriented toward the inevitable conversation and debate, discernment, and understanding that must mark the movement of the nations. Unity is a set of enacted practices, not a static condition. Nothing in the history of the Church has supplanted this orientation, at least as a compelling alternative to Babelic fragmentation.

Practice

If the soul of a nation lies in its integration of tradition and present faithfulness, the Church's soul is something identified within the ongoing forms by which the Scriptures are communicated and received by the nations themselves. Put another way, this soul takes shape such that translated distinctions can be coordinated and integrated. This is why Scripture lies at the root of the Church's life. It is also why the Church's ministry and counsel are given in terms of an ordered approach to its engagement, an approach that follows the forms of Jesus' own apostolic service as the Son sent into the world and traversing it on his way to the Father.

I have stated that this constitutes a kind of "tutelage" of the nations. For Israel, this is expressed in terms of being a "holy nation" among other nations (Exod 19:6; Lev 19:2), applied in continuity to the Church (1 Pet 2:9; cf. Matt 5:48). In a way, the frame of the Church's ordering in faith, hope, and love is exactly *what* the Church seeks to shape its people into embodying, for it is the apostle who is first called to this life, and the great Apostle, Jesus, who is its perfection. To this extent, the Church's ministry, traditionally conceived, is essential to the Church's fullness of life, and any dissonance between ordering ministry or decision-making and "Christian life" for the whole people has historically led to the dissolution of the Church's mission and health.

The form of Christian life, given in holiness, prayer, and the common service of the nations, constitutes the "way" of the Church's existence in time. Traditionally, this was laid out in the forms of catechesis that marked out the "two ways" of life and death offered to all peoples. Catechesis, which simply means "teaching," refers to the primary shape of the Christian life as that of a "learner" or "disciple" (*mathetes*). Apostles, evangelists, and teachers encouraged new Christians to pursue life according to the catechetical map provided by the Church and received from Israel (cf. Deut 30:15; Eph 2:1–3; Col 1:10–13, etc.). Some of this had already been well established in the formation of the nations according to the "laws of Noah," viewed as a universally revealed framework of righteousness, given first to Adam. These laws—e.g., against murder (Gen 20:11), adultery (Gen 39:9), infidelity (Gen 39:8f)—were seen as applicable to the nations as a whole, and as Israel's vocation to enunciate for the sake of others. Just on this basis, Amos could articulate divine judgment on all nations, including Israel.

Within Christianity these laws were not eliminated but profoundly adapted to the wider scriptural depiction of Christ's apostleship, handed over to his own apostles (Matt 28:19–20). The Noahic Law and then the fuller Mosaic Law were assumed in Christ, as he became the embodied vehicle for the nations' salvation.[9] The exact elements in Christian teaching varied and developed from broad discussions in early Christian documents like *The Letter of Barnabas* and *The Didache* to what became an almost universal format in the Western Church, including the Apostles' Creed, the Ten Commandments, and the Lord's Prayer. In practice, these outlines were but frameworks for extended, elaborated, and necessarily enacted practices of truth-telling about God (Creed), holy living (the Commandments), and worship (the Lord's Prayer, but often tied to sacramental liturgy), which would envelop familial life, toil, and generational apprenticeship and dying. Their historical power was understood in much the same terms as

---

9. See Donaldson, *Paul and the Gentiles*, on the especially Pauline theology of how Christ assumed the role of Torah for the redemption of the Gentiles.

Crummell's vision for the "peculiar" vocation of African Americans in late nineteenth-century America: the transformation of one nation through the transfiguration of another in contact with it.

There was nothing mysterious about the content and aim of this catechetical tradition, either. In most cases, both in the East and West, in European and in non-European missionary contexts, the discipled life that was to emerge from this tutelage was scripturally grounded in most details, and its precise form was deliberately gauged according to the dynamics of popular translation. The limitations of such tutelage were the same as those affecting scriptural translation in general across cultures. But in an even more visible way, the deliberate catechesis of the nations has, until recently, proved among the most astonishing embodiments of Christian peopling in the history of the Church. In addition to verbal language, the process has included music, visual artifacts, familial traditions, liturgical styles, and radical experiments and developments in pedagogy itself.[10]

The form of the Church's life as a nation, then, was determined by the Church's own Adamic—First and Last—vocation to bring all nations, in their distinctive kinds, to God's fulfilled purpose as Lord. Chosen among nations by its assumption in the being of Christ, this one nation would lead human particularity away from cacophony into a divine resolution of common praise. Deuteronomy notes the strange way that the nations were, for a time, given over by God to the tutelage of lesser gods (cf. Deut 29:25; 32:8, esp. in the Greek translation), even while Israel was chosen as an object of divinely personal formation. Yet Israel's purpose, as we have seen, was to move from this singular position so as to gather up all in the new Adam, a work fulfilled in God taking human flesh, as Israel's body becoming itself the Body of the nations. The conglomeration of texts here draws this together:

> And he said to me, "You are my servant, Israel, in whom I will be glorified." ... He says: "It is too light a thing that you should be my servant to raise up the tribes of Jacob and to restore the preserved of Israel; I will give you as a light to the nations, that my salvation may reach to the end of the earth." (Isa 49:3, 6 RSV)

---

10. A proper history of catechesis has yet to be written. The work of diverse Christian witnesses from Augustine to Isaac Watts to Bernardino de Sahagún to Francis Blanchet to John Veniaminov opens up a vision of Christian history among the nations—and hence, of the church—that requires new work.

What has been called "supercessionism," the persistent Christian refusal to accept the Church's continuity with Israel, has itself poisoned the formative tutelage of the nations, largely because it has severed Christ from the one body that he has always possessed and that he has given for all nations. We shall turn to this issue in the next chapter. For now, however, we need to emphasize the positive ecclesiological aspect of overcoming the supercessionist heresy. The very recent recognition of this fact, whereby Christ has been re-acknowledged as the head belonging to that one body—of Israel, the Church, and the Nations—marks the renewal of a profound cosmic hymn. For Watts, it sings of how *ethnogenesis*, the origin of peoples, has been transfigured into *ethnokatallage*, the reconciliation of peoples in their multiplied diversity:

> People and realms of every tongue
> Dwell on His love with sweetest song;
> And infant voices shall proclaim
> Their early blessings on His name.
>
> In Him the tribes of Adam boast
> More blessings than their father lost.
>
> Let every creature rise and bring
> Peculiar honors to our King,
> Angels descend with songs again,
> And earth repeat the long Amen.[11]

Watts wrote this, having listened in on the deeper strain:

> After this I looked, and behold, a great multitude which no man could number, from every nation, from all tribes and peoples and tongues, standing before the throne and before the Lamb, clothed in white robes, with palm branches in their hands. (Rev 7:9 RSV)

---

11. Watts, *Psalms of David*, 186–87 (Ps 72).

Further Reading

Anderson, Benedict. *Imagined Communities: Reflections on the Origin and Spread of Nationalism*. Rev. ed. London: Verso, 2006.
Borst, Arno. *Der Turmbau von Babel: Geschichte der Meinungen über Ursprung und Vielfalt der Sprachen und Völker*. 4 vols. Stuttgart: Hiersemann, 1957–63.
Carpenter, Charles Blake. "Sunday in an Eskimo Village." *Churchman* (Oct. 20, 1894) 32–33 (484–85).
Cohen, Shaye. *The Beginnings of Jewishness: Boundaries, Varieties, Uncertainties*. Berkeley: University of California Press, 1999.
Donaldson, Terry. *Paul and the Gentiles: Remapping the Apostle's Convictional World*. Minneapolis: Fortress, 1997.
Eisen, Robert. *The Peace and Violence of Judaism: From the Bible to Modern Zionism*. New York: Oxford University Press, 2011.
Eyl, Jennifer. "Semantic Voids, New Testament Translation, and Anachronism: The Case of Paul's Use of *Ekklesia*." *Method and Theory in the Study of Religion* 26 (2014) 315–39.
Greenberg, Moshe. "Mankind, Israel, and the Nations in Hebraic Heritage." In *No Man Is Alien: Essays on the Unity of Mankind*, edited by J. Robert Nelson, 15–40. Leiden: Brill, 1971.
Hengel, Martin. *Jews, Greeks, Barbarians: Aspects of the Hellenization of Judaism in the Pre-Christian Period*. Philadelphia: Fortress, 1980.
Kaiser, Walter. *Mission in the Old Testament: Israel as a Light to the Nations*. Grand Rapids: Baker, 2000.
Katz, Jacob. *Exclusivism and Tolerance: Jewish-Gentile Relations in the Medieval and Modern Times*. New York: Oxford University Press, 1961.
Morgenstern, Mira. *Conceiving a Nation: The Development of Political Discourse in the Hebrew Bible*. University Park: Pennsylvania State University Press, 2009.
Okoye, James Chukwuma. *Israel and the Nations: A Mission Theology of the Old Testament*. Maryknoll: Orbis, 2006.
Radner, Ephraim. *The End of the Church: A Pneumatology of Christian Division in the West*. Grand Rapids: Eerdmans, 1998.
Rafael, Vicente L. *Contracting Colonialism: Translation and Christian Conversion in Tagalog Society under Early Spanish Rule*. Ithaca, NY: Cornell University Press, 1988.
———. *The Promise of the Foreign: Nationalism and the Technics of Translations in the Spanish Philippines*. Durham: Duke University Press, 2005.
Raisin, Jacob S. *Gentile Reactions to Jewish Ideals with Special Reference to Proselytes*. New York: Philosophical Library, 1953.
Renan, Ernest. *Qu'est-ce qu'une nation? Et autres essais politiques*. Paris: Presses Pocket, 1992.
Sanneh, Lamin. *Translating the Message: The Missionary Impact on Culture*. 2nd ed. Maryknoll: Orbis, 2009.
———. "The Yogi and the Commissar." In *Disciples of All Nations: Pillars of World Christianity*, 131–62. Oxford: Oxford University Press, 2008.
Wells, Samuel, and George R. Sumner. *Esther and Daniel*. Grand Rapids: Brazos, 2013.

Church

Discussion Questions

1. Why is it important for understanding the Church to insist that nations have "histories" and thus are not static entities?

2. In what ways, positive and negative, is the Church a "nation" like other nations?

3. In what way is the Church *not* "like other nations"? What elements are peculiar to the Church's nationhood, and why are they important in terms of the Church's election by God?

6

The Church as Israel

The Repentant Missionary

Some Twentieth-Century Developments in Ecclesiology: People of God and Communion

Looking at the Church as a "people" is a mostly twentieth-century theological development, but not one divorced from a long tradition. Augustine famously spoke of the "City of God" much earlier, and the notion of the Church as a Christian "commonwealth" of some kind became established in the West. Bellarmine's famous comparison of the Church to the "Republic of Venice" draws from this stream of discussion as it developed in the Middle Ages especially and engaged a range of political reflections. But the political aspects came to predominate, focusing ecclesiology on offices and order. Even as Protestants, with their reactive congregationalism, sought to return to the "gathering" aspect of the *ecclesia*, they did so in a way that was also swept up into political self-identities, as the development of Puritan and then Baptist notions took off in the directions of explicitly democratic popular constructions. These were hardly abstract developments either, as the experiments and struggles of Protestant groups in the American colonies demonstrated.

The twentieth-century turn in ecclesiology to the category of peoplehood was driven by at least two responses to this earlier set of traditions. One was a desire to escape the pull of what was seen as a rigidified religious institutionalism. The other was a renewed self-consciousness about the Church as a fundamentally missionary entity. Talk of the "people of God" seemed to return the Church to a kind of pre-political construal without abandoning its collective identity. Furthermore, this pre-political aspect was informed mostly by the scriptural account of Israel as a specifically de-institutionalized people. In the twentieth-century versions of "the People of God," the long period of the Israelite *kingdoms* was deliberately pushed into the shadows, and the exodus and wilderness aspects of Israel were lifted up. Interestingly, the time of Israel's life as a kingdom, with a temple and officers, laws and courts, was of far greater interest in the Middle Ages and early modern period, while the exodus and desert life of the people had far less interest for them. As "people of God," the Church was to be seen in terms of a kind of *movement*, from slavery to a promised end, led directly by God but never settled in an institutional rest or stability. This outlook was marked by the use of qualifiers like "the pilgrim people of God," or "the wilderness people of God." Released from the trappings of established power, the Church could travel lightly in a world seeking new hope, which the Church was called to serve, aiming always at a future promise rather than at a given fullness.

This eschatologically driven, institutionally divested vision made a certain sense in the wake of the world wars. The Church understood how inept it had been in restraining human (mostly Western) madness and now sought to position itself on the side of confused populations caught up in the dizzying political and economic reconfigurations of an ever more divided postwar and decolonizing world. The Church was to be humble in this service of hope, a mission that came to define the heart of ecclesial existence itself. Generation-shaping books from this perspective were written by Lesslie Newbigin, the ecumenical missiologist, whose leadership in the new united Church of South India gave him a frontline position in gauging the Church's life in this new context. Newbigin continues to challenge Christians; and the general postwar perspective on the "people of God" has remained consistent in much contemporary ecclesiology. It can be seen in widely noted volumes by Gehard Lohfink (Catholic) and more recently Stephen Pickard (Anglican).

Institutional humility and mission have been among the great gains in recent "people of God" ecclesiologies. But their somewhat vague relation to actual peoples, indeed the deliberate attempt to detach the Church from *organized* peoples and identify it with a more abstracted notion of peoplehood, has carried with it some problems. One problem that was prominently identified among Catholics especially was that the Church's journeying peoplehood can easily be swept up by the concrete "peoplehood" of those among

The Church as Israel

whom the Church lives. This was why, with the popular work of Hauerwas and Willimon, "being alien" could easily replace peoplehood itself: better to be distinct from every popular movement, than be appropriated to its false character. So, for instance, in 1964 the radically reforming Vatican II Council of the Catholic Church issued, among its many influential decrees, a decree on the Church known as *Lumen Gentium* ("Light to the Nations"), or "The Dogmatic Constitution of the Church." Chapter 2 of the decree contains a famous discussion of the Church as "The People of God." Much was made of this focus, with its clear Old Testament resonances and its shift away from thinking about the Church in primarily institutional categories. But very quickly the phrase got caught up in ecclesial struggles. In 2001, then Cardinal Ratzinger (later Pope Benedict XVI) summarized some of the challenges. He had positive things to say about the "people of God" concept, and noted that it arose in the earlier part of the twentieth century among biblical theologians, and was then taken up by Catholic theologians as a more adaptive way of talking about the Church—compared with the more static or fixed character of the older "image" for the Church as the Body of Christ. A people-oriented concept for the Church was better able, Ratzinger said, to explain the relationship of non-Catholic Christians to the Church (in communion with, if not actually members of it), as well as that of non-Christians ("ordered to" the Church, though not necessarily without salvific hope). Finally, the "people of God" concept was more historically rendered, and could make sense of the Church's experientially imperfect character, since it was, like a "pilgrim," still on its way.

All this was good, and surely Ratzinger was quite right to underscore these elements. But he also noted how the "people of God" concept could be taken, and was in fact taken by many Catholic theologians and leaders, in highly political directions—"people" vs. "authority" or institution, Marxist analysis, liberal ideals of "democratization." Ratzinger, along with others, was particularly concerned with Latin American Christians' generally Leftist orientation, known as "Liberation Theology." Nor was this rendering of the Church a simple slipping into political or sociological reductionism, he thought. From a practical or moral standpoint, when "people" becomes the focus in the Church's self-understanding, it is too easy for the Church to succumb to the enclosing web of competing human interests and organizations. In theory, Ratzinger insisted, Vatican II's notion of "the Church as People God" was meant to focus on the "vertical" aspect of God, and this focus was too easily lost. Again, Ratzinger was probably right here. The capturing and appropriating of the abstract by the tendentious concrete is one reason why some Catholic theologians, like Dulles, preferred to relegate "people of God" to one of a number of "images of the Church," to be applied as hortatively useful, rather than to describe the Church in any essential fashion.

Still, "people" remain a stubborn aspect of the Church as well; and rather than demote the "concept" as being too hard to assimilate to a divine economy, the question to answer is how this aspect is in fact "vertically" bound to God, as Ratzinger (reticently) suggested it was. Theoretically, we could say that "people" is the material concern of the Church; and God is the one who establishes the formal truth of this concern in its very being. Even more precisely, as we will see, we should say that God has established the Church's popular concern as its very being because God has identified himself with that concern. God himself becomes the people who are oriented to their creator. "People," then, is not just an image of the Church, but its constituent matter as bound to God. What we call an "image" of the Church, in its turn, applies rightly only as it explicates somehow the truth relationship between the Church's people and God. But "images" or "concepts" of the Church cannot escape the popular grounding of their application. It is this grounding, furthermore, that challenges Christian witness with its unavoidable insistence: Why are there different churches, often vying? Why is there not in historical practice "one people"? The historical reality that goes with creatureliness, one that defines why there is a Church at all, means that the Church is always facing two inevitable demands that ecclesiology can never escape: to be a people is to press collective distinction, and to be a people for the sake of other peoples is to wade into the waters of deep political struggle.

This is one reason why the ecumenical leaders, despite the rise of "pilgrim" terminology and anti-institutional language among modern ecclesiologists, have never quite been able to let go of the more political aspects of the Church. The gathering of the World Council of Churches in New Delhi in 1961 articulated as clearly as possible what had always been at the heart of the ecumenical vision:

> We believe that the unity which is both God's will and his gift to his Church is being made visible as all in each place who are baptized into Jesus Christ and confess him as Lord and Saviour are brought by the Holy Spirit into one fully committed fellowship, holding the one apostolic faith, preaching the one Gospel,

breaking the one bread, joining in common prayer, and having a corporate life reaching out in witness and service to all and who at the same time are united with the whole Christian fellowship in all places and all ages in such wise that ministry and members are accepted by all, and that all can act and speak together as occasion requires for the tasks to which God calls his people. It is for such unity that we believe we must pray and work.[1]

The Council itself now calls this "probably the greatest run-on sentence in ecumenical history." The sentence itself has become the classic statement of ecumenism's commitment to "visible" "organic unity," in which confession, baptism, gathering, teaching, Eucharist, prayer, ministry, and witness are somehow "common" among all Christians. With such an understanding in mind, the concrete questions of congruent teaching, mutual recognitions, integrated ministries, coordinated decision-making, and finally, actual worship together became the bread and butter of ecumenical obligation. Yet this view of the Church, informing the efforts of dialogue and discussion, did not square with the developing looseness with which "people of God" conceptions were being self-consciously deployed.

Just out of this tension arose the second great ecclesiological movement of recent times, so-called "communion ecclesiology." More than anything, this was an ecumenical development that arose (or so it seems in retrospect) as a way to soften the hard institutional challenges of something like the New Delhi vision, sublating them into thoroughly divine and hence non-concrete dynamics, not unlike those in the relationships among the three persons of the Trinity. Initially in the Catholic context, this was less obvious. The Church's character as "communion" was defined in terms of the communion existent among its members and with God, in a kind of "sacramental" sense. Hence, the Eucharist was viewed as the most crystalline expression of the Church in this aspect.[2] This way of looking at communion—often using the Greek word *koinonia*—was certainly trinitarian, in the sense that it acknowledged the active role of all three persons of the Trinity in the life of the gathered eucharistic people. To speak of "the Church as Communion" fit seamlessly with a certain vision of the Church as the "people of God," moving in mission toward a full life with God, who is in fact Father, Son, and Holy Spirit:

---

1. World Council of Churches, "New Delhi Statement."
2. See the Congregation for the Doctrine of the Faith, *Letter to the Bishops*.

Church

> Communion implies that the Church is a dynamic reality moving towards its fulfilment. Communion embraces both the visible gathering of God's people and its divine life-giving source. We are thus directed to the life of God, Father, Son and Holy Spirit, the life God wills to share with all people. There is held before us the vision of God's reign over the whole of creation, and of the Church as the firstfruits of humankind which is drawn into that divine life through acceptance of the redemption given in Jesus Christ.[3]

Furthermore, this way of looking at the Church's communion was seen as completely congruent with standard notions of popular Christianity—that is, with the elements that define the nationhood of the Church:

> [The Church is founded on] the confession of the one apostolic faith, revealed in the scriptures, and set forth in the creeds. It is founded upon one baptism. The one celebration of the Eucharist is its pre-eminent expression and focus. It necessarily finds expression in shared commitment to mission entrusted by Christ to his Church. It is a life of shared concern for one another in mutual forbearance, submission, gentleness and love; in the placing of the interests of others above the interests of self; in making room for each other in the body of Christ; in solidarity with the poor and the powerless; and in the sharing of gifts both material and spiritual (cf. Acts 2:44). Also constitutive of life in communion is acceptance of the same basic moral values, the sharing of the same vision of humanity created in the image of God and recreated in Christ and the common confession of the one hope in the final consummation of the Kingdom of God. For the nurture and growth of this communion, Christ the Lord has provided a ministry of oversight, the fullness of which is entrusted to the episcopate, which has the responsibility of maintaining and expressing the unity of the churches.[4]

But the "internal" nature of God as a relationship of three persons in unity soon became viewed as a good way to look at the Church itself. Spurred by theological work on what became known as "social trinitarianism"—work done by all strands of the Christian tradition—trinitarian "relations" came to be seen as the source, foundation, or model for the proper relations of humankind, perfected in the communion of the Church. The Church was to be (or "is" in fact) the "image" of the Trinity's own divine

---

3. Anglican–Roman Catholic International Dialogue, "Church as Communion," para. 3.

4. Ibid., para. 45.

life, and its historical existence must be measured by this trinitarian self-existence. The World Council of Churches' Faith and Order Conference devoted itself to this topic in 1993, stating clearly that the communion (*koinonia*) of God's trinitarian nature *is* the communion of the Church.

> This koinonia which we share is nothing less than the reconciling presence of the love of God. God wills unity for the Church, for humanity, and for creation because God is a koinonia of love, the unity of the Father, Son and Holy Spirit. This koinonia comes to us as a gift we can only accept in gratitude.[5]

Local Anglican–Roman Catholic dialogue groups began saying the same thing, as did Lutherans, and, most fully, the Anglican-Orthodox dialogue. As a reflection of the Trinity, the Church is a communion of diverse persons characterized by "mutuality," "relationality," "openness" "service," and "unity in diversity."

The terms were not so much false as politically flaccid, incapable of application and traction. In the face of matters of common confession and teaching, shared sacramental life, oversight, and decision-making, trinitarian communion talk could not deliver. Anglicans and Roman Catholics (and Orthodox) are arguably further apart than before; the same is true for Anglicans and Lutherans, despite some concrete though finally superficial mutual recognitions of ministry. This is so because Anglicans themselves, proud of their very ordering as a "communion," have descended into a spectacular dynamic of mutual separation.

The reason for the failure of communion ecclesiology to change the way the Church actually lives is simple. Because communion ecclesiology locates the Church's life in the inner life of God as its reflection, it leaves the Church bereft of access to the human demands that its actual existence must struggle with. God's person has no need to overcome anything, for it is perfect. God's life—unless one wants to reduce it to a creaturely process itself—has no need to engage the distinctions of creation as they list and topple on one another; it has no need to negotiate, to compromise, to sacrifice, to forgive and trust. God's life has no need of these things because it is not burdened with the edges of created difference and the sin that has sharpened these. Divine mutuality can be adored, but it cannot be modeled. To be the Church, one must figure out how to be, and at least submit to being, an actual people.

---

5. World Council of Churches, "Message," para. 4.

The Church as Israel:
Figural Ecclesiology

Communion ecclesiology, along with the looser "pilgrim" aspects of peoplehood, have dominated ecclesiology in the past four decades, engaging theologians as diverse as John Zizioulas and Jürgen Moltmann. Yet they have never quite worked, largely because neither approach could make sense of the Church's actual life of historical sin, suffering, and the demands of collective or popular formation. The limitations go back specifically to the question of Israel. The Church is not simply an *aspect* of Israel—the wandering Aramean and pilgrim people, living only from the manna of the desert and seeking a promised home, nor the integrated people ordered in ranks before God. The Church is also the Israel who battled, betrayed, rebelled, built and ordered its life, had censuses and civil wars, was faithless and feckless, was besieged and battered, exiled, enslaved and indentured. Here we see the *Totus Christus*, the whole Christ, given in the *Totus Israel*, the whole Israel.

The idea that the Church is Israel—and vice versa—is one we have been working with in a general way thus far in this volume, in large measure because it has always been a Christian presupposition, however ill-formulated or aberrantly applied. In the context of contemporary discussions such as those just mentioned, it was George Lindbeck who first proposed that ecclesiology be renewed in the form of "Israelology," in part to stabilize some of the floating elements we have just noted. Lindbeck's proposal was motivated by various concerns. One of them was his clear sense that the Church's deliberate decoupling of itself from Israel was bound up with a range of stunted self-identities and eventually sinful attitudes. Reaffirming its Israel-identity, the Church could face itself responsibly, take account of its actions, repent, and be renewed.

Accountability becomes paramount in the present discussion. The Church as a people is, like any people, responsible for its popular or national temptations and sins, as well as its collective reordering. With a specific national vocation, these responsibilities are both unique and acute. The ecclesial flight from Israel has had the effect of obscuring what it is that a people must do: political struggle. With respect to the particular vocation of the Church, the obscuring has rendered the Church not only incapable of fulfilling her vocation *as* Israel, but has also made the Church too much *like* Israel in just the areas Israel has herself rebelled against her divine calling. The Church is like any other nation in many respects, not all good; as Israel, that likeness is exactly the place where ecclesiology exposes a divine truth.

The failures of peoplehood more broadly are legion and well known. They are one of the grounds upon which the search for ecclesiodicy, in its more dogmatic forms, has been pursued, in an effort to articulate an "inner" or "essential" and certainly stable nature for the Church that can somehow transcend such failures. If the Church is not what it claims to be in terms of historical witness, then surely we must seek the Church's truth in some ahistorical and certainly spiritual realm. Almost all modern observers of the Christian Church are at least dimly aware—often acutely so—of Christian division, rancor, and sometimes gross complicity in socialized suffering and violence. One of the most common things one hears from the children of pastors, children who in adulthood have left the church, is that they were disillusioned and even angry at seeing what congregations did to their fathers and families. We can write that on a large scale with respect to the Church and her members.

But disenchantment need not end in loss of faith, and in general it has not in any consistent way. Christians have continued to "love" the Church. The reality of Christ Jesus' own life and divine power in his Spirit has always remained present in the Church somehow, although explaining this often involves appeals to "mystery" (more Catholic) and to transcendent or "invisible" realities (Protestant) that are difficult to identify historically. Usually, however, faith in the Church has been maintained by local and personal commitments taking precedence over the worrying concerns of the Church's popular failures. Still, these failures have proven hard to avoid at some point, and in fact much of the character of modern Christian apologetics has been driven by this question of how to resolve these failures in the face of a divinely given Church that one loves. If nothing else, the very discipline which we now call "ecclesiology," which developed for the most part (as we have seen) only in and after the sixteenth century, is at root an attempt to answer the challenge. That is to say, ecclesiology is really a form of ecclesiodicy—a "justifying of the Church," a discipline that is itself a peculiarly Christian form of *theodicy*, the justification of God in the face of seemingly contradictory evidence from within the world. Ecclesiology developed as Christians proclaimed the Christian church as "one, holy, catholic, and apostolic," even while the world was seeing something that did not conform to this claim. To this day Christians affirm that Jesus really *is* Lord, and Lord of his Church, which is his body. How do we make sense of all these inescapable facts at once?

What Lindbeck and others began to see is that there is no simple answer to this in terms of a conceptual theory that could be propositionally articulated, as was once done in scholastic handbooks of both Catholic and Protestant form. Those answers tended to strike out some of the claims that we must hold concurrently: if the Church is "one," then there really is *no* division of the Church, only sinful heresy and schism (a common Catholic response that supported a view of the Church's fundamental "infallibility"). Again, if what we see are visible failures of Christians, then what we should conclude is that there really is *no* visible "real" Church to contradict our claims of faith (a common Protestant response, relying on the hidden agglomeration of the predestined saints to define the Church). Finally, a more liberal response has been that, given the failures of the Church, Jesus really is not Lord of the Church, but rather of something else, like the struggle for justice. These kinds of answers, which undergird traditional ecclesiology, sound increasingly hollow. But holding *all* the claims together—the oneness, holiness, catholicity and apostolicity of the Church, their contradiction in historical terms, and the Lordship of Christ—doesn't really compute in scholastic terms. Indeed, one of the directions Lindbeck pointed to was locating "the ecclesiological" in the realm of scriptural reading, and with it the whole issue of ecclesiodicy. That is, to understand the Church is to read Scripture a certain way. Put ontologically, the Christian Church is given to us in the forms of Scripture's reference, logically prior to the Church's actual historical embodiment. History is given by Scripture. One cannot distill the Christian Church *out of* Scripture as the theoretical conclusion to a set of scriptural propositions. Rather, the Church's temporal contours match what Scripture says about the life of the people of God in the world, so that how the Scriptures speak of the Church *is* in fact the Church's life. Finally, the way the Scriptures speak of this is in speaking about Israel.

This approach, which I call a "figural" ecclesiology, depends on reading Scripture and apprehending the forms or figures of Israel's life within it. This constitutes a discipline of engaging the Bible in an ongoing fashion, rather than seeking out propositions that would timelessly identify the Church apart from the actual life of Israel, scripturally described. To approach ecclesiology in this way is to reframe, at least in this instance, both its theological task and more importantly the apologetic task that has been so central to the historic discipline of ecclesiology. For a scriptural-figural ecclesiology cannot tell anybody why the Church should be believed; or why this or that church should be followed. It can only say: here is the Church—Israel!—and look what is happening to it. At that point, the Christian can only then say, "and here is what I must do." It is much like Peter's sermon in Acts 2 to the assembled people of Israel itself, as it were, gathered in Jerusalem on the day of Pentecost. This is who you are, O Israel! Here is what Joel says, here is what David says, and here is Jesus: I lay it out before you. What then? Repent and be baptized! Peter's sermon is constantly being repeated in the history of the world, in different ways, among the nations, and thus with adjusted outcomes. But the framework has remained basic: I speak to you of Israel and the Christ; and this is what the Church now is, and what is hence our calling.

From this follow a good many things that are traditionally matters of ecclesiological concern: worship, order, ministry, teaching. These follow, however, insofar as they are the constituting elements of Israel's scriptural life, lived as the Church for the nations. Christians deal with these elements and make decisions about them on the basis of what they both see as Israel, and what they live as Israel, often reluctantly and recalcitrantly. The theological tension between seeing the Church as a "universal" reality and seeing it as a "particular" set of local congregations has hounded both Catholics and Protestants. The Church as Israel in the Scriptures does not resolve this tension, but at least it locates the place to grapple with it: the fate of Israel in the world, elected and subjected to the forces of temporal choices and divine ordering. There is only one people called Israel, with one calling, given one set of gifts. This is a "universal" referent. But that people has done this and that, and been taken here and there, and been given the responsibility to repent and follow in this and that way and at such and such a time. These "particulars" are not simply parts of the one Church; they are that Church as it *is* the Israel of the Word of God, as she in fact lives in the time of God's creation.

Israel, Jew, and Gentile

The Church is a people, a nation of a certain kind, that exists on behalf of all nations in their distinctive kinds, and for their multiplied reconciliation. The Church's mission, order, and formative life is distinct in some way, and is thus common to the "kind" that is the Church. Yet that distinctiveness, paradoxically, is able to maintain and burnish the distinctiveness of the nations whom the Church helps gather into Christ. This paradox and its difficult navigation in practice have been at the root of ecclesiology's scar-marked form. The Church's failure as a people lies in her failure properly to engage and reconcile the peoplehood of the nations. This leads us back to the more standard themes of the Church: her form, her ministry, her practices. Although each of these elements, as they now present themselves to observers, has been determined fundamentally by her particular national destiny, they have also been shaped by the specific ways that destiny has been resisted by the Church's people from the start. In this sense, ecclesiology is not defined simply by what the Church has been called to do, but by the history of that vocation's popular receipt and God's response. This is exactly the story of Israel.

The unity of the Old and New Testaments is fundamental and exhaustive. It is given in Jesus Christ, who is the single carrier of one people across time, for the sake of all peoples. If there is a distinction between Old and New Testaments, as their designations indicate, it is in the way this one story is *shown* to be the case within history. Paul will speak of a "revelation of a mystery" that was held in "secret" since the world began (Rom 16:25). Yet the mystery is nonetheless the truth of the world since its beginning, and therefore the truth to which Old and New Testaments are equally bound, indeed bound as one. Only the manifestation of this truth, its obviousness, marks a distinction in time, in the way that it can be "seen" and "touched" (1 John 1:1-2). To see, hear, and touch Jesus is to understand Old and New together, and to see the identity in time of Israel and the Church.

The distinction between Israel and the Church, which both Jew and Gentile have insisted upon over the centuries, is the mark of a terrible blindness, though one long noted by God. Israel is just such a place of blindness: "Son of man, thou dwellest in the midst of a rebellious house, which have eyes to see, and see not; they have ears to hear, and hear not: for they [are] a rebellious house" (Ezek 12:2 KJV). Isaiah's similar claim (Isa 6:9-10) becomes a common New Testament trope, used by Jesus (e.g., Mark 4:12) and taken up by Paul (Acts 28:25-28; Rom 11:7-8). But Jesus can apply this warning directly to his disciples: "Having eyes, see ye not? and having ears, hear ye not? and do ye not remember?" (Mark 8:18 KJV). A line of continuity from Isaiah to the Church is established around blindness, one that cannot see Jew and Gentile given their reconciled form through the ministry of Israel.

The Church as Israel

I emphasize all this because such blindness is the original ecclesiological scar. On the one hand, the early church entered into a debate over who constituted the "true" Israel—Jews or the (now Gentile) Church. That the Church *was* "Israel" was a given, as the earliest Christian apologists insisted, identifying Israel with Christ himself.[6] But the distinction between the "Jewishness" of the Israel from the past and the Gentileness of the Israel of the Church was now established. The claim of Ephesians 2:14–18 seemed but a momentary threshold, one that once crossed could be left behind. The Jews had been rejected, that much was clear. And this rejection was then read back into the Old Testament itself, so that "Israel," for the Christian Church, became a spiritual entity whose integrity as the referent of divine revelation in the Scriptures could only be grasped in ways that transcended the actual story of her life as a nation. The difficult relationship with God given in faithfulness and faithlessness was a problem faced by Jews, not so much by Christians. The Israel of the Old Testament, in other words, had little to say concretely to the Church of the New. This meant, in practical terms, that the Church no longer consistently read the Old Testament as a place where she could see herself reflected directly in its narrative, in judgment and mercy both. Romans 11:21—Paul's warning to Gentiles on the basis of God's dealing with Israel's people—was a hollow plea. Despite holding on to the title of Israel, the Church had detached it from the Old Testament's actual historical reference.

The results of this decoupling are well known and lamentable. Jews became the original "other" to the Church, the one nation that stood as a contrast to the Church's being, the example of a stubborn "carnal" nationalism in its own right.[7] One can speculate on the psychosocial aspects of this—Judaism as the reminder of the Church's own susceptibility to historical dissolution, the shadow of Christianity's flight into her own form of Gnostic spiritualism and (false) liberation from the demands of historical mission. Anti-Semitism, in any case, proved to be the Church's fundamental rebellion against her own mission as a "light to the nations," having abandoned the very national soul of her own divine creation.

In our day, after the acknowledgment of Christian crimes against the Jews became unavoidable in the wake of World War II, a kind of reverse

---

6. Justin Martyr, *Dialogue with Trypho*, c. 130. On the struggle over who owned the "true Israel," see Marcel Simon's classic text, *Versus Israel*.

7. More recently, Jewish scholars have begun to study the way the Jews altered their own self-understanding in response to Christianity as *their* defining "other." See Yuval, *Two Nations in Your Womb*.

rejection of the Jews has taken place, in the form of missionary paralysis or even denial. Having murdered the Jews over the centuries out of a failure to heed the gospel, Christians since the 1950s have tended to place them in a category of indigenous reserve, where they are to be protected from the gospel altogether. *This* nation will be withheld from Christ's revealed word, as a kind of penance for past Christian misdeeds. Theological rationales have been offered for this. There are, for example, "two covenants" that God has made, one with the Jews and one with the Christian Church, and there is thus no need to confuse the two. This of course means that ecclesiology is basically a study of the Gentiles. Another approach has been to press religious pluralism yet more widely, allowing for "many paths" to God that would include the religions of the Gentiles themselves—Hinduism, Buddhism, and Islam, among others. This provides an ecclesiology that is roundly pluralistic in its own right, and founded mostly on individual choice or happenstance.

To point out these outcomes is not to say that the way in which Israel and the Church are to be properly identified is obvious. The statement "the Church is Israel" somehow needs to take into account the fact that the Israel that is made up of Jews is not self-evidently a part of the Christian Church in experiential terms, and that Christians (Jewish and Gentile in national origin) and Jews are clearly two distinct groups with respect to theological claims and the order of common life before God. In a basic way, "Israel" has been divided for centuries, analogously to the split between Judah and Israel (or Ephraim or Samaria) after the reign of Solomon: there is a Christian part of Israel, "the Church," and a Jewish part ("the Jews"). One might even wish to root this division in fundamental patterns of human sin, whose apportionment could vary, shifting weight decidedly to the side of the Church. But, as the Jewish Christian theologian Jakob Jocz insists, "There can be no plural to Israel. The idea of another Israel is utterly alien to the N.T., as alien as the idea that beside the God of Israel there can be another God."[8] Division is not multiplication; it is simply brokenness.

But division, just because it is bound to sin, obscures reality. Paul himself struggles to keep the thread clear, in part because of this obscuring, in the key passage of Romans 9–11 that discusses the strange confrontation of Jew and Gentile that then becomes the confrontation of Israel and the Church. As Paul tries to explain how Israel has failed to acknowledge the Christ in faith, yet is still the Israel of God's election, his terms seem to

---

8. Jocz, *Theology of Election*, 120.

The Church as Israel

shift: he can speak of Israel as "children" after the "flesh" (unbelieving) in contrast to an Israel after the "Spirit" (Rom 9:8; cf. Gal 4:29). After all, being an Israelite (by flesh) does not make one a *true* Israelite (cf. Rom 9:6). Does this mean, then, that Paul considers unbelieving Jews to be in fact false Israelites, and *not* part of the people elected by God and called by God "Israel"? This is by no means clear. For he also calls those Israelites who are his own "flesh" *just these Israelites* whom God has adopted, and covenanted with, and promised (9:4). Just these Israelites of the "flesh" are those whom Paul seeks to bring to Christ, and to whom, at the end of this long and complex passage, he applies an ultimate promise of "reconciliation" and "life from the dead" (11:15). The promise, finally, is expanded beyond potentiality or partiality to some mysterious purpose of God, by which Israel's great unfaithfulness is turned and used by God for Gentile conversion and her own final ingathering. "And so all Israel shall be saved" (11:26 KJV), and this because in the end, "the gifts and calling of God are without repentance" (11:29 KJV). It is a claim that Paul presses to an astonishing inclusivity: "For God hath concluded them all in unbelief, that he might have mercy upon all" (11:32 KJV).

Barth was able to draw from this a claim that, in God's own time, all Jews would be saved in a kind of corporate divine act. It was a conclusion that other theologians like Jocz believed might undermine the demand for individual repentance and conversion, if taken too broadly. In this, Jocz was surely correct. *Jewish* believing in Christ's Lordship is not only a necessary calling, but an inevitable one given who God is in Christ Jesus and given the very ordering of the Church from her manifest source in Christ, where Jew and Gentile are gathered. So-called "Messianic Jews" today—Jewish believers in Christ, mostly in an evangelical form, who nonetheless maintain Jewish identity and a range of Jewish practices—represent a key witness to the ongoing reality of this divine work. So too do the often-overlooked Jewish Christians in more established churches, both Catholic and Protestant. But leaving aside the question of conversionary mechanics, which are potentially quite complex, the point for both Barth and Jocz was that God was using Jewish Israel for a purpose that would at some point be made clear in its integration with the Church as a whole. Barth, in any case, saw the relationship of Church and Jew to be an "ecumenical" issue, not an interreligious one, indeed as he said late in life to the pope, the "ultimately only one truly great ecumenical question."[9] That the "true Israel" could in

---

9. Quoted in Johnson, "New Testament Understanding," 236.

some way also be filled with Jewish unbelievers had been made abundantly clear, after all, under National Socialism in Germany. Being a *Jew*, whether or not a Christian at the same time, was a mark of indelible solidarity with Israel, and in this case with her smiting.

One inadequate way to handle this difficult knot of identity would be to take up an admittedly negative contrast from the Middle Ages—Church and Synagogue—and subvert it by turning it into a matter of nations more particularly: Gentile Church and Jewish Synagogue, making each an aspect of the Ekklesia or Church of Israel itself. Both *are* Israel, and as such both are subject to the judgment and mercy of God as nations among nations, yet as called to a reconciled place within the people of God. Another approach, perhaps more consistent even if conceptually difficult, is to speak of the Church as Israel under a certain aspect. She is "Israel-on-the-way"—the way by which the nations, beginning with the Jews, are gathered into Christ. This aspect is distinct from other aspects of Israel, in particular from her Jewish self-ordering in the world. Identity in this case is founded in historical location and practice, in *how* the nations are gathered with Israel. Jocz attempted something like this, although altering the terms somewhat, when he described Israel as existing both as Church (the Christian Church, which is in a kind of collective identity of visible bonds defined by faith in Christ), and as Mission, that is, as the object of God's address, judgment and mercy at once, a people in the process of being converted. Israel as "mission," in this case, would include Jew and Christian both, whatever the condition of their faith, for it would always be a faith in need of some kind of conversion.

The Church-as-Israel is not easily parsed, perhaps no more easily than the nature of Christ. But it involves a relationship of Jew (believing or non-Christian) and Christian believer (whether Gentile or Jewish) that is ordered *together* to an obedience of God that will finally give rise to a common praise, as the vision of Revelation 7 indicates. From the standpoint of ecclesiology, Catholic and Reformed Christians have always insisted on this eschatological goal of divine glorification, gazing upon the Lamb, as it is founded in the event of Pentecost in Acts 2. But such a goal does not demand that the Church be viewed as a single stream, a single "people" growing from the Abrahamic current into a widening river that finally sweeps all into its midst—a reverse universal deluge. This vision, among certain modern proponents of the "people of God" theology, can sometimes simply reproduce, if in more dynamic terms, a monolithic cultural understanding of the Church. "Properly speaking, the Church is just the people of God, just humanity remade in Christ," Newbigin wrote.[10] This entails diversity in a certain way, "as much variety as the human race," but no "segregation" according to "temperaments" and "traditions." Newbigin, after all, had come to worry about the invasive and destructive effects of particular cultures on the gospel (especially forms of "enlightenment" in Western culture) and wanted to press for a specific *Christian* distinctiveness that was, in a sense, ranged against the array of particular fallen human cultures in the world. Christianity was itself "alien" to these cultures in many fundamental ways, as he and others began to insist,[11] in a way that finally acted as a subversion of peoplehood itself.

This emphasis made a lot of ethical sense, given the inherent popular sinfulness embedded in humanity's Babelic spirit. Yet it was also problematic, for in practice it is hard to maintain faithfully. First, there is the alternative ethical demand: the pressure to erase national distinctions has had its own horrendous effects. This is most obvious, as we have seen, in the attempt to exile from God's redemptive reach Jewish particularity. One result of this attempt and its consequences has been to drive Jews themselves—one thinks of Emil Fackenheim—to posit a new divine covenant that is simply bound to Jewish *survival* in its particularity, pure and simple. It is a plausible claim, furthermore, that now stands as a towering challenge to Christian universalizing ambitions. Even someone like Elie Wiesel, committed to the universal ethical demands of human rights, locates that demand's historical efficacy in a *particular* Jewish covenant that itself requires acknowledgment. But the moral burden of popular survival is not the only thing that opposes national erasures. Second, an even more fundamental affirmation of ongoing national specificity is the divine Adamic character of the Son as Creator of the nations who includes himself within that which he creates, both the Jewish-Gentile and Gentile-Gentile distinctions. This reality will always press against monolithic identities that go beyond Christ's own work and person. The Church is literally "patient" of these distinctions (she "suffers" them) and lives with and waits upon them. To be sure, since the purposes of God involve a common confession of Christ (Phil 2:10–11), the conversion to faith in Christ of Jew and Gentile is always at the center of the Church's mission. But because Israel is itself an object of

---

10. Newbigin, *Faith for This One World?*, 83.

11. See Newbigin's later works, especially *Foolishness to the Greeks*, as well as Hauerwas and Willimon's *Resident Aliens*.

mission, the Church must always include herself within her conversionary aspect. To be "missionary" is, as Jocz insisted, to be "repenting."[12] But this is precisely what the excision of Israel—"Jewish" Israel as it turned out in concrete practice—from her identity has prevented the Church from being.

The Missionary Church as Repentant Israel

We need to be clear about the outcome to this primordial rejection of Israel's life as the Church's own, including the consequences of the Church's modern worries over her treatment of the Jews. In the first instance, the demeaning of the Jews became a long descent into the degradation of other nations in an attempt to assimilate them to the Church. The descent was neither universal nor consistent. Still, with "Jewish" Israel rendered problematic, the already profound challenge of coordinating unity and diversity among the nations in the mission of the Church was turned toward a default mode of subjugation.

Without peoples, there is no genocide of course; only murder, usually forgotten. Elie Wiesel's notion of "witness" thus really only works among peoples; general murder usually disappears in the dark ocean of sin's forgetfulness. A witness requires a people. Or a God. With Israel, both.

The fourth-century Roman emperor Julian, re-embracing his pagan heritage, is among the first to complain about the way Christians eviscerated longstanding cultures; and the great eighteenth-century historian of Rome, Edward Gibbon, made the charge stick, at least with respect to the classical world. There is an irony at work in this judgment, in that, by the early twentieth century, scholars like Adolf Harnack claimed that Christianity's fourth-century dogmatic roots were *all* "Hellenistic" and that its appropriation of a Greek conceptual apparatus has shackled theology to a cultural outlook ever since. Hence, more recent efforts have been made to throw off such classical (in this case, literally "Nicene") conceptions about God and aim for more local forms of articulating Christian truth.

My argument here, however, has little to do with theological terms and their background, but with the material forms of distinct cultural artifacts, deployed in common life among peoples who, in one fashion or another, became members of the Church. Apart from such discussions, arguments about the relevance of this or that bit of philosophical

---

12. Jocz, *Christians and Jews*, 5.

nomenclature may be beside the point. Actually, we know little about how cultures in Northern Europe were transformed or perhaps even obliterated by the Church's expansion in that direction, although we can assume this must have happened frequently. Historians can argue as to how much cultural (and religious) "adaptation" the Church accepted, given the remnants of paganism in Europe centuries later. But we have records of what Charlemagne and others did in the course of imposing a Christian culture, and it is hardly pacific. Only after the early modern expansion of Christianity from the sixteenth century on do we have documented evidence from which to draw concrete conclusions, and here the record is decidedly ambivalent. David Stannard's *American Holocaust* (1992) laid out in its closing chapters an argument against Christian mission as a form of cultural and biological genocide, and that argument has since become standard. Stannard's numbers on aboriginal American deaths in the wake of the European contact and conquest are debated but generally accepted as to their sweeping magnitude: whole peoples simply disappeared through disease, hunger, dislocation, and violence. In many respects, Stannard was drawing on a well-stocked scholarly pool. Critics lined up, however, to question his wholesale application of diverse and unconnected Christian Eurocentric and racist tropes to explicate the real nature of mission in the Americas. Others complained that European conquest was no different in its extirpating breadth than other conquests, from the distant past to the Persians or Romans, or Mongols and Japanese. But although the Americas were, after all, depressingly different in this respect from the arena of missions in other parts of the world, details and comparative differences miss the point. The Church was not called to be *like* the nations, but to lead them into their own healing. Even if it is limited, unavoidable and detailed evidence of how this healing did not happen in too many cases is now impossible to overlook.[13] Cultural deconstruction that has come about through the Church's mission, intentional or not, has led to death, not life.

This is obviously not the whole story. In the Americas itself, the ways that Christian truths and practices given in and through the Church entered into the cultures and distinctions of local nations are profound and moving. They acted as transfigurative realities, not simply destructive ones; and ignoring these also marks a real blindness to God's work. The

13. See the recent Truth and Reconciliation Commission work in Canada, on the activities of Catholic and Protestant churches in running residential schools for native children. The claim that these schools resulted in "cultural genocide" of native peoples may be too strong; but negative judgments that attach to that phrase are not misplaced.

work of Sanneh, already mentioned, has demonstrated two things. First, the Church's mission in its translating and vernacularizing thrust has also been real. It has in fact empowered resistance to the worst kinds of cultural and popular dismantlings, and has done so explicitly through the exercise of an intrinsic Christian vocation. In this vein, scholars are beginning to explore how the Church often worked to push back against the very sins of its enabling nationalisms—its colonial supports—on the basis of the gospel itself; or how the process of cultural encounter moved in multiple and complex directions that cannot be reduced to unilateral impositions. Sanneh, among others, has also shown how "Western guilt" about Christian mission is not the appropriate response to the misdeeds of the Church. It is in fact a further act of pride that assumes its own cultural program was the prime initiating power in the Church's mission in the first place. It was not, and could not have been, simply because the soul of the Church lies with its Lord. The Church's sins are real; but they are against its own divine mission at its root. They are sins against the Church's own soul.

The Church's lapse into local forms of nationalism stands as another reaction to the rejection of Israel's more fundamental national vocation. That is to say, when the Church loses her positive and hence divinely accountable connection to Israel—and not just her sharing of Israel's national election—Christians in this or that place are prone to assuming local national interests as somehow reflecting ecclesial character itself. In this, the Church becomes "like the nations" around her (cf. Deut 17:14; 18:9; Ezek 20:32). Instead of the Church as Israel, we find for instance America as the Chosen Nation. The alignment of Church and particular nations—from Rome and Byzantium to the Concordats of the Catholic Church in the nineteenth and twentieth centuries, to the civic Christian claims of Britain and America, to the partnerships in Moscow and China—have over and over again pushed the church into "phyletic" arrangements (to use an Orthodox term meaning "tribalist") that have constrained at best, and at worst perverted, her own vocation as Israel. Leaving the nations as they are, she has become "like them," either actively advancing their own unredeemed interests herself, or simply ignoring them while resting "at ease in Zion" (Amos 6:1).

Turned in on herself, the Church in either case has directed the animosity of otherness against her own members, erasing differences or setting one against another. The long history of the Church as a struggle against heretics, or self-orderings according to nation, race, or class, has given rise to the denominational structures of the Church that we consider to be specific fodder for ecclesiology. But these structures are at best of secondary interest. H. Richard Niebuhr's classic work on *The Social Sources of Denominationalism* (1929) helped to de-dogmatize these structures and show them for what they are: the product of an obscured vocation, driven by the crude dynamics of unconscious social striving, and clothed in often sophisticated theological self-justifications.

The Church and the Nations: Jacob and Esau

The obscuring itself is of interest, but only so as to indicate what God is doing with the Church, how she is being changed, and where she is being led. This is the burden of a figural reading of the Church; and in this case, it points us more fully to the fulfillment of her actual mission. For if the Church is a nation for the nations, what is happening to her in the world is the story of her conversion and repentance. This is the foundation of her mission and as such, on any given day, this is properly her ecclesial nature. In light of our discussion above, regarding the Church as Israel who has turned against her own national identity, the Church's mission can be described for instance in terms of Obadiah 10–15. These verses, taken from a small book that is entirely devoted to a vision of "what the Lord says concerning Edom," are ecclesiologically rich because they tell us what Israel-on-the-way is now engaging:

> For the violence done to your brother Jacob,
> shame shall cover you,
> and you shall be cut off for ever.
> On the day that you stood aloof,
> on the day that strangers carried off his wealth,
> and foreigners entered his gates
> and cast lots for Jerusalem,
> you were like one of them.
> But you should not have gloated over the
>   day of your brother
> in the day of his misfortune;
> you should not have rejoiced over the
> people of Judah
> in the day of their ruin;
> you should not have boasted

> in the day of distress.
> You should not have entered the gate
> > of my people
> in the day of his calamity;
> you should not have gloated over his disaster
> in the day of his calamity;
> you should not have looted his goods
> in the day of his calamity.
> You should not have stood at the parting
> > of the ways
> to cut off his fugitives;
> you should not have delivered up his survivors
> in the day of distress.
>
> For the day of the LORD is near upon all
> > the nations.
> As you have done, it shall be done to you,
> your deeds shall return on your own head.
>
> (Obad 10–15 RSV)

Edom's sin, as Obadiah tells us, lay in standing aside as other nations mistreated Israel. The depth of the sin, however, is given in the figure of their brotherhood as Esau and Jacob. "Your brother Jacob" is the object here of relational failure—violence, "standing on the other side," looking away or gloating as the brother became a "stranger"; following in after Jacob's enemies have broken down her gates, and picking up the leftover spoils; even standing at the crossroads and blocking the way of Jacob's escape. And thus, "as you have done, it shall be done to you" (15).

The figure of the two brothers obviously goes deep, back to the story of their birth in Genesis, and then the account of their struggles and tensions, with Jacob taking Esau's place as the firstborn, and then quite literally stealing their father Isaac's blessing. The relationship between the two is obviously complicated—filled with enmity and menace, anxiety, forgiveness and reconciliation, to the point where Jacob himself offers his displaced brother a blessing of his own (Gen 33:11), even while Esau enjoys a subsequent blessing from his father that will place him somehow above his brother at some point. Esau and Jacob represent a long and tortured story.

Part of this story—for it is told in Genesis for just this reason, as the genealogies tell us—is given in the subsequent enmity between Israel and the peoples of Edom, Esau's descendants. The prophets are filled with divine denunciations and curses against the Edomites, often couched in eschatological colors (e.g., Isa 34). It is Paul, finally, who uses the figure of the two brothers in Romans to express the stark mystery of God's choices, in this case the choice of the wicked Jacob over the firstborn Esau, quoting Malachi: "Jacob have I loved, but Esau have I hated" (Rom 9:13 KJV). For Malachi, these words are God's answer to the complaining Israelites, for whom God asserts love despite Edom's present prosperity. For Paul, they are a sign of God's choice of the "younger" over the older, of the Gentiles in Christ over the Jews in the flesh. In each instance, it *is* the case that this is who Israel is in relation to the nations, and who this particular nation is in relation to Israel—Jacob and Esau *are* something insofar as they are thus described.

Although Augustine, not without reason, will take Paul's figure here mostly as an image of election and predestination to salvation more broadly, the larger tradition into the Middle Ages and even beyond will still focus on the embedded notion of "peoples." It will go back and forth as to who is who. For the Jewish exegetical tradition, Esau stands for the Christian Gentiles—lifted high today, brought down tomorrow. For the Christians, Esau symbolizes the Jewish synagogue, exalted long ago, debased today. Not until modernity, with people like Blake, is there any attempt to break this opposition open, although only by creating new ones (e.g., organized religion, as it were, to be denounced over and against enlightened and embattled spirit).

But what Obadiah presses us into engaging is precisely what Genesis insists upon as well: Jacob and Esau are *brothers*—"your brother," he tells Edom—and the history of their relationship is made profoundly problematic precisely in their brotherhood. At the core of their relationship are their rivalries, as René Girard would point out (although, curiously, he has little interest in Esau and Jacob), the jealousies and the submerged and frightened angers, the desperate losses—and, most deeply, the betrayal that this brings with its incomprehensible violence years later as Israel is given over to Assyria and Babylon. You stood aside; you blocked my way; you took advantage of my misfortune; you laughed. Yes, there is also the pathetic historical figure, making use of the biblical figure, in which Jew and Christian for centuries apply the figure in contradictory ways—*you're* Edom; no, *you're* Edom!—precisely in order to prove, unwittingly, that the scriptural figure is right. It is *there*, it seems to me, that Paul's mysterious deployment of the brothers is actually displayed in its shocking meaning—God chooses in the midst of our own perverted choices.

The Jewish-Christian heretical disjunction is, as I have insisted, paradigmatic for all Christian division. As the Jew became the Christian Church's primordial heretic—explicitly using this language—he provided a ground upon which "brother" could become "heretic" as a kind of definitional identity. Edom (or the Jew) becomes Judas, lurking about and then breaking forth from time to time and going out and forming new conventicles. But, given something like Obadiah, I think it is better to see the Jewish-Christian / brother-brother division as a figure—God's historical description—of the Church herself. In the Church brothers become the brothers of the Lord, as is their calling certainly. Their calling is also the judgment continually brought upon their unresolved and frequently hostile relationship. In this struggle which now issues in the call to repentance, the full panoply of the nations is unfolded, and the Church's mission is laid bare.

There is an odd aspect to the Old Testament judgments against the nations. Israel is being punished, God leaves no doubt; but that is not the business of the nations, not of Edom, Moab, Ammon and the rest. That is not *your* business, God seems to say to the nations—you can be judged for how you treat Israel even if God is the ultimate agent of Israel's suffering, and Israel the cause of her own demise, through her sin and unfaithfulness. Divine judgment on Israel is not an excuse for the unrighteous acts of Israel's neighbors against her (cf. Ezek 25:6–7; Zeph 2:8, 10; Isa 10:12–15; Jer 50:4–7). In the end, the prophetic denunciations of the nations that we tend to skim over have at least this point: all are guilty. Israel and the nations fall into one pit, as it were. Esau and Jacob are taken up in the same dynamic judgment. This "allness" is something that is brought into relief by Paul obviously, and by Jesus himself earlier and the New Testament more broadly. This "allness" is also one of the reasons why typical ecclesiologies of the past—ecclesiodicies as I have called them, or "apologetic" ecclesiologies as others have described them—always fall short of their explanatory hopes. Every "image of the Church," taken as a window for clarifying her character, cannot embrace how each nation, including Israel herself, reverts to the flood, lingers at Babel, roams the fields of Megiddo (Judg 5:19; Rev 16:16). Only a figural reading of Scripture with respect to the Church is properly inclusive of multiple texts and referents. The Church is Israel, yes;

The Church as Israel

but the Church is Edom also, and Ethiopia, and Nineveh, and Moab. We are to find her there, where Adam walks and the Last Adam returns.

Given this "allness," the division of the Church is both easily engaged by Scripture and is also subversive of all sorts of ecclesiodicies at the same time. It is difficult to justify the Church with precision, if our very being is tied up with a history of unjustifiable figural hostility. Although this *is* a theological problem in a technical sense, it is more importantly an exegetical problem, in the sense of trying to understand what it means that such and such is happening, particularly what is happening to the Church given who she is. The problem is to find a place for the Church in history that can be understood scripturally. The problem and the answers given to it have a long tradition, one that moves from the Bible, of course, through certain early Fathers like Salvian and then Bede, and then through the Middle Ages, winding its way into the corners of both Protestant and Catholic reflection—Puritan, Jansenist and Jesuit, and even Anglican, all of whom have sought to engage scripturally the reality that God judges the Church, not just individuals. Modern theologians, drawing on elements of scholastic disdain, have tended to siphon off this kind of reflection as being somehow bound to a "prophetic" genre that has no place in serious academic discussion.

We should resist this temptation. We know the church in her scriptural identity: the Israel of God, a people bound up in the Person of Jesus Christ. We describe the church—her history, her division, growth, shrinkage, challenges, martyrdoms, shafts of light and glory—and we see in what ways the scriptural identity is described as somehow inclusive of what we know of the church today. Hence we learn of God. If there is a prophetic aspect to this kind of theology, it is not of a predictive kind. Rather it unveils the present, in the form of Christ and his own movement through time. On the one hand, we see Israel as the man Jesus: *Ecce homo!* in the (Latin) words of Pilate displaying his prisoner before the mob. On the other hand, the passage of Jesus through time, which is the way that Israel moves as the Church, is the visage of divinity. In terms of method, this kind of discipline falls into the category of "theological phenomenology."

Phenomenology is a broad category of study that seeks to get at reality, not through a consideration of reality's essence or nature, but through the way we apprehend or experience reality. Phenomenological studies, as applied to the discipline of ecclesiology, have tended to be shunted aside or placed in the position of introductions to the more dogmatic work of explicating the Church's nature or essence. Even among modern ecclesiologists, they are secondary to a more fundamental demand for ethical direction. And modern theology is fueled by an activist fire, as the apologetic impulse of ecclesiology demonstrates. Our modern goal is to show and explain the "true Church" so as to set people to the tasks that will achieve the goals of truth. That is the activist desire of modern ecclesiology; and theological phenomenology, describing the scriptural church in this case, does not fulfill it. This worry about uselessness, nonetheless, should not be overwhelming. To *see* the Church, to use this example, in her scriptural place is also, as I indicated earlier, to see the people of the Church in the place where they are properly addressed by God. The Church of Israel, driven and obscured, is properly called to repentance. That is what her being Israel demands, and in Jocz's phrase, it is what allows her to do mission at all among the nations she is set to serve. That is "who we are," from a purely descriptive perspective: *Ierusalem, Ierusalem, convertere ad Dominum Deum tuum*, in the famous words of Lamentations, taken up in the Holy Week liturgies of the Middle Ages and early modern period ("Jerusalem, Jerusalem, return [or convert] to the Lord thy God!"). By the same token, that repentance is given in actions that themselves embody the redemptive grace of Christ given just there, such that repentance is itself renewal and becomes the ministry of the Church among the Children of Adam, just as first this ministry was given supremely in the act of Jesus' own self-giving to his enemies, the Son of Man as the Perfect Penitent.

We can place some of the traditional elements of ecclesiology within this work. In the end, they come down to the resolution of any given scriptural figure of Israel's life, such as this one, embodied in Jacob *sharing* with Esau in a way that establishes the future:

> Jacob said [to Esau], ". . . if I have found favor in your sight, then accept my present from my hand; for truly to see your face is like seeing the face of God, with such favor have you received me. Accept, I pray you, my gift that is brought to you, because God has dealt graciously with me, and because I have enough." Thus he urged him, and [Esau] took it. (Gen 33:10–11 RSV)

Further Reading

Anderson, Braden P. *Chosen Nation: Scripture, Theopolitics, and the Project of National Identity*. Eugene, OR: Cascade, 2012.

Anglican–Roman Catholic International Dialogue. "The Church as Communion." 1991. http://www.vatican.va/roman_curia/pontifical_councils/chrstuni/angl-comm-docs/rc_pc_chrstuni_doc_19900906_church-communion_en.html.

Anglican-Orthodox Dialogue. "The Cyprus Statement: The Church of the Triune God." London: Anglican Communion Office, 2006. http://www.anglicancommunion.org/media/103818/The-Church-of-the-Triune-God.pdf.

Assis, Eliyahu. *Identity in Conflict: The Struggle between Esau and Jacob, Edom and Israel*. Winona Lake, IN: Eisenbrauns, 2016.

Berend, Nora, ed. *Christianization and the Rise of Christian Monarchy: Scandinavia, Central Europe and Rus' c. 900–1200*. Cambridge: Cambridge University Press, 2007.

Congregation for the Doctrine of the Faith. *Letter to the Bishops of the Catholic Church on some Aspects of the Church Understood as Communion*. Rome, 1992. http://www.vatican.va/roman_curia/congregations/cfaith/documents/rc_con_cfaith_doc_28051992_communionis-notio_en.html.

D'Costa, Gavin, ed. *Christian Uniqueness Reconsidered: The Myth of a Pluralistic Theology of Religions*. Maryknoll: Orbis, 1990.

Ellis, Marc H. *O, Jerusalem! The Contested Future of the Jewish Covenant*. Minneapolis: Fortress, 1999.

Fletcher, Richard. *The Barbarian Conversion: From Paganism to Christianity*. Berkeley: University of California Press, 1997.

Fuchs, Lorelei F. *Koinonia and the Quest for an Ecumenical Ecclesiology: From Foundations through Dialogue to Symbolic Competence for Communionality*. Grand Rapids: Eerdmans, 2008.

Hauerwas, Stanley, and William H. Willimon. *Resident Aliens: Life in the Christian Colony*. Nashville: Abingdon, 1989.

Jocz, Jakob. *Christians and Jews: Encounter and Mission*. London: SPCK, 1966.

———. *A Theology of Election*. New York: Macmillan, 1958.

John Paul II. *Ecclesia de eucharistia*. Acta Apostolicae Sedis 95 (2003) 433–75. http://www.vatican.va/holy_father/special_features/encyclicals/documents/hf_jp-ii_enc_20030417_ecclesia_eucharistia_en.html.

Johnson, John J. "A New Testament Understanding of the Jewish Rejection of Jesus: Four Theologians on the Salvation of Israel." *Journal of the Evangelical Theological Society* 42.2 (2000) 229–46.

Kasper, Walter. "On the Church: A Friendly Reply to Cardinal Ratzinger." Translated by Ladislas Orsy. *America* 184 (2001) 8–14.

Kinzer, Mark S., and Jennifer M. Rosner, eds. *Israel's Messiah and the People of God: A Vision for Messianic Jewish Covenant Fidelity*. Eugene, OR: Cascade, 2011.

LaCugna, Catherine M. *God for Us: The Trinity and Christian Life*. San Francisco: Harper, 1993.

Lassiter, Luke, et al. *The Jesus Road: Kiowas, Christianity, and Indian Hymns*. Lincoln: University of Nebraska Press, 2002.

Lindbeck, George A. "Confession and Community: An Israel-like View of the Church." *Christian Century* 107 (1990) 492–96.

———. "The Gospel's Uniqueness: Election and Untranslatibility." *Modern Theology* 13 (1997) 423–50.

Lohfink, Gerhard. *Does God Need the Church? Toward a Theology of the People of God.* Translated by Linda M. Maloney. Collegeville: Liturgical, 1999.

Longenecker, Bruce W. "Different Answers to Different Issues: Israel, the Gentiles and Salvation History in Romans 9–11." *Journal for the Study of the New Testament* 36 (1989) 95–123.

Martyr, Justin. *Dialogue with Trypho.* Translated by Thomas B. Falls, in *The Fathers of the Church: Saint Justin Martyr.* Washington, DC: Catholic University of America Press, 2008.

Moseley, Carys. *Nationhood, Providence, and Witness: Israel in Protestant Theology and Social Theory.* Eugene, OR: Cascade, 2013.

Newbigin, Lesslie. *A Faith for This One World?* London: SCM, 1961.

———. *Foolishness to the Greeks: The Gospel and Western Culture.* London: SPCK, 1986.

Moltmann, Jürgen. *The Open Church: Invitation to a Messianic Lifestyle.* Translated by M. D. Meeks. London: SCM, 1978.

Niebuhr, H. Richard. *Social Sources of Denominationalism.* New York: Hold, 1929.

Pickard, Stephen. *Seeking the Church: An Introduction to Ecclesiology.* London: SCM, 2012.

Radner, Ephraim. *Brutal Unity: The Spiritual Politics of the Christian Church.* Waco, TX: Baylor University Press, 2012.

Ratzinger, Joseph. "The Ecclesiology of Vatican II." *Conference of Cardinal Ratzinger at the Opening of the Pastoral Congress of the Diocese of Aversa (Italy).* 15 September 2001. L'Osservatore Romano, weekly edition in English, 23 January 2002, 5.

———. "A Response to Walter Kasper: The Local Church and the Universal Church." *America* 185 (2001) 7–11.

Robert, Dana L., ed. *Converting Colonialism: Visions and Realities in Mission History, 1706–1914.* Grand Rapids: Eerdmans, 2008.

Sanmark, Alexandra. *Power and Conversion: A Comparative Study of Christianization in Scandinavia.* Uppsala: OPIA, 2004.

Simon, Marcel. *Verus Israel: A Study of the Relations between Christians and Jews in the Roman Empire (135–425).* Translated by H. McKeating. New York: Littman Library / Oxford University Press, 1986.

Stannard, David. *American Holocaust: The Conquest of the New World.* Oxford: Oxford University Press, 1992.

Torrance, Alan. "Jesus in Christian Doctrine." In *The Cambridge Companion to Jesus,* edited by Markus Bockmuehl, 200–219. Cambridge: Cambridge University Press, 2001.

Truth and Reconciliation Commission. http://www.trc.ca/websites/trcinstitution/index.php?p=9.

Walls, Andrew F. *The Cross-Cultural Process in Christian History: Studies in the Transmission and Appropriation of Faith.* Maryknoll: Orbis, 2002.

World Council of Churches. "Message from the Fifth World Conference of Faith and Order, 1993." http://www.oikoumene.org/en/resources/documents/commissions/faith-and-order/x-other-documents-from-conferences-and-meetings/message-from-the-fifth-world-conference-on-faith-and-order-1993.

World Council of Churches. "New Delhi Statement on Unity." 1961. https://www.oikoumene.org/en/resources/documents/assembly/1961-new-delhi/new-delhi-statement-on-unity.

The Church as Israel

Yuval, Israel Jacob. *Two Nations in Your Womb: Perceptions of Jews and Christians in Late Antiquity and the Middle Ages.* Translated by Barbara Harshav and Jonathan Chipman. Berkeley: University of California Press, 2008.

Zizioulas, John. *Being as Communion: Studies in Personhood and the Church.* Crestwood, NY: St. Vladimir's Seminary Press, 1997.

Discussion Questions

1. Why did it take until the twentieth century to talk about the Church as the "People of God"? Similarly, what factors in the twentieth century led to the rise of "Communion Ecclesiology"? Do these historical contexts offer illumination on the true character of the Church?

2. What concerns lay behind George Lindbeck's argument for understanding the Church "as Israel"? How does this understanding constitute a "figural ecclesiology"?

3. How might we conceive of non-Christian Jews being part of the "one Israel" with believing Christians? What important aspect of the Church is affirmed in such a conception?

4. What is a "repentant missionary," if the phrase is applied to the Church? Is the Church Jacob or Esau in this sense?

7

The Figure of the Church

THE CHURCH IS A people called and animated by God in Spirit to gather all peoples in Christ together in praise of their Creator.

Theologians may well observe that the divine character of this simple definition is intrinsically trinitarian: God the Creator and Caller, Christ who assumes the nations to himself, and the Spirit who indwells and moves the people. This is a necessary and sometimes useful thing to stress. As many modern ecclesiologists have noted, the trinitarian character of God's relationship to the Church was in the past often ignored in favor of other aspects. We have also seen how, in recent years, so-called communion ecclesiology has embraced this trinitarian reality as somehow broadly explanatory of the Church's own form.

I am not sure that the way this has happened has been altogether helpful. If the trinitarian reality of the Church's life is to be identified, it must inform and elucidate the peculiarities of the Church's life: the forming of this collective, the calling, the animation, the gathering, and the praising, which are all the defining elements of what it means to be the Church *coram Deo*, before God and from the hand of God. The trinitarian Church before God is precisely the people assumed by the Son, the Second Adam who takes up the First Adam and brings him and his children to their divinely created end. On one level, a trinitarian Christology is at work in understanding how this happens. But more specifically, we describe the Church by describing the life of the assuming Son. This happens fundamentally in the scriptural description of Israel and Jesus. The Church as a people, called and animated by God in Spirit to gather all peoples in Christ together in praise of their Creator, is very specifically what we see in the genealogical outworking and experience of Israel. From them the Christ is born, and he takes them to himself and sends them in his Spirit to the nations.

In the previous chapter, I explained this claim finally in terms of a "figural ecclesiology," in which we must say that the Church *is* the people that we see scripturally figured in Israel and Jesus, and that the Church's relationship with other peoples in her calling is figured there as well. Such an approach does not do away with traditional elements that have made up various theologies of the Church; but it does try to locate them within a certain framework. Here, in this final chapter, I want to indicate some of how this can be done, mostly in a descriptive way. But simply doing that will sound some notes of how things "ought" to be.

A People Called

To be a people, there must be members; but what makes a person a member of a people? This question has had to be engaged legally, not only with questions of national citizenship, but in terms of membership of a given tribe, to whom perhaps rights and obligations pertain. The Jewish rabbis and the contemporary nation of Israel have different laws in this regard. Judaism is unusual in that it combines genealogical and religiously conversionary aspects of membership. Most ethnically identified peoples, however, also have forms of special entrance into membership, often understood in terms of "adoption," analogous to adopted members of a family. The history of adoption into Israel is well rehearsed. The Christian Church in this context is a people constituted by adoption as a whole.

Paul, obviously, seems to speak of this in his discussion of being made "heirs" through "adoption" (Rom 8:15, 17). Some writers have turned adoption into an exhaustive ecclesial characteristic, capable as well of explicating new familial relationships within modernity's altered views of sexuality. This would be a mistake, however. Adoption for Paul is only one way of expressing the gracious act of God's calling and animating of his people. In particular, it applies to Israel as a whole (Rom 9:4). Thus the Church as a people of adopted children is exactly what Israel is, not something other than Israel. That is, Gentiles are not "adopted" into Israel; rather, Israel is "adopted" into Christ, as children by flesh of the First Adam are made children by grace of the Second. The "seed of Abraham" is an *ex nihilo* reality— created purely by the grace of God (Matt 3:9). To be adopted into Christ is to share in that creative grace (Gal 3:29).

There is a tension in this language. Jesus is genealogically drawn from the seed of Abraham (Matt 1:1; Gal 3:23) and of Israel (Rom 9:5, 1:3; 2 Tim 2:8; Rev 22:16). The relationship is vital but also paradoxical. He lives out, in the constraints of the flesh, the grace of a people made *ex nihilo* by his own hand. Human redemption is given *ex nihilo* by the grace of adoption into—and assumption by—the Son of God, who nonetheless is born of the flesh of Israel, his child by grace. Christian peoplehood derives from and embodies this paradox. It is founded on the grace of adoption into Christ's "sonship," but the Church also carries with it the genealogical contours of Israel's shared familial life. Individuals are baptized (1 Cor 1:14); so are whole "households" (Acts 16:33). Decisions are made in a moment (Acts 2:41); lives are shaped over time (Eph 6:1–9). A good bit of the division between infant-baptizers and believer-baptizers (or adult-baptizers) in the Church is driven by the unresolved nature of this paradox and by what is, from a historical perspective, its intrinsic irresolvability. Those who are adopted are nonetheless formed in their created life by the breadth of their filiated existence, in families or in contexts of discipline.

Baptism has certainly been, uniformly in the Church's life, the entry point into the Church as a people. But its meaning, apart from the way that grace and filiated discipline come together variously, is hard to pin down. The Church is a people called by God; and baptism marks the hearing of that call and its receipt and recognition all at once. Baptism is not without the Church—that is, Israel as its presupposition and presence. It is not without the articulation of a word whose substance must be comprehensible, and hence translated through the work of a range of other persons and their applied knowledge and skills. It is not without some kind of response that has been ordered and is recognized by the people themselves and that has some coherence with the very person of the individual who is joining this new nation. Hence, baptism's divine graciousness and adoptive power is inextricably bound up with the concrete collective and its temporal existence.

Thus, this calling by God that constitutes the entry of a person into the Church casts a wide historical net. We can place within its figural reach Abram and the Ethiopian Eunuch, Ruth and David, Mary Magdalene and Paul. But once we do this, we are acknowledging that, however necessary a singular moment of entry may be to identity, that moment cannot exist apart from a complex and varied range of events, influences, learning, and provocations. The Church herself is not apart from all this but involved. Yet all this in turn cannot and should not be systematized apart from the clear parameters that inform the entry point itself. Those parameters include the assumptive embrace of Jesus through the fullness of his gifted life—his death and resurrection (e.g., Rom 6:3–6) and the ordering reality of this embrace in its movement before God, through the Spirit to the Father (John 16:4–33). Baptism in water, in the name of Father, Son, and Holy Spirit, enunciates the nexus of all this, and has therefore become universally recognized as the divinely given threshold of peoplehood.

But the threshold has a voice. This is absolutely critical to recognize. Since membership in the people of Israel comes from a divine calling, the divine voice must be heard as articulate speech. This happens in the message of the gospel being spoken and its welcoming reception being articulated. Traditionally, this has been done in terms of the Church's preaching or catechism, then in an individual's repentance and confession of faith and commitment in following Jesus. While all this once again presumes Israel's collective life as the Church, it does not do so in a uniform fashion. What one preaches or teaches in the call to membership, how one repents and confesses, what degree of concreteness in following Christ is assumed—none of this has ever been laid out with exactitude, even in the more detailed forms of baptismal preparation used by some churches, which, in any case, have predictably varied over time and place.

It is just the changes and chances of this collective's life in informing the flesh of baptism that has made baptism itself a source of contention among Christians. In the early days of the Reformation—and for quite some time after that in normal life, despite clear doctrinal teaching to the contrary—Catholics and Protestants often did not recognize each other's baptisms. This was based on the wider issue of popular antagonisms, involving this or that view of sacrament or doctrine. That has changed in a formal way. But, as with Judaism's internal disagreements on who is a Jew, the wider breadth of what is required for the threshold of popular membership in Christian Israel is still a source of division. There is, however, a general consensus that in the West at least, sources of wider baptismal formation have dried up, particularly those provided by the Christian people themselves in family and society. The places where the divine calling has been articulated have therefore been reduced, with the result as well that the response of commitment itself has less scope for informed enunciation. What this people is, and what membership is about, is more thinly understood.

The issue of baptism for the Church, then, is not so much a matter of "who is this people," but knowledge and hence faithfulness. A figural ecclesiology will locate this in teaching of a certain kind, about which Israel is consistently called to account, and because of which her life is subjected to divine rejection and even destruction: "My people are destroyed for lack of knowledge: because thou hast rejected knowledge, I will also reject thee, that thou shalt be no priest to me: seeing thou hast forgotten the law of thy God, I will also forget thy children" (Hos 4:6 KJV; see also Isa 5:13, and thus Jer 5:21 and Matt 5:14). In some ways, ecumenical consensus has moved away from trying to figure out "what happens" in baptism to asserting a fuller claim about baptism's lived context. This has meant a movement toward an affirmation of "believer's baptism" in its *purpose*—membership in a divinely ordered people with a specific mission. This could be applied among children and thus their families or among adults, but only on the basis of a profound and engaged preparation, which involves not just the informing of consciences, but the missionary mentoring of all the newly baptized. Short of this, the Church—while still the Church—subjects herself to "destruction."

Animated by God

This key claim about the Church, as I have argued, is associated with a people's "soul," and thus the formation of its "we-ness." The issue here is not to isolate the divine agency in this collective life, but to identify how the Church's specific acts and collective life are in fact congruent with God's agency.

The way that individuals are able to become a "we" is hard to trace, and we have noted philosophers and sociologists who struggle to understand this domain of reality. For some collectives it happens unconsciously, as children quietly grow into an understanding of their place within a people (which is one reason why the Christian people need not assume the incongruity of children as members of their nation). In many contemporary cultures, however, membership in anything is a matter of choice, and thus the transformation from "I" to "we" cannot be left to chance.

One thing we have learned about nations in general is that this transformation is a process rather than a moment. This points back to the thick and often wide boundary for which baptism is only an indicating line. Becoming a nation, furthermore, is not only a matter of individual transformation, but of continual collective transformation as well, so that collective identities and agencies become re-formed as individuals in different ways join in. The pioneering work of a sociologist like Norbert Elias in studying a slice of European nation-forming in the late Middle Ages and early modernity—the "civilizing process" as he called it—demonstrates on how many levels, and with what multitude of inputs, the "we" is made. It involves everything from how children are taught to eat at dinner to ways in which the aged dispense of their money.[1]

It is not enough, then, to delimit the work of the Spirit in the Church to this or that specific activity—sacrament or council or godly admonition. God animates the Church insofar as the people as a whole is formed *by* God. This must include the range of her blessings and curses. One general thing that can be said of the Church's animating life in God, then, is that the wholeness of Christ, or *totus Christus* as the Augustinian tradition deployed the phrase, is here not only pointing to the coincidence of Christ and Church, but designates the Spirit working through the breadth of the Church's existence according to the full figure of Christ. The figural history of the Church *is* its peoplehood, because all the happenings of the Church and her people constitute the way that God animates his people, as Christ Jesus assumes them in his person—including those who join and those who fall away as well as those who are raised up anew and sent out.

We can be relatively specific here, in a way that traces the figures of Israel and Christ himself. There are some similarities in this approach to the standard post-Reformation concerns with delineating the "marks of the Church," whether understood in Protestant forms (word, sacrament, discipline) or Catholic ones (mostly given in creedal terms). In fact, though, the tradition of the "marks" was a classic exercise in ecclesiodicy, aimed at distinguishing the true Church (or individual congregations) from her counterfeits, and offering a grid for personal judgment. When we speak of the divinely animating features of the Church, by contrast we are simply saying "what is" the case. Our judgments about the Church in this light are aimed at understanding our location, not at inventing new locations for the Church.

The Scripture: Cradle of the Church

Jesus is born, in a real sense, out of the Scriptures (Luke 1); and he orders the Church according to that which gave him birth (Luke 24:44-48). In

---

1. Norbert Elias, *Civilizing Process*. This monumental work was written in the 1930s but did not become well known until much later.

like manner, Israel is a child of the Scriptures, and the Church is continually raised up within the Scriptures. We have already mentioned this with respect to the formational dynamic of the Church as a people: God's calling word becomes the shaping force of Israel's ongoing life in the crystalline sense of Deuteronomy 6:1–9 (cf. also 8:2; 32:10). The Word is the ground of God's animating presence, and this takes form in the generational pedagogy of what is "written" (1 John 2:12–14). The written word in turn is bound to the literal *paradosis* or "handing down" of what one has "received," learning and teaching in a continual stream of historical life within the community. At this point, what is important to stress is that this notion of tradition (cf. 1 Cor 11:23; 15:1) must be located in the one thing that God offers as the animating sphere itself of the Church's life: the Word uttered by God in creating, ordering, and fulfilling (Col 1:15–19). The Protestant claim to *sola Scriptura* is not denied by Catholics or Orthodox so long as its integrating reach is acknowledged. The Word that is written is the Word at work in the breadth of God's creative life. We could point here to another formulation of the *totus Christus* more in tune with Origen's and Maximus the Confessor's ideas of a multiple set of epiphanies of the Word in creation, incarnation, and Scripture, within which the Church is given its form.

The Church, in any case, does not stand outside Scripture in ways that Protestants have sometimes pressed, often going against their own claim that it is the *creatura verbi* ("creature of the word"), subordinate to Scripture. To be accountable to something does not presuppose that one is separate from that which holds one to account, any more than the health of our hearts is subject to the frame of our larger bodies. The Church is not accountable to Scripture as a human institution of autonomous value is measured by some agent according to an external standard. As Israel, the Church is wholly Scripture, no matter what she does. Hence there is no alternative space to inhabit except Scripture's when it comes to ecclesial existence.

It is possible to draw prescriptions from such a claim, like the more Protestant elements in Barth's proposed list of twelve "marks." They include the expected proclamation of the gospel, but Barth adds explicitly "the study of the Bible."[2] Such proposals represent positive callings. But even when the Church fails to do this, as noted below, it is still the Church ordered by the Word and animated by God, although in a different mode.

---

2. Barth, *Church Dogmatics*, 4.3.2.

The Figure of the Church

The Living Bequest of the Past

Jesus is formed within the life of the law and the worship of Israel, including the temple and sacrifice (Luke 2:22-52). I have mentioned that membership in a people presupposes the people itself. Israel is its own presupposition. "All Israel" or "all the churches of the saints" (1 Cor 14:33) is an inclusive referent that extends to the past as well as the present. Creedally, this past-present inclusion has been referred to as "the Communion of Saints." To be sure, much of the Old Testament as well as the New refers to "the fathers" negatively—they are the ones who sinned against the Lord for generation after generation (see, among dozens of examples, Jer 7:25-26). Yet they are also those to whom the promises and presence of God has been given infallibly (cf. Deut 32:7; Rom 11:28). In their midst stand those in whom these promises are manifested triumphantly—Abraham, Isaac, Jacob, the prophets, all gathered in the kingdom of God, into which even the Church is heading (Luke 13:28). This living manifestation holds sway in the Church's life even now (Luke 20:37-38), for their witness "lives" insofar as God is "the God of the living"; and in Christ they continue to speak of him (John 8:56-58; 5:45-57).

The search for origins and for a way to conform to these origins—what in the history of the Church has been called "primitivism"—can mislead us if the origins stand as an external measure of the present. But when the origins remain a living aspect of the present, their measuring rod becomes a source of creative power and renewal. The reality of the living God of the saints clearly raises up the past as an authoritative tradition of sorts, yet not in any atavistic sense. Because of the Word's creative integrity, all Israel remains as a witness to God's work in Christ, and thus even in her wickedness, she "rises up"—as do all the nations—to speak to the present of God's truth, as even Nineveh does (Matt 12:41).

Israel's and the Church's past is endlessly populated, and the Church is a people within and made up of this vast population. Chesterton famously called tradition "the democracy of the dead," a democracy that speaks to the outspoken demands of the past. One should also speak of the "culture of the dead" with respect to their formative embrace. There has been much recent discussion about the frameworks by which "belonging" is nurtured among a people—common myths of origins, formative canons of value, shared popular rituals and manners—*mores* and morals more generally. Attempts to invent such "traditions" in newly formed political entities, something the European Union has sought in creating a pan-European popular identity, have faced obvious challenges, and are arguably bound for failure. "Belonging" to a people involves a network of practices that are *engaged*, of course, but that are engaged as something that has been received in a continuum of life across time. By severing the temporal life of popular existence from the past, much modern national identity eviscerated itself, existing as polities with laws but without norms.

The proliferation of diverse and often antagonistic "traditions" within divided churches, built up simply over time, has been a longstanding problem for Christians. But it is one that is perhaps disappearing as an obstacle to peoplehood. More problematic is the Church's captivity to the de-traditionalized polities of modernity. This is particularly true in the West. The animated "we" of the Church has dissolved because there is no place for it to be encountered. The demise of a culturally supported Christian framework—schools, institutions, family—leaves the we-ness to the temporal space of one hour and a half, perhaps two times a month. Here, the life of the past not only withers but is utterly suppressed; and with it, the network of practices elicited from their cultural gifts and pressures disappears. Within this context, a different mode of divine animation orders the church.

Rebellion

As Jesus makes his rounds, he observes around him a "wicked and perverse generation" (Luke 9:41). In this, he names Israel and the Church (Deut 32:5). From the midst of this people arises the hostility that aims to destroy him. "The same day there came certain of the Pharisees, saying unto him, Get thee out, and depart hence: for Herod will kill thee" (Luke 13:31 KJV).

Most of the failures of the Church with respect to integrating the living presence of the past into its present life give rise to immediate forms of perversity. This does not mean that this formational area of the Church's life is the only one that counts, but rather that its absence functions most clearly as the cause of collective disintegration. Rebellion is the primary figure of Israel's life in this regard, since it constitutes a turning away from the animating life of God's living servants. Such rebellion does not indicate simply an absence of God, however, but unveils the presence of a peculiar animation bound to Israel and her body, given in divine judgment.

The Figure of the Church

We see this unveiling over and over again among the prophets, but Revelation 2–3 offers a version of this as the Spirit speaking to the churches. Israel is beleaguered, reduced, even tormented by wicked leaders and miscreant nations. Ecclesial disarray is likewise a straightforward divine movement of judgment, whose double form as testing does not undercut the sentence of God. At the same time, the judgment of God upon Israel is a service to the nations, and hence even in this odd way a part of her mission: "Even all nations shall say, Wherefore hath the LORD done thus unto this land? what [meaneth] the heat of this great anger? Then men shall say, Because they have forsaken the covenant of the LORD God of their fathers, which he made with them when he brought them forth out of the land of Egypt" (Deut 29:24–25 KJV). Israel cries out against this: "We are become a reproach to our neighbours, a scorn and derision to them that are round about us . . . Wherefore should the heathen say, Where [is] their God? let him be known among the heathen in our sight [by] the revenging of the blood of thy servants [which is] shed" (Ps 79:4, 10 KJV). Yet it is also part of the Lord's grace, chastising the one he loves (Jer 31:18–20; Heb 12:5–6).

What is important to see in God's judgment against the Church's rebellion is how the very "body of Christ" is thereby unveiled as the nature of the Church herself. Chastisement becomes his own form (Isa 53:5); and the "delivering up" of Adam to his own passions (Rom 1:28) becomes the delivering up of the Second Adam again to the cross and the Father's mercy (Matt 27:26; Luke 24:7). The ability to grasp this, and thus to receive it finally with hope, is bound, as I have argued insistently, to maintaining the identity of the Church with Israel, in the most intimate and challenging of ways.

Division

The deepest form of rebellion for Israel lies in turning against herself. As her families align themselves in mutual conflict (Judg 20; 1 Kgs 11:29–33), so too do the disciples begin disputes that turn to a final scattering (Luke 9:46; 22:24; Mark 14:50). Division is, for Jesus, a final loneliness (Ps 88:18).

Though an aspect of the Church's rebellion, division is worth setting apart within the animating work of God, because it so characterizes the Church's life in our era. It is also one of the ways God turns evil into good. It leads to Israel's actual confrontation with her deep sense of loss, such that she cries out (Ps 79:8–13; Luke 15:17–18), and seeks forgiveness (Neh 9).

Division leads Israel to a series of exiles, as different tribes are taken away at different times and in different ways. Her common life is rent more deeply through its serial disintegration. Life in the diaspora, on the other hand, serves to strengthen the ties of peoplehood over the centuries, and devotion to the Law and to prayer among the people expands rather than contracts. Within the divided Church, one begins to hear voices—one is the movement of "receptive ecumenism"—seeking to understand the "gifts" that diverse and separated streams of Christianity have ended by disclosing: scriptural study, musical devotion, the pneumatic empowerment of otherwise excluded social classes, evangelism.

Perhaps most powerfully active in the division of the Church has been the call, heard out of the posture of repentance, to submit to the needs of the broken body. Paul is adamant on this matter (Phil 2:30; Rom 12:10; 1 Cor 12:26), which he insists upon just in the midst of the stresses of division. It is, of course, Jesus who embodies this, the Lord who became "slave of all," indeed of those most rebellious and conflicted (Mark 10:45; 1 Tim 2:6). Division calls forth sacrifice, not as a necessary outcome, but as the gift of God that animates the body of Christ and that thus outlines the dark precincts from which new creation appears. It is not surprising that the most powerful recent plea for the unity of the Church, John Paul II's encyclical *Ut unum sint* ("That they may be one") begins with martyrdom—both Catholic and Protestant for Christ's name—as its ecclesial foundation; and this martyrdom is the site of utter reconciliation, that is, the "we" that is in fact perfectly taken up by Christ. Without confronting her division, the Church tarries in obscurity, awaiting the opportunity to be "taken where she does not wish to go" (John 21:18), which is precisely the "death by which" she might "glorify God" (21:19).

Martyrdom

Israel finds her life in the giving of her life as servant. The strange transition of referents in Isaiah 49–53 testifies in a single series of verses to the historical passage that God's life enacts within Israel. The text moves from Jacob, battered and then encouraged, to Israel the servant of God, to a single servant of Israel herself, who transforms the whole people in the bearing of sin. A similar movement, now explicitly joining Christ, the Church, and her servants, is given in Colossians 1:18–24. Jesus is the One Witness, or Martyr, to whose life as Israel the Church is joined. Granted, Jesus' *martyria* or testimony is unusual, for in pointing to the Father, it points back to him, through his works (John 5:36). But this work, to be shared with the Church (John 14:12), is the Father's work in him (John 4:34), which is accomplished on the cross (John 17:4; 19:30).

As God animates the Church, the Church is taken by Christ to this perfect place of union. It is the place where the Spirit is disclosed as the soul of the Church (Heb 9:14), for it is the Spirit who gives up the Son to the Father, and so announces this work in the Church's life at this moment supremely.

Luther pointed to this in one of his own later elaborations of the "Marks of the Church." Having listed several of the expected marks—word, baptism, the "sacrament of the altar" (Eucharist), as well as the "office of the keys" (related to repentance and forgiveness), ministry, and worship—Luther adds a seventh mark. The Church "must endure every misfortune and persecution, all kinds of trials and evil from the devil, the world, and the flesh (as the Lord's Prayer indicates) by inward sadness, timidity, fear, outward poverty, contempt, illness, and weakness, in order to become like their head, Christ."[3] He goes on to emphasize the animating center of this reality: "This too is a holy possession whereby the Holy Spirit not only sanctifies his people, but also blesses them."[4] Luther links this, of course, to the true preaching of the gospel, which is the message of the cross, folly and stumbling block to Israel and the Nations both. Luther himself is often a full-blown exemplar of writing ecclesiodicy in its most blatant form, and his remarks in this case are in the context of trying to locate the "true church" as opposed to (especially) the false Roman version. Still, his notion that the sufferings of Christ are brought on by human sin (which includes the Church's), and that these sufferings are somehow to be shared with his Body (that very Church), is figurally exacting; and it ecclesiologically upends even some of Luther's own impulses.

The line between suffering the divine judgment on sin and the experience of self-offering is not easily drawn. This is most challenging in periods of vying martyrdoms, like the Reformation and post-Reformation, when Christians killed each other and various groups lifted up their own dead as "martyrs" to the true Church. While no one should doubt the courage and faith of these various witnesses—Protestant (of several kinds) and Catholic both—faith and fallenness coincide tragically in the circumstances of such

---

3. Luther, *On the Councils and the Church*, 164–65.
4. Ibid.

testimony. It coincides in Jesus as "sin" (2 Cor 5:21) and "curse" (Gal 3:13) "for us," so that in Israel's life the distinction can be made through God's own mercy. This is one reason why division itself is such a dangerous place in which Christians seek to make decisions, for they inevitably confuse judgment and offering over and over. Yet when the Church embraces the former for the sake of the latter, then the Spirit is unveiled. In doing this, the gifts of the Spirit become visible.

Renewal

The shape of this movement is spoken of by Jesus in pointing to the grain that falls to the ground and dies, only then bearing fruit (John 12:24). Cross and resurrection are figures of ecclesial life in this regard, locating the renewal of the Church in ways that the Prophets repeatedly emphasized for Israel, epitomized in the great thirty-first chapter of Jeremiah. From the judgment of the cross comes new creation. From the blood of martyrs springs the new life of the Church, in Tertullian's famous phrase.[5]

Many of the great movements of renewal do indeed emerge just in this context, from monastic gathering to Franciscan self-offering to African American devotion and Chinese conversion. As we noted above, even the judgments of rebellion and division, when given in the crucible of sacrifice, have borne an array of spiritual gifts. The charisms of so many of the Church's special groups and saints are thus hardly arbitrary in their appearance, but follow the particular figural logic of Israel's own life in Christ. Discernment and testing of spirits—and thus testing for the animating Spirit of the Church—is given in part by tracing this line.

Mission

The shape of this figural line is important. The mission of the Church is, as I have been arguing, the central feature of the Church as a people: a people sent to the Peoples, a nation for the Nations. Enough has been said already about this, and recent writing on the Church has rightly embraced this focus.[6]

---

5. Tertullian, *Apology*, 50.

6. Guder has been a leader here in our generation; see his *Called to Witness*. See also Wright, *Mission of God*.

Furthermore, the apostolic or "sending" character of the Church is granted through the Spirit in the apostolic reality of Christ Jesus, who has assumed Israel in the flesh. John 20:21 is regularly cited in this context, as well it should be: "Then said Jesus to them again, Peace [be] unto you: as [my] Father hath sent me, even so send I you" (John 20:21 KJV). But this sending in the Spirit (20:22) is the *fulfillment* of a figure, not an independent event in its own right to be decoupled from the person of Christ and inserted here and there in the Church's life as a prod or hortatory demand. Here the prescriptive form of a figural ecclesiology can perhaps be better seen. The Church's mission grows out of her life with Christ as it is fully integrated into the passage of his form through time. The Church cannot fulfil this mission apart from her scripturally formed life, having traversed her sins and judgments in the forms of penitential sacrifice, in the power and blessing of the Spirit's offering. Here the baptismal threshold is elongated and stretched across the frame of Christ:

> And James and John, the sons of Zebedee, come unto him, saying, Master, we would that thou shouldest do for us whatsoever we shall desire. And he said unto them, What would ye that I should do for you? They said unto him, Grant unto us that we may sit, one on thy right hand, and the other on thy left hand, in thy glory. But Jesus said unto them, Ye know not what ye ask: can ye drink of the cup that I drink of? and be baptized with the baptism that I am baptized with? And they said unto him, We can. And Jesus said unto them, Ye shall indeed drink of the cup that I drink of; and with the baptism that I am baptized withal shall ye be baptized . . . (Mark 10:35–39 KJV)

Gathering

The gathering of the nations can, from one perspective, be equated with the very acts of the animating Spirit of Christ in the Church. So, for instance, we could trace the line of Christian martyrs across time and find in it the animating movement of sacrifice that flows from missionary to new Christian, and see in this just the gathering that the Church *is*. Organizations like Voice of the Martyrs have, in a sense, done just this. There are in this story anywhere from ten thousand to one hundred thousand Christians who currently die for their faith each year. The discrepancy in estimations is significant, at least insofar as it points to some of the figural discernments that are required to make sense of this phenomenon ecclesially. But the numbers are large. The twentieth century alone was a Christian bloodbath—as it was for other peoples, including Jews in particular. Work by the statistician David Barrett provides some summary. He puts the number of Christians systematically exterminated in Nazi Germany at a million, while he estimates the number of Orthodox Christians and others murdered in Russia between 1917 and 1950 to be fifteen million. In China at least two hundred thousand Christians and foreigners were killed in the Boxer Rebellion of 1898–1901. Another seven hundred thousand were killed in communist China between 1950 and 1980. The number of Catholics killed in Mexico from the late 1800s to 1930 is estimated at 107,000, while 300,000 Christians are believed to have been killed under Idi Amin in Uganda between 1971 and 1979.[7]

Just as significantly, however, the documentation of Christian martyrdom maps a burgeoning faith around the world, taking in dozens and dozens of nations whose place within the Church's life is relentlessly growing in stature, from Mongolia to Cape Verde.[8]

The movement among the central elements of the figure of Scripture, living tradition, and the animating Spirit of Christ, then, constitutes the gathering of the nations itself. This has to continue in any church, and will in some fashion. But the Church as gathering also speaks to the enduring aspect of this movement, and thus to the character of toil involved in its ongoing enactment. We can speak of tasks, but we must also speak of commitments that inform these tasks so that they are carried through. Gathering the nations, then, reveals for the Church prescriptive, and not only descriptive, aspects of her life.

The Ongoing Communicative Act of Translation

We have already pointed to translation as a fundamental aspect of the Church's missionary being. According to the prominent Bible translation organization now known as the Wycliffe Global Alliance, in 2015 there were full translations of the Bible in 554 languages, with New Testament translations in 1,333 languages.[9] These figures do not include many more

---

7. Martin, "70 Million Christians."
8. See the significant work of Voice of the Martyrs, https://www.persecution.com/public/aboutVOM.aspx?clickfrom=%3d6d61696e5f6d656e75.
9. See Wycliffe Global Alliance, "Statistics," http://www.wycliffe.net/statistics.

languages in which portions of the Bible have been translated. But given the approximately seven thousand global languages currently spoken, the work of scriptural translation continues to face enormous challenges.

Translation, however, as the wider act of communicating the scriptural fullness of God's truth in Christ, involves not just single linguistic projects or the collection of such acts and artifacts. It includes the whole context of Christian life and encounter that makes this possible and that makes use of these acts and artifacts. Describing this aspect of translation as the gift of endurance in communication indicates the breadth of what is involved. Even in its most personal examples from isolated missionary contexts in the sixteenth or seventeenth centuries, translating the Scriptures requires interpersonal engagement, conversation, observation, reordering of thinking and listening and behaving among participants over years. The remarkable work of translation today through Bible societies, Scripture unions, Wycliffe translators, and ecclesial commissions around the world is intensely and expansively communal, often ecumenically based, and takes place over long periods of time. The texture and extent of the commitment and ordering of diverse human skills and attitudes in these projects puts most civil political programs to shame. In pursuing this work, furthermore, Christian lives are transformed and bring back to the process gifts and understanding that in turn water new and ongoing efforts and re-translation. Even the most traditionalist advocate of this or that translation in a given context cannot overlook how the reformable aspect of translation grows out of an extraordinary commitment to an enduring life together.

Take away this commitment and its enactment, and the communicative act itself withers. Communicative action involves not just the formal acts of scriptural translation, but the whole array of related applications of these acts and their enabling practices, involving living together, listening across divides of culture, teaching, conversing, serving together, and indeed praying together. That is to say, if the scriptural gospel is the core of the Church's missionary offering, then enduring encounter among nations must continue consistently and deeply, within the Church and of course by the Church outwards. The danger facing segregated Christian communities—segregated by nation, tribe, or family—is obvious: as iniquity abounds, it stifles the already limited faith of many, and love "waxes cold" (Matt 24:12). Every part of the Church where the lines between the nations have ceased to be crossed in an enduring fashion, or to be built into the fabric of daily Christian life, faces its own disintegration. That is to say, those who are gathered have thus endured.

The great debates over "inculturation" or "contextualization" in the Church are generally products of gathering, rather than of disintegration.[10] They arise only because and where the Church has indeed sought to endure in her translating existence. But because gathering involves endurance in encounter, all such debates can be evaluated at least in terms of such endurance in life together, as opposed to life apart. Just here, we confront the difficult and often troubling character of the Church's peoplehood in relation to the nations themselves. The enduring encounter associated with the communicative act of sharing the gospel—Christian translation—is transformative of all those involved. The Church, in its empowering of the cultural integrities of the nations, also changes them, even as the cultural character of all the Christian members of the Church are also thereby transformed as well.

One can see an analogue to this today in some of the dynamics at work in multicultural nations. The very ideal of the multicultural nation, touted by countries like Canada, has been challenged on a number of bases. One of them is the simple fact that, however much a political system may attempt to carve out spaces within a nation for multiple (usually immigrant) cultures, these cultures are subjected to a host of transformative pressures (e.g., common laws regarding moral pluralism on the one hand, and single educational and legal systems that impose monolithic attitudes) that inevitably alter their character and, arguably, subvert them. Nonetheless, minority or immigrant cultures find ways of maintaining key aspects of their identities. Studies of so-called "diaspora" cultures—not just Jews, but African groups who have moved and perhaps lived for several generations in Europe or the Americas—reveal creative patterns of "nesting," whereby original national languages and customs are "nested" within a range of larger linguistic and cultural forms. Immigrants learn to navigate the various levels of their nested existence, even while they become new people in the process.

The Christian nation is itself a nation in diaspora, for she is Israel. The Church exists not in one place but around the world, entering into and then gathering the places of many. It is a kind of invitational diaspora, which both takes in and rattles into new forms the cultural bequests of

---

10. For a Catholic perspective, see Shorter's *Toward a Theology of Inculturation*; for a Protestant one, see Bosch's *Transforming Mission*, part 3.

many peoples. Augustine himself captures this in a famous section of the *City of God*. He describes the way that the human race itself, ordered finally by God according to two "societies" of love, one for self and the other for God, moves through time to its end. The Church is identified with the "city of God," but relates to the earthly city in a way that mixes in, with, and among its members, integrating within itself what is good from the nations for the sake of worshiping God truly:

> So long, then, as the heavenly city is wayfaring on earth, she invites citizens from all nations and tongues, and unites them into a single pilgrim band. She takes no issue with that diversity of customs, laws, and traditions whereby human peace is sought and maintained. Instead of nullifying or tearing down, she [the heavenly city] pressures and appropriates whatever in the diversity of nations is aimed at one and the same objective of human peace, provided only that they do not stand in the way of the faith and worship of the one supreme and true God.[11]

This is not "cosmopolitanism," in the sense of creating a new culture that is a single new way of organizing the nations and their cultures. The Church does not really have a single culture. On the other hand, it has a single transformative energy, the Spirit of Christ figured in the Scriptures, which, in the process of time, is constantly assimilating, perhaps strengthening, perhaps reordering the multiple cultures of Adam's children.

In the passage quoted above, Augustine himself speaks about politics in particular—the politics of the nations that are driven by their diverse cultures. For him, it is "peace," a peace found in God's deepest creative will, that must prove a criterion for the Church's embrace of cultural diversity. This point, which moves the discussion of ecclesiology in a new direction of political theology, nonetheless bears noticing: the gathering of the nations, in its enduring aspect, is one that is founded on peace among nations and within them. The Church properly enters into the particularities of national life in this or that place. It does so for the sake of the peace of God willed for the nations themselves. The danger of such a political engagement by the Church is obvious. Commitment to peoples in their distinctive political struggles can easily swallow up the Church into the rushing currents of violence *against* the nations, including sometimes other Christians. Even when Christian pacifism becomes a guard against such a slide, the danger is always real, and almost always overwhelming. Hence, *this* aspect of

---

11. Augustine, *City of God*, 19.17 (228).

gathering inevitably thrusts the Church back upon the figural movement of her Lord, of his passage and end.

In short, the translation involved in gathering means that cultures are changed, yet not into a single culture so much as into a cultural openness—something that necessarily characterizes peace in this world—to something yet unknown, but given in Christ.

Order

The implied political aspects of gathering do point to something explicit that cannot be ignored in the Church's actual life: decision-making. To be gathered is to make decisions together. This constitutes the great challenge of ecclesial "order" that has been at the center of most ecclesiologies since their long gestation and birth. From a systematic perspective, however, it is important to see that the question of order falls within the life of the gathered nations, not elsewhere. The order of the Church is not given statically in a divine institutional establishment; and twentieth-century ecclesiology, including Catholic ecclesiology, has been right to acknowledge this. Decision making, and hence authority in its executive function, is what the Church does as a gathering of Nations, even in that gathering's dynamic expansion.

If we list authorities within the animating movement of the Church's figural life, we see an array of traditional elements—Scripture, prophets, apostles, teachers. These might easily be rejigged in terms of orders of ministry. But the movement we have outlined also follows a certain larger figure, that of Christ's own self-offering and its fruit. There is surely something to be learned from this with respect to the enduring aspects of decision-making among the nations. First, peoples themselves in their distinctive self-orderings are involved in the Church's common discernment; and second, that discernment and decision is given through the martyrial form of subjection and sacrifice.

Leaving aside competing ways of organizing these features, there has been a common understanding in the Church, across time and divisions, that gathering and decision-making within the fullness of Christian distinctions properly takes the form of "council." The term "conciliarity" has been used to describe this basic approach. The latter term has some particular historic connotations, pointing to a period in the Western Church in the later fourteenth through early sixteenth centuries when, in the face of a weakened and divided Papacy, many Christians argued for the alternative governance of a widely representative "council" that would be central to the Church's order. But before and after this period, among Protestants as much as among Catholics, conciliar decision-making in the form of synods or sessions or conventions and convocations has been the natural means of making decisions for most Christians, at least in theory. The rationale for this, and its many forms, have varied. But for most, these forms have traced their roots back to the apostolic gathering of the Twelve and to the more basic *ekklesia* of Israel itself.

The fact, however, that such councils have become in a sense smaller and smaller in their representation, as churches have become more and more divided or insular, stands as a contradiction to gathering itself. The Orthodox at least have stood firm on the issue of an "ecumenical" council as the only real locus of authority for the Church, even if they assume that the fullness of the Church in fact excludes most Protestant Christians. Yet we should assume that the council of the nations will look very different from the councils of the embattled churches of today. We should assume that any gathering will be inclusive of the nations in their truly Adamic diversity, even among Christians; we should assume that it will be gathered by those who have touched the nations through their own self-offering; we should assume that they will be ordered to sacrifice rather than gain; we should assume that they will open the storehouses of many gifts, not shut them away. We can assume all this, and in so doing see the signs of gathering where these aspects, more locally and more fitfully, emerge. They are and will be the threads of endurance among the peoples of the earth.

Praise

The Church is the gathering of the nations that sings praise before God and the throne of the Lamb, in many tongues. They join their song to that of angels and cherubim. Their number includes those from long ago, in historical terms, and those whose lives perhaps we touch today in daily intercourse. Their song, in however many languages, is a translated singularity: "Salvation to our God, which sitteth upon the throne, and unto the Lamb!" "Blessing and glory, and wisdom, and thanksgiving, and honour, and power, and might, be unto our God for ever and ever. Amen!" (Rev 7:9–12 KJV). The English here is but one vocalization. The words, furthermore, coincide with other heavenly songs: "Holy, holy, holy, Lord God Almighty, which was, and is, and is to come!" (Rev 4:8; cf. Isa 6:3). The description given in these texts needs to be seen as part of the figure of Christ's own traversal of time, however transcendent of history the picture in Revelation seems. The Lamb on the throne *is* the Jesus who walks in Galilee. The Lamb is also he who most perfectly *adores* the Father, Son, and Spirit together, as the seventeenth-century theologian Bérulle insisted, "glorified and glorifying," most especially in the cross itself (John 13:31–32).[12] Given the ordering of the scriptural canon, this movement of Jesus also looks back to the opening of Genesis, where the Word emerges for us in our encounter with our own creation and with the world's peoples themselves. The full figure is given in compressed form in Philippians 2:5–11. The passage, which begins with the "form" and "equality" of God and proceeds through the cross, ends with every creature in heaven and on earth bowing in confession before Christ Jesus as Lord, "to the glory of God the Father." Jesus is the perfect adorer as well: he is the Lamb that praises the Father, the "glorifier."

Most "Marks of the Church" include sacraments. Some, like Luther's and Barth's, include "worship." From the standpoint of the Church's figural life, the song is the summit of her being, bound up with the ascended person of Christ. Most "eschatological" versions of ecclesiology include something like it. Yet the summit is not simply a final moment. It *is* the Church as the Church lives her life of gathering in Christ. So it is important to understand the normal and perhaps quotidian acts of worship and praise that are rightly associated with the Church as being firmly set within the context of her mission among the nations. The Church sings to God as she sings together in many tongues.

There are many practical issues that arise in thinking this way. Matters of inculturation we have already noted; other issues involve the styles (often segregated) of musical worship, spatial orderings of congregational devotion, and the Anglican concern with "common prayer." But most central, it seems to me, is the single reality of the Eucharist. This is, in fact, the one song of adoration that is most commonly sung today among the nations. Its center is given in the acclamation of the thrice-holy being of God. Its actual form articulates the full figural breadth of Christ Jesus in his transformative assumption of Adam's diversified life. When Orthodox, Catholic, and even some Protestants announce that, in the great thanksgiving to God indicated by the word "Eucharist," Christians join in a universal and heavenly liturgy, they are asserting something that is intrinsic to the Church's self-identity.

---

12. Thompson, *Bérulle and the French School*, 126–30.

The Figure of the Church

The Church, they proclaim, comprises the common life given through grace by the God of the living, of Abraham, Isaac, and Jacob. This God joins heaven and earth in his Son, so that the voices of all creation sing together before him in joy. When the song is sung today, it is *in fact* sung with all the "kinds" that populate heaven and earth; it is furthermore sung so that this song can be heard. The Church lives and is ordered for this singing.

The distinction between the Church Militant ("here on earth") and the Church Triumphant ("in heaven"), which dates from the Middle Ages, can easily obscure what is at work here as a figural movement. The movement from Baptism to Eucharist, which is given in the figure of Christ that orders the Church, is a very clear one. It is a movement that conforms to the Church's general way of arranging these two sacraments. It is a missionary movement. It is, most importantly, the movement that Christ himself assumes for the sake of the nations he has created in Adam. Protestants who either diminish or even ignore the Eucharist have obscured their own place in this movement. By the same token, Catholics who have made the theological articulation of the Eucharist a shibboleth of peoplehood have misconstrued its power as something ordered by the spirit of Christ. Its proper figural meaning is inclusive of the very movement by which Christians not only have come to be from among the nations, but also have rebelled, divided, and been given life again by grace in the body of Jesus. In this regard, the Eucharist is the offering, from the side of the Church, of self to others in Christ. But in Christ too the liturgy of heaven proceeds, even while the Church only haltingly and sporadically joins in. The Eucharist does not belong to the Church. We join and are joined to it in the course of our redemption.

Further Reading

Augustine. *The City of God, Books XVII–XXII*. Translated by Gerald G. Walsh and Daniel J. Honan. Washington, DC: Catholic University of America Press, 2010.

Barth, Karl. "The Holy Spirit and the Sending of the Christian Community: Part 4, The Ministry of the Community." In *Church Dogmatics*, edited by Thomas F. Torrance and Geoffrey Bromiley, 4.3.2. Peabody: Hendrickson, 2010.

Bonhoeffer, Dietrich. *The Cost of Discipleship*. Translated by R. H. Fuller. New York: Macmillan, 1959.

Bosch, David. *Transforming Mission: Paradigm Shifts in Theology of Mission*. Maryknoll: Orbis, 2011.

Burke, Trevor. *Adopted into God's Family: Exploring a Pauline Metaphor*. Downers Grove: InterVarsity, 2004.

Corbon, Jean. *The Wellspring of Worship*. Translated by Matthew J. O'Connell. San Francisco: Ignatius, 2005.
Croucher, Sheila. *Globalization and Belonging: The Politics of Identity in a Changing World*. Lanham, MD: Rowman & Littlefield, 2004.
Elias, Norbert. *The Civilizing Process*. 2 vols. Translated by Edmund Jephcott. New York: Pantheon/Urizen, 1978.
Etzioni, Amitai. "Bottom-Up Nation Building." *Policy Review* 158 (2009–10) 51–62.
Gregory, Brad S. *Salvation at Stake: Christian Martyrdom in Early Modern Europe*. Cambridge: Harvard University Press, 1999.
Guder, Darrell L. *Called to Witness: Doing Missional Theology*. Grand Rapids: Eerdmans, 2015.
Harrington, Bobby, and Alex Absolom. *Discipleship That Fits*. Grand Rapids: Zondervan, 2016.
John Paul II. *Ut unum sint*. *Acta Apostolicae Sedis* 87 (1995) 921–82.
Luther, Martin. *On the Councils and the Church*. Translated by Charles M. Jacobs. In *Luther's Works*, vol. 41, edited by Eric W. Gritsch, 3–178. Philadelphia: Fortress, 1966.
Martin, Cath. "'70 Million Christians' Martyred for Their Faith since Jesus Walked the Earth." *Christianity Today*, June 25, 2014. http://www.christiantoday.com/article/70.million.christians.martyred.faith.since.jesus.walked.earth/38403.htm.
Murray, Paul D., and Luca Badini-Confalonieri, eds. *Receptive Ecumenism and the Call to Catholic Learning*. New York: Oxford University Press, 2008.
Ndhlovu, Finex. *Becoming an African Diaspora in Australia: Language, Culture, Identity*. New York: Palgrave Macmillan, 2014.
Radner, Ephraim. *Brutal Unity: The Spiritual Politics of the Christian Church*. Waco, TX: Baylor University Press, 2012.
Scott, James M. *Adoption as Sons of God: An Exegetical Investigation into the Background of ΥΙΟΘΕΣΙΑ in the Pauline Corpus*. Tübingen: Mohr Siebeck, 1992.
Shorter, Aylward. *Toward a Theology of Inculturation*. Maryknoll: Orbis, 1999.
Swaan, Abram de. *The Killing Compartments: The Mentality of Mass Murder*. New Haven: Yale University Press, 2014.
Tertullian. *Apology*. Translated by T. R. Glover. Loeb Classical Library 250. Cambridge: Harvard University Press, 1998.
Thompson, William M., ed. *Bérulle and the French School: Selected Writings*. Translated by Lowell M. Glendon. New York: Paulist, 1989.
Voice of the Martyrs. https://www.persecution.com/public/aboutVOM.aspx?clickfrom=%3d6d61696e5f6d656e75.
Watson, Cynthia. *Nation-Building: A Reference Handbook*. Santa Barbara, CA: ABC-CLIO, 2004.
Wright, Christopher J. H. *The Mission of God: Unlocking the Bible's Grand Narrative*. Downers Grove: InterVarsity, 2006.
Wycliffe Global Alliance. "Scripture and Language Statistics 2015." http://www.wycliffe.net/statistics.

The Figure of the Church

Discussion Questions

1. How does the Church "figure Christ"? Where does any of this coincide or not coincide with traditional markers of the "true Church"?

2. How does looking at the Church figurally, in the way this chapter outlines, resolve some of the traditional apologetic debates and antagonisms among Christians about the Church?

3. Why is there a Church at all?

Conclusion

A Longing People

THE ECCLESIOLOGICAL GOAL OF defending the true Church is one I want to give up. Instead, I have tried simply to describe the Church as this one people of Israel who exists for the sake of all peoples, so that all might be taken up by Christ for the purposes of God's praise. I have tried to describe in a broad way how this happens. In doing so, finally, I have tried to pick my way through the various clamorings of particular ecclesial self-justifications. Though I do not reject them, I believe that they must find their meaning only within the larger movement of Christ's assumption of Israel in his flesh.

A crucial aspect of being the people of God is being judged by God. I have tried to insist that this reality does not negate the Church, but that it is simply a part of the actual reality of the Church's life. Still, we can discern criteria for God's judgment, and these criteria *do* constitute measures for the Church's integrity. The descent of Israel into competing kingdoms and finally dispersal, and the fragmentation of the Church into competing churches and their withering, while truly descriptive of the Church, are still matters of judgment. The dynamics of this descent can and should be examined and identified; and the Church should seek to reorder her witness and her common life in ways that rectify these dissolutions. This testing, accountability, and correction is also what it means to be the Church. *Ecclesia semper reformanda*—the Church as always a people to be reformed—has been a claim associated with Protestants most famously up to Barth. But it is drawn from Augustine, and it describes the figural calling of the Church in a pointed fashion.

Conclusion

In the previous chapter, I began to hint at some of the ways in which a more "prescriptive" approach to the Church could indeed emerge from its figural description. In a way, this approach follows that of much traditional ecumenical discussion, which moves from description to recognition, and only somewhat obliquely in the end to suggestions for reform. The great 1982 agreement on "Baptism, Eucharist, Ministry," forged by the work of the World Council of Churches' Faith and Order Commission, proceeded in this fashion. It first describes, with a good deal of scriptural and ecclesial detail, what baptism, Eucharist, and ministry look like and mean across the spectrum of Christianity. It then indicates how most churches do indeed conform their practices in this regard to key scriptural guides. On this basis, the document seeks to offer a framework for mutual "recognition" among divided churches, so that they can affirm that just these essential aspects of the Church are genuinely held across the spectrum. Finally, where they are not held or not wholly, the document encourages change, to bring churches to this common, if broadly understood, set of practices and understandings. While, for instance, Pentecostals do not generally have "bishops" who order the ministries among congregations, they often *do* have "supervisory" ministries that fulfill episcopal functions in many key New Testament ways. Having recognized this, the diverse terminologies we apply to ministries may mask deeper and genuine continuities. And where they do not, then churches are called to consider forging such continuities in new ways.

In talking about the Church as Israel in her scripturally-given mission and vicissitudes, I therefore do not wish to rule out the need to articulate the grounds upon which Israel is being called to account, over and over. But, having only hinted at some of this, I leave the task for others. What I wish to stress, however, is that the task itself needs to be properly construed, not as identifying the true church, but as nation-building. Christians are already members of the true Church. That is why we love her, secretly and implicitly, but truly. It is why we ever seek her well-being and the fulfillment of her promise, however misguidedly at times.

Nation-building today is usually viewed as a task pursued after the wreckage of civil disorder. One definition says starkly that "nation-building" aims at

> ending military conflict and rebuilding economic and political infrastructures, along with basic services, to include the armed forces, police, government, banks, transportation networks,

communications, health and medical care, schools, and the other basic infrastructure.[1]

Nation-building assumes that a nation has been torn up, often in complex ways that touch the rich texture of the civil sphere of people's lives. Just here the difficulties and debates arise: how can we "build up" the common identity and "we-ness" of a people that has been ripped apart? There is a sense in which the Church is such a nation, and ecclesiology then an expression of tornness. There is probably much that the Church can learn from secular attempts at nation-building in their success and failures. For instance, the notion that nations are more successfully rebuilt not from the top down, through uniformly imposed systems, but "from the bottom up," through local leaders and along the seams and energies of diverse tribes and groups, is something the Church's nation-of-nations can learn from as well as teach. There is much too that the Church can learn simply from the dynamics of national breakdown and the reverse process of "de-civilizing," which picks apart the genuine sinews of civil life, often through coercive technocratic or bureaucratic systems of social control. The search for analogies here to the Church's life as a nation has barely begun, but it needs to move forward if accountability and renewal are to happen. I have tried to indicate a few directions this might go.

But the analogy only goes so far. After all, the Church is *not* like any other nation; it is ordered by a divine spirit and toward an assumptive relationship with the body of Christ, taken up by God to himself. This is why the modern State of Israel is not simply an extension or landed embodiment of Israel. To this degree, whatever happens to the Church *is* the Church, and its truth is given in the Scriptures according to the Spirit of Christ at work in his body. This era, and all eras, belong to God. The temptation to deny the process of national breakdown for the Church, or to stand quiescently before it, is thus also the temptation to assert (falsely) that "whatever is, is right." Hence, we must end here by trying to be more precise about the kind of love the Christian holds for the Church—a love that both holds us close to our people and also motivates our honesties and service in ways that maintain the Church's people as Christ's own, and not our invention.

Christians love the Church, we can say, because Christ loves the Church. This has always been a directional presupposition, as in Paul's discussion in Ephesians 5:22–33. It has always been a matter of puzzlement that Paul speaks of husbands "loving" their wives, but wives instead

1. Watson, *Nation-Building*, 10.

Conclusion

"reverencing" or "honoring" their husbands. Should not each spouse "love" the other equally? It is not, of course, that wives cannot and do not love their husbands. But here the figure of Christ and his Church takes over the nuptial discussion: Christ first loves the Church. That initiating and founding love is prior and primary. We love "because he first loved us" (1 John 4:19; cf. 4:10). We *are* the Church because of this love. It is not that we cannot or do not love the one who loves the Church (cf. Isa 5:1). But "in Christ" we are always engaging that love from the perspective of one whose love given in return is never quite congruent with its origin. We cannot love the Church as Christ loves the Church, his own body. For us, to love the Church is to *long*, that form of love whose grasp cannot match the reach of its hopes, and thus it waits in desire.

The Church is not like other nations in this regard. As a figure of Christ, this nation itself is not fully ordered. It is on its way, as we have seen, engaged in mission. Encountering and gathering other nations, it works its way through time and history, mired in failures, pulled from them, imagining or approaching not-yet futures. The whole of the figure is given in Christ as he assumes Israel and carries it with him. But the carrying is, from our perspective, a movement. We *do* speak of "building up the Church," and Paul especially makes use of the image (cf. 1 Cor 3:9–23). But, as a people assumed by Christ in the world, this cannot mean that we do any more than follow up on our longings, within the ordering that is given us in the scriptural Christ, the "foundation" in Paul's image. Here we build by moving, the "rock" moving alongside us (1 Cor 10:4). The Church, bound to the peripatetic Christ, loves by moving with him in his circulation and his aim, even while she cannot assess the fullness of that which is already his. Her love is colored by obscurity itself, even as it is wholly given over to the one she loves. "La civilisation n'est pas encore terminée"—civilization is still not finished—as the Baron d'Holbach said in his progressivist view of enlightenment culture. One might say the same thing of the Church, except that, in Christ, her ending is absolutely given in this movement; progressivism is denied; there is only the rise and fall of faithfulness, and the stirring of desire. Shaped in and by Christ, the Church learns to yearn in response, and her members grow in this kind of love.

This brings us back to the Bride, with whom we began this volume. We have stressed in this book the collective aspect of the Church as her fundamental character. This is something that has become difficult for modern people to grasp. But the world in its novel forms—its Anthropocene revolution—is certainly not a place where individuals as such can survive, nor was it ever. Yet it is not as if human individuals do not exist or that somehow they do not, as individuals, hold a primary place in God's creative concern. God knows us each "by name," not only by kind, and on this basis also calls us (John 10:3; Exod 33:17; cf. Ps 147:4). Those written in "the Book of Life" are written individually (Phil 4:3; Rev 21:27). This individuality, however, precisely as *redeemed* individuality, derives from the Church's formative peoplehood. Made a member, the Christian individual is given a "new name" (Isa 62:2; Rev 2:17), and from this life together a new individual identity arises. That identity, furthermore, is given in the very figural mode by which the Church herself exists: the "disciple" becomes "like the master" (Luke 6:40), and "conformity" to Christ describes the shape of this likeness (Rom 8:29). Individual and people both "look like" each other, for both are apprehended figures of Christ Jesus, who "gave his life for the many" (Mark 10:45). When Paul writes that "I live, yet not I, but Christ liveth in me" (Gal 2:20 KJV), he speaks of this unique identity that is given through the self-giving of Christ, which, taken as a whole, constitutes the "we" of the Church. When Christ "gives himself" for the Church, he does so through the baptismal purification of her members (Eph 5:25–26). Each is made to become his "body," his own "flesh and bones," the bride to his espousal; and the "I" takes form in the "we" that is the single identity of Christ.

The figural conformance of this collective and individual identity is, in part, what Orthodox theology has indicated in its profound notion of "theosis" or "divinization" (drawing on the trembling and elusive promise of 2 Peter 1:4 regarding "sharing the divine nature"). "Discipleship" is a currently popular focus for Christian ministry, largely because, in an era of increasingly indistinct Christian identity, training individuals to live as distinct a Christian life as possible seems critical. Much of this training has become highly individualized itself, involving tasks of intense personal devotion and moral focus, as in Oswald Chambers's classic *My Utmost for His Highest* (1924). Recent books on discipleship, however, have begun to grasp the collective aspects more and more. Eastern Orthodoxy far more traditionally has always understood that the Master's disciple, even in the recesses of an isolated hermitage, is such only because, in prayer as much as anything, he or she is bound to the Church's body, whose form is first of all Christ's own. If there is a task to be performed in making disciples, it is first of all a divine task, which is displayed most fully and literally in the "divine liturgy" of the Eucharist.

Conclusion

The intimate apprehension of human*kind* by God in Christ, as Christ moves forward through time, changes us. "Holiness" is the name given to that specific act of transformation that turns "I's" into a "we" whose single identity is granted by Christ. Bonhoeffer, who so agonizingly struggled to coordinate individual faith with the Church, spoke of first being *stripped* of our original and unredeemed collective commitments—leaving family and friends for the sake of Christ—only to be remade into a new collective. "Though we all have to enter upon discipleship alone, we do not remain alone. If we take him at his word and dare to become individuals, our reward is the fellowship of the Church."[2] Perhaps Bonhoeffer offers his own figural indication here: the Anthropocene era is hardly one that bodes well. Although we cannot and should not speak as if we knew, it may be that the Church's mission goes its way "each in its own order," ecclesiologies each falling away; and now in our very era "comes the end" (1 Cor 15:23, 24), when Christ himself "delivers the Kingdom to God the Father." In this case, surely our "faithfulness" is not some work we do *on* ourselves. In our stripped and refashioned "we," we are already part of a work God has been doing. We breathe it insofar as God has given us this particular life itself—*plebs sancta Dei*, God making holy his people, in Dix's famous eucharistic phrase. Our faithfulness is only our "yes" to the work God does on us within his people. That this "yes" is most clearly identified with Mary in her divine conception (by both Catholics and Protestants like Luther; cf. Luke 1:38) explains why, in so much of the Christian tradition, the Church is spoken of as Bride in conjunction with Mary's name, the Eve from and by Christ's side.

Mary is waiting, longing, desiring. She awaits uncertainly the end of her Son's mission; she longs to see his vindication; she desires his safety and protects his future (cf. Rev 12). The Church—Israel the Bride—thus yearns to be utterly *with* her Lord, and hence like him, though this utter likeness is something given only in its full figure, not in a moment (1 John 3:2). She forms her members, not as complete, but as filled with this receptive longing; and their peopled lives, whatever their individuality, do the same. They are committed not to the moment but to the horizon of all peoples, the fullness of Adam's race, where Christianity has spilled out of its confines now and covers the world. The Church longs, she does not hold. On that distinction all human ecclesiologies, Catholic and Protestant, must give way to divine grace in repentant and humble expectation.

2. Bonhoeffer, *Cost of Discipleship*, 113.

Christians love the Church because they recognize that their own lives are oriented in longing response to Christ's love for what he has made his own Body. "When they therefore were come together, they asked of him, saying, Lord, wilt thou at this time restore again the kingdom to Israel?" (Acts 1:6 KJV). There is only one thing that the Church *does*, and those who do it do so as the Church: the Church prays, *as her savior Christ has taught her.*

The Church prays: "thy kingdom come." The Church receives: "give us this day our daily bread . . . forgive us our sins." The Church reaches out to all the children of Adam: "as we forgive those who have sinned against us." The Church gives herself away: "for thine is the kingdom, the power, and the glory." The Church does this in and through Jesus Christ, which becomes the spectacular movement of the human race's history: the Last Adam (1 Cor 15:45) loves his own body (Eph 5:23, 28–30), the Church, such that in Christ the Church becomes the whole Adam who is finally God's own, a Bride joined to her Husband. This movement is both the means and the measure by which God judges the Church, and by which we are her members. Thus is she indeed the broken and restored body, the true Bride of the Bridegroom, the one who ever longs for the one who loves her.

Discussion Questions

1. The traditional linkage of the Church with Mary and with the Bride of Christ carries with it certain theological implications. What are some of these theological implications, in light of this volume's figural ecclesiology?

2. How might this way of understanding the Church be positively suited to the present era of human affairs?

Bibliography

Afanasiev, Nicholas. *The Church of the Holy Spirit*. Translated by Vitaly Permiakov. Notre Dame: University of Notre Dame Press, 2007.
Anderson, Benedict. *Imagined Communities: Reflections on the Origin and Spread of Nationalism*. Rev. ed. London: Verso, 2006.
Anderson, Braden P. *Chosen Nation: Scripture, Theopolitics, and the Project of National Identity*. Eugene, OR: Cascade, 2012.
Anglican-Orthodox Dialogue. "The Cyprus Statement: The Church of the Triune God." London: The Anglican Communion Office, 2006. http://www.anglicancommunion.org/media/103818/The-Church-of-the-Triune-God.pdf.
Anglican–Roman Catholic International Dialogue. "The Church as Communion." 1991. http://www.vatican.va/roman_curia/pontifical_councils/chrstuni/angl-comm-docs/rc_pc_chrstuni_doc_19900906_church-communion_en.html.
Arias-Maldonado, Manuel. *Environment and Society: Socionatural Relations in the Anthropocene*. Cham, Switzerland: Springer, 2015.
Assis, Eliyahu. *Identity in Conflict: The Struggle between Esau and Jacob, Edom and Israel*. Winona Lake, IN: Eisenbrauns, 2016.
Auburn Seminary Record 12:7 (Feb 1917).
Augustine. *The City of God. Books XVII–XXII*. Translated by Gerald G. Walsh and Daniel J. Honan. Washington, DC: Catholic University of America Press, 2010.
———. "Sermon 267." Translated by Edmund Hill. In *Sermons III/7 (230–272B) on Liturgical Seasons*, edited by John E. Rotelle, 271–74. Hyde Park, NY: New City, 1993.
Barth, Karl. *Dogmatics in Outline*. Translated by G. T. Thomson. London: SCM, 1949.
———. "The Holy Spirit and the Sending of the Christian Community: Part 4, The Ministry of the Community." In *Church Dogmatics*, edited by Thomas F. Torrance and Geoffrey Bromiley, 4.3.2. Peabody, MA: Hendrickson, 2010.
Bellarmine, Robert. *De conciliis*. In *Opera omnia*, 12 vols., edited by J. Fèvre, II:187–507. Paris: Vivès, 1870–74.
Berend, Nora, ed. *Christianization and the Rise of Christian Monarchy: Scandinavia, Central Europe and Rus' c. 900–1200*. Cambridge: Cambridge University Press, 2007.
Bonhoeffer, Dietrich. *The Cost of Discipleship*. Translated by R. H. Fuller. New York: Macmillan, 1959.

Bibliography

———. *Sanctorum Communio: A Dogmatic Inquiry into the Sociology of the Church*. Translated by Ronald Gregor Smith. London: Collins, 1963.

Borst, Arno. *Der Turmbau von Babel: Geschichte der Meinungen über Ursprung und Vielfalt der Sprachen und Völker*. 4 vols. Stuttgart: Hiersemann, 1957–63.

Bosch, David. *Transforming Mission: Paradigm Shifts in Theology of Mission*. Maryknoll: Orbis, 2011.

Breuilly, John. "Nationalism and the Making of National Pasts." In *Nations and Their Histories: Constructions and Representations*, edited by Susana Carvalho and François Gemenne, 7–28. New York: Palgrave Macmillan, 2009.

———, ed. *The Oxford Handbook of the History of Nationalism*. Oxford: Oxford University Press, 2013.

Bulgakov, Sergius. *The Bride of the Lamb*. Translated by Boris Jakim. Grand Rapids: Eerdmans, 2002.

Burke, Trevor. *Adopted into God's Family: Exploring a Pauline Metaphor*. Downers Grove: InterVarsity, 2004.

Calhoun, Craig. *Nations Matter: Culture, History, and the Cosmopolitan Dream*. London: Routledge, 2007.

Calvin, John. *Institutes of the Christian Religion*. Edited by John T. McNeill. Translated by Ford Lewis Battles. Louisville: Westminster John Knox, 1960.

Carpenter, Charles Blake. "Sunday in an Eskimo Village." *Churchman* 32/33 (Oct 20, 1894) 484–85.

Carvalho, Susana, and François Gemenne, eds. *Nations and Their Histories: Constructions and Representations*. New York: Palgrave Macmillan, 2009.

Catechism of the Catholic Church. Vatican: Libreria Vaticana, 1993. http://www.vatican.va/archive/ENG0015/_INDEX.HTM.

Cicero. *On Divination*. Translated by W. A. Falconer. In *On Old Age; On Friendship; On Divination*. Loeb Classical Library 154. Cambridge: Harvard University Press, 1923.

———. *On Ends*. Translated by H. Rackham. Loeb Classical Library 40. Cambridge: Harvard University Press, 2014.

Clarke, Elizabeth. *Politics, Religion and the Song of Songs in Seventeenth-Century England*. New York: Palgrave Macmillan, 2011.

Clericus Connorensis. *Ecclesiologism Exposed: Being the Letters of "Clericus Connorensis," as Originally Published in the Belfast Commercial Chronicle*. Belfast, 1843.

Cohen, Shaye. *The Beginnings of Jewishness: Boundaries, Varieties, Uncertainties*. Berkeley: University of California Press, 1999.

Congar, Yves. *L'Église de saint Augustin à l'époque moderne*. Histoire des dogmes 20. Paris: Cerf, 1970.

Congregation for the Doctrine of the Faith. *Dominus Iesus*. Declaration on the unicity and salvific universality of Jesus Christ and the Church. Rome, 2000. http://www.vatican.va/roman_curia/congregations/cfaith/documents/rc_con_cfaith_doc_20000806_dominus-iesus_en.html.

———. *Letter to the Bishops of the Catholic Church on some Aspects of the Church Understood as Communion*. Rome, 1992. http://www.vatican.va/roman_curia/congregations/cfaith/documents/rc_con_cfaith_doc_28051992_communionis-notio_en.html.

Corbon, Jean. *The Wellspring of Worship*. Translated by Matthew J. O'Connell. San Francisco: Ignatius, 2005.

Bibliography

Croucher, Sheila. *Globalization and Belonging: The Politics of Identity in a Changing World*. Lanham, MD: Rowman & Littlefield, 2004.
Crummell, Alexander. *The Greatness of Christ and Other Sermons*. New York, 1882.
Crutzen, Paul J. "Geology of Mankind." *Nature* 415 (2002). doi:10.1038/415023a.
Currie, Archibald. *God's Bottle for Believers' Tears, by One Who Has a Tear for Others as Well as Himself*. Edinburgh, 1854.
Daniel, David P. "Luther on the Church." In *The Oxford Handbook of Martin Luther's Theology*, edited by Robert Kolb et al., 333–49. Oxford: Oxford University Press, 2014.
D'Costa, Gavin, ed. *Christian Uniqueness Reconsidered: The Myth of a Pluralistic Theology of Religions*. Maryknoll: Orbis, 1990.
Dewey, John. "The Historic Background of Corporate Legal Personality." *Yale Law Journal* 35 (1926) 655–73.
Dix, Gregory. *The Shape of the Liturgy*. London: Dacre, 1964.
Donaldson, Terry. *Paul and the Gentiles: Remapping the Apostle's Convictional World*. Minneapolis: Fortress, 1997.
Dorrien, Gary J. *The Making of American Liberal Theology: Imagining Progressive Religion, 1805–1900*. Louisville: Westminster John Knox, 2001.
Dulles, Avery. *Models of the Church*. Expanded ed. New York: Image, 2002.
Durham, James. *Clavis Cantici; or, An Exposition of the Song of Solomon*. Edinburgh, 1723.
"Ecclesialogist v. Ecclesiologist." *Ecclesiologist* 1 (1843) 74–75.
"Ecclesialogy." Anonymously written review article. *British Critic Quarterly Theological Review* 22 (1837) 218–48.
Ecclesiological (Cambridge Camden) Society. *Handbook of English Ecclesiology*. London, 1847.
Eisen, Robert. *The Peace and Violence of Judaism: From the Bible to Modern Zionism*. New York: Oxford University Press, 2011.
Elias, Norbert. *The Civilizing Process*. Translated by Edmund Jephcott. 2 vols. New York: Pantheon/Urizen, 1978.
Ellis, Marc H. *O, Jerusalem! The Contested Future of the Jewish Covenant*. Minneapolis: Fortress, 1999.
Etzioni, Amitai. "Bottom-Up Nation Building." *Policy Review* 158 (2009/2010) 51–62.
Evans, Hugh Davey. "The Reformation." *American Church Monthly* 2.1 (1857) 4–18.
Eyl, Jennifer. "Semantic Voids, New Testament Translation, and Anachronism: The Case of Paul's Use of *Ekklesia*." *Method and Theory in the Study of Religion* 26 (2014) 315–39.
Field, Richard. *Of the Church: Five Books*. Cambridge: Cambridge University Press, 1847–52.
Fletcher, Richard. *The Barbarian Conversion: From Paganism to Christianity*. Berkeley: University of California Press, 1997.
Forsyth, P. T. *Theology in Church and State*. London: Hodder and Stoughton, 1915.
Fuchs, Lorelei F. *Koinonia and the Quest for an Ecumenical Ecclesiology: From Foundations through Dialogue to Symbolic Competence for Communionality*. Grand Rapids: Eerdmans, 2008.
Gignac, J. "Anathema." In *The Catholic Encyclopedia*. New York: Robert Appleton. http://www.newadvent.org/cathen/01455e.htm.
Gilbert, Margaret. *Joint Commitment: How We Make the Social World*. New York: Oxford University Press, 2014.

BIBLIOGRAPHY

———. *On Social Facts*. London: Routledge, 1989.

———. *Sociality and Responsibility: New Essays in Plural Subject Theory*. Lanham, MD: Rowman and Littlefield, 2000.

Goldman, Alvin I. *Knowledge in a Social World*. Oxford: Clarendon, 1999.

Greenberg, Moshe. "Mankind, Israel, and the Nations in Hebraic Heritage." In *No Man Is Alien: Essays on the Unity of Mankind*, edited by J. Robert Nelson, 15–40. Leiden: Brill, 1971.

Gregory, Brad S. *Salvation at Stake: Christian Martyrdom in Early Modern Europe*. Cambridge: Harvard University Press, 1999.

Guder, Darrell L. *Called to Witness: Doing Missional Theology*. Grand Rapids: Eerdmans, 2015.

Haight, Roger. *Christian Community in History*. 3 vols. New York: Continuum, 2004–8.

Harrington, Bobby, and Alex Absolom. *Discipleship That Fits*. Grand Rapids: Zondervan, 2016.

Hauerwas, Stanley, and William H. Willimon. *Resident Aliens: Life in the Christian Colony*. Nashville: Abingdon, 1989.

Hawn, C. Michael. *Gather into One: Praying and Singing Globally*. Grand Rapids: Eerdmans, 2003.

Healy, Nicholas M. *Church, World, and the Christian Life: Practical-Prophetic Ecclesiology*. New York: Cambridge University Press, 2000.

Hengel, Martin. *Jews, Greeks, Barbarians: Aspects of the Hellenization of Judaism in the Pre-Christian Period*. Philadelphia: Fortress, 1980.

Iriye, Akira, ed. *Global Interdependence: The World after 1945*. Cambridge: Belknap of Harvard University Press, 2014.

Jáki, P. Stanislas. *Les tendances nouvelles de l'ecclésiologie*. Rome: Herder, 1957.

Jakim, Boris, and Robert Bird, trans. and eds. *On Spiritual Unity: A Slavophile Reader*. Hudson, NY: Lindisfarne, 1998.

Jocz, Jakob. *Christians and Jews: Encounter and Mission*. London: SPCK, 1966.

———. *A Theology of Election*. New York: Macmillan, 1958.

John Paul II. *Ecclesia de eucharistia*. Encyclical letter on the Eucharist in its relationship to the Church. *Acta Apostolicae Sedis* 95 (2003) 433–75. http://www.vatican.va/holy_father/special_features/encyclicals/documents/hf_jp-ii_enc_20030417_ecclesia_eucharistia_en.html.

———. *Ut unum sint*. Encyclical letter on commitment to ecumenism. *Acta Apostolicae Sedis* 87 (1995) 921–82. http://w2.vatican.va/content/john-paul-ii/en/encyclicals/documents/hf_jp-ii_enc_25051995_ut-unum-sint.html.

Johnson, John J. "A New Testament Understanding of the Jewish Rejection of Jesus: Four Theologians on the Salvation of Israel." *Journal of the Evangelical Theological Society* 42 (2000) 229–46.

"Joint Catholic-Orthodox Declaration of His Holiness Pope Paul VI and the Ecumenical Patriarch Athenagoras I." December 7, 1965. http://w2.vatican.va/content/paul-vi/en/speeches/1965/documents/hf_p-vi_spe_19651207_common-declaration.html.

Kaiser, Walter. *Mission in the Old Testament: Israel as a Light to the Nations*. Grand Rapids: Baker, 2000.

Kärkkäinen, Veli-Matti. *An Introduction to Ecclesiology: Ecumenical, Historical & Global Perspectives*. Downers Grove: InterVarsity, 2009.

Kasper, Walter. "On the Church: A Friendly Reply to Cardinal Ratzinger." Translated by Ladislas Orsy. *America* 184 (2001) 8–14.

Bibliography

Katz, Jacob. *Exclusivism and Tolerance: Jewish-Gentile Relations in the Medieval and Modern Times.* New York: Oxford University Press, 1961.

Kessler, Edward. *An Introduction to Jewish-Christian Relations.* Cambridge: Cambridge University Press, 2010.

Kimbrough, S. T., Jr., ed. *Orthodox and Wesleyan Ecclesiology.* Crestwood, NY: St. Vladimir's Seminary Press, 2007.

Kinzer, Mark S., and Jennifer M. Rosner, eds. *Israel's Messiah and the People of God: A Vision for Messianic Jewish Covenant Fidelity.* Eugene, OR: Cascade, 2011.

Koessler, Maximilian. "The Person in Imagination or Persona Ficta of the Corporation." *Louisiana Law Review* 9.4 (1949) 435–49.

Kolakowski, Leszek. *Chrétiens sans église: La conscience religieuse et le lien confessionnel au XVIIe siècle.* Paris: Gallimard, 1969.

LaCugna, Catherine Mowry. *God for Us: The Trinity and Christian Life.* San Francisco: Harper, 1993.

Lassiter, Luke, et al. *The Jesus Road: Kiowas, Christianity, and Indian Hymns.* Lincoln: University of Nebraska Press, 2002.

Lewis, David. *On the Plurality of Worlds.* Oxford: Blackwell, 1986.

Lindbeck, George A. "Confession and Community: An Israel-like View of the Church." *Christian Century* 107 (1990) 492–96.

———. "The Gospel's Uniqueness: Election and Untranslatibility." *Modern Theology* 13 (1997) 423–50.

Lohfink, Gerhard. *Does God Need the Church? Toward a Theology of the People of God.* Translated by Linda M. Maloney. Collegeville: Liturgical, 1999.

Loisy, Alfred. *L'Évangile et l'église.* Paris: Picard, 1902.

Longenecker, Bruce W. "Different Answers to Different Issues: Israel, the Gentiles and Salvation History in Romans 9–11." *Journal for the Study of the New Testament* 36 (1989) 95–123.

Luther, Martin. *On the Councils and the Church.* Translated by Charles M. Jacobs. In vol. 41 of *Luther's Works*, edited by Eric W. Gritsch, 3–178. Philadelphia: Fortress, 1966.

Martin, Cath. "'70 million Christians' Martyred for Their Faith since Jesus Walked the Earth." *Christianity Today*, June 25, 2014. http://www.christiantoday.com/article/70.million.christians.martyred.faith.since.jesus.walked.earth/38403.htm.

Martyr, Justin. *Dialogue with Trypho.* Translated by Thomas B. Falls. Washington, DC: Catholic University of America Press, 2008.

Mathetes. *Epistle to Diognetus.* Translated by Alexander Roberts and James Donaldson. In vol. 1 of *Ante-Nicene Fathers*, edited by Alexander Roberts et al. Buffalo, NY, 1885.

Matter, E. Ann. *The Voice of My Beloved: The Song of Songs in Western Medieval Christianity.* Philadelphia: University of Pennsylvania Press, 1990.

McNeill, John T. *Unitive Protestantism: The Ecumenical Spirit and Its Persistent Expression.* 2nd ed. Richmond: John Knox, 1964.

Mersch, Emile. *The Whole Christ: The Historical Development of the Doctrine of the Mystical Body in Scripture and Tradition.* Translated by John R. Kelly. 1938. Reprint, Eugene, OR: Wipf and Stock, 2011.

Michaud-Quantin, Pierre. *Universitas. Expressions du mouvement communautaire dans le Moyen Âge latin.* L'Église et l'État au Moyen Âge 13. Paris: Vrin, 1970.

Miller, Kiri. *Traveling Home: Sacred Harp Singing and American Pluralism.* Urbana: University of Illinois Press, 2008.

Bibliography

Minear, Paul. *Images of the Church in the New Testament.* Louisville: Westminster John Knox, 2004.

Moltmann, Jürgen. *The Open Church: Invitation to a Messianic Lifestyle.* Translated by M. D. Meeks. London: SCM, 1978.

Morgan, Timothy C. "Why Muslims Are Becoming the Best Evangelists." Interview with Dave Garrison. *Christianity Today*, April 22, 2014. http://www.christianitytoday.com/ct/2014/april-web-only/why-muslims-are-becoming-best-evangelists.html.

Morgenstern, Mira. *Conceiving a Nation: The Development of Political Discourse in the Hebrew Bible.* University Park: Pennsylvania State University Press, 2009.

Moseley, Carys. *Nationhood, Providence, and Witness: Israel in Protestant Theology and Social Theory.* Eugene, OR: Cascade, 2013.

Murray, Paul D., and Luca Badini-Confalonieri, eds. *Receptive Ecumenism and the Call to Catholic Learning.* New York: Oxford University Press, 2008.

Ndhlovu, Finex. *Becoming an African Diaspora in Australia: Language, Culture, Identity.* New York: Palgrave Macmillan, 2014.

Nelson, Samuel, and Philip Gorski. "Conditions of Religious Belonging: Confessionalization, De-parochialization, and the Euro-American Divergence." *International Sociology* 29 (2014) 3–21.

Newbigin, Lesslie. *A Faith for This One World?* London: SCM, 1961.

———. *Foolishness to the Greeks: The Gospel and Western Culture.* London: SPCK, 1986.

Niebuhr, H. Richard. *Social Sources of Denominationalism.* New York: Holt, 1929.

Okoye, James Chukwuma. *Israel and the Nations: A Mission Theology of the Old Testament.* Maryknoll: Orbis, 2006.

Ormerod, Neil. "Recent Ecclesiology: A Survey." *Pacifica* 21 (2008) 57–67.

Partridge, George E. *The Psychology of Nations: A Contribution to the Philosophy of History.* New York: Macmillan, 1919.

Pew Research Center. "Global Christianity: A Report on the Size and Distribution of the World's Christian Population." Forum on Religion and Public Life, December 2011. http://www.pewforum.org/2011/12/19/global-christianity-exec.

Philaret. "A Protest to Patriarch Athenagoras: On the Lifting of the Anathemas of 1054." December 1965. http://orthodoxinfo.com/ecumenism/philaret_lifting.aspx.

Pickard, Stephen. *Seeking the Church: An Introduction to Ecclesiology.* London: SCM, 2012.

Pius XII. *Mystici corporis Christi.* Encyclical letter on the mistical [sic] body of Christ. *Acta Apostolicae Sedis* 35 (1943) 193–248. http://w2.vatican.va/content/pius-xii/en/encyclicals/documents/hf_p-xii_enc_29061943_mystici-corporis-christi.html.

Radner, Ephraim. *Brutal Unity: The Spiritual Politics of the Christian Church.* Waco, TX: Baylor University Press, 2012.

———. *The End of the Church: A Pneumatology of Christian Division in the West.* Grand Rapids: Eerdmans, 1998.

Rafael, Vicente L. *Contracting Colonialism: Translation and Christian Conversion in Tagalog Society under Early Spanish Rule.* Ithaca: Cornell University Press, 1988.

———. *The Promise of the Foreign: Nationalism and the Technics of Translations in the Spanish Philippines.* Durham: Duke University Press, 2005.

Raisin, Jacob S. *Gentile Reactions to Jewish Ideals with Special Reference to Proselytes.* New York: Philosophical Library, 1953.

Ratzinger, Joseph. "The Ecclesiology of Vatican II." Conference of Cardinal Ratzinger at the opening of the Pastoral Congress of the Diocese of Aversa (Italy). 15 September 2001. *L'Osservatore Romano*, weekly edition in English, 23 January 2002, 5.

Bibliography

———. "A Response to Walter Kasper: The Local Church and the Universal Church." *America* 185 (2001) 7–11.
Renan, Ernest. *Qu'est-ce qu'une nation? Et autres essais politiques.* Paris: Presses Pocket, 1992.
Reventlow, Henning Graf. *The Authority of the Bible and the Rise of the Modern World.* Philadelphia: Fortress, 1985.
Robert, Dana L., ed. *Converting Colonialism: Visions and Realities in Mission History, 1706–1914.* Grand Rapids: Eerdmans, 2008.
Robinson, H. Wheeler. *Corporate Personality in Ancient Israel.* Edinburgh: T. & T. Clark, 1981.
Sanmark, Alexandra. *Power and Conversion: A Comparative Study of Christianization in Scandinavia.* Uppsala: Uppsala University, 2004.
Sanneh, Lamin. *Translating the Message: The Missionary Impact on Culture.* 2nd ed. Maryknoll: Orbis, 2009.
———. "The Yogi and the Commissar." In *Disciples of All Nations: Pillars of World Christianity,* 131–62. Oxford: Oxford University Press, 2008.
Scott, James M. *Adoption as Sons of God: An Exegetical Investigation into the Background of ΥΙΟΘΕΣΙΑ in the Pauline Corpus.* Tübingen: Mohr Siebeck, 1992.
Serle, Ambrose. *The Church of God; or, Essays upon Some Descriptive Names and Titles Given in the Scriptures.* London, 1793.
Shorter, Aylward. *Toward a Theology of Inculturation.* Maryknoll: Orbis, 1999.
Simon, Marcel. *Versus Israel: A Study of the Relations between Christians and Jews in the Roman Empire (135–425).* Translated by H. McKeating. Oxford: Oxford University Press, 1986.
Stannard, David. *American Holocaust: The Conquest of the New World.* New York: Oxford University Press, 1992.
Stoermer, Eugene F. "The 'Anthropocene.'" *IGBP Newsletter* 41 (2000) 17–18.
Swaan, Abram de. *Killing Compartments: The Mentality of Mass Murder.* New Haven: Yale University Press, 2014.
Tertullian. *Apology.* Translated by T. R. Glover. Loeb Classical Library 250. Cambridge: Harvard University Press, 1998.
Thompson, William M., ed. *Bérulle and the French School: Selected Writings.* Translated by Lowell M. Glendon. New York: Paulist, 1989.
Torrance, Alan. "Jesus in Christian Doctrine." In *The Cambridge Companion to Jesus,* edited by Markus Bockmuehl, 200–219. Cambridge: Cambridge University Press, 2001.
Turnbull, Stephen, ed. *Japan's Hidden Christians, 1549–1999.* 2 vols. Surrey, UK: Japan Library, 2000.
Tyndale, William. *An Answer to Sir Thomas More's Dialogue.* Cambridge: Cambridge University Press, 1850.
Vansittart, William. *A Statement of the Argument respecting Abel's Sacrifice and Faith.* London, 1826.
Walls, Andrew F. *The Cross-Cultural Process in Christian History: Studies in the Transmission and Appropriation of Faith.* Maryknoll: Orbis, 2002.
Watts, Isaac. *The Psalms of David.* London, 1719.
Watson, Cynthia. *Nation-Building: A Reference Handbook.* Santa Barbara, CA: ABC-CLIO, 2004.
Wells, Samuel, and George R. Sumner. *Esther and Daniel.* Grand Rapids: Brazos, 2013.

BIBLIOGRAPHY

World Council of Churches. "Message from the Fifth World Conference of Faith and Order, 1993." Santiago de Compostela, Spain, August 1993. http://www.oikoumene.org/en/resources/documents/commissions/faith-and-order/x-other-documents-from-conferences-and-meetings/message-from-the-fifth-world-conference-on-faith-and-order-1993.

———. "New Delhi Statement on Unity." December 31, 1961. https://www.oikoumene.org/en/resources/documents/assembly/1961-new-delhi/new-delhi-statement-on-unity.

Wright, Christopher J. H. *The Mission of God: Unlocking the Bible's Grand Narrative.* Downers Grove: InterVarsity, 2006.

Yuval, Israel Jacob. *Two Nations in Your Womb: Perceptions of Jews and Christians in Late Antiquity and the Middle Ages.* Translated by Barbara Harshav and Jonathan Chipman. Berkeley: University of California Press, 2008.

Zizioulas, John. *Being as Communion: Studies in Personhood and the Church.* Crestwood, NY: St. Vladimir's Seminary Press, 1997.

Subject Index

Africa, 2, 49, 54, 85–87, 111
African-Americans, 85–87
Anabaptists, 44–45
Anglicans, 17–18, 35, 44–45, 54, 121, 164
Anthropocene, 2–3, 171
anti-Semitism, 127–28
apologetics, 14, 15–23, 123, 138, 140
Asia, 2, 56, 57, 158
authority, 16–17, 36–37, 47, 108, 117, 162–63

baptism, 45, 53–54, 145–48, 157
Baptists, 44, 45, 115
body (of Christ), 7, 14, 25, 69, 75–79; corporate personality, 65, 70–72, 75–78
bride (of Christ), 5–6, 53, 67, 77, 171–75

Calvinism, 43–44, 45
canon law, 13, 38, 44, 76
Charismatic movement, 49, 50
Christocentrism, 36, 38
church: as abstract/concrete: 60–61, 72, 79, 82; as Adam, 79–81, 85, 92, 111; as alien, 117, 131; as congregation, 59, 62–65, 92, 115; as disciples, 26, 110–11, 172; etymology of, 55–58; images of, 22–27, 118; as institution, 24–25, 38, 42, 55, 62, 101–7, 162–63; as (in)visible, 14–15, 24–25, 42–47, 124; as Israel, 10, 115, 122–45; as Jacob/Esau, 135–40; as kerygma, 25–26; marks of, 17, 149, 150–51, 155, 164; medieval, 78, 81, 84, 115, 133; as mystery, 14, 23, 25, 123; patristic, 39, 47, 132; as people, 55, 59–67, 69–88, 115–21, 145, 168; as pilgrim, 116–18, 122; as proper name, 61–62; as "real," 6, 53–54, 64, 73–76, 124; as sacramental, 15, 25, 119, 165; as servant, 26, 47, 154; as soul of world, 47
Church of England. *See* Anglican
Church of the East, 39–40
collectives, 9–10, 75–80, 148
conciliarity, 162–63
congregationalism, 44, 45–46, 115
contextualization, 60, 66, 160
councils: 16–17, 38, 162–63; of Chalcedon, 39; of Florence, 31; of Jerusalem, 78; of Trent, 21; of Vatican II, 70, 117
creed, 50, 57, 81, 110

Eastern Orthodox, 29–37, 38, 163, 172; vs. Roman Catholic, 37–39; vs. Protestant, 33, 37, 150

Subject Index

ecclesiology: 15–28, 115–24; "apologetic," 15–23, 123, 138, 140; "communion," 119–22, 144; congregational, 44–46, 115; Eastern Orthodox, 30–36, 163; figural, 10, 98, 124–25, 135–40, 147–48, 157; medieval, 15–16, 25, 50; origins of, 15–20; Pentecostal, 48–49, 169; Protestant, 23–26, 40–51, 124, 150; Roman Catholic, 117, 119–20
ecumenism, 118–19, 129, 154, 169
election, 81–85, 87, 128, 137
evangelicalism, 44, 45, 47, 57
Eucharist, 14, 25, 41, 107, 118–20, 164–65; Orthodox views, 36, 172; Protestant views, 42, 44, 155, 165; Roman Catholic views, 7, 14, 25, 165
exegesis: allegorical, 5; figural, 98, 124–25, 135–40; historical-critical, 98; literal, 5; of Jacob and Esau, 135–40

figural ecclesiology, 10, 124–25, 135–40, 147–48, 157

globalization, 3, 46, 48–49

Hegelianism, 47
heresy, 16, 26, 32–33, 64, 123

inculturation, 160, 164
individual(ism), 22, 45, 47, 75–78, 171–73
infallibility, 14, 47, 124, 151
Islam, 2, 16, 30, 37, 40, 128
Israel: as Church, 10, 115, 122–45; covenant with, 70, 128–29, 131; election of, 82–83; vs. Gentiles, 94–95, 99, 125–32, 153; as Jacob/Esau, 135–40

Judaism, 94, 99, 127, 145, 147

kerygma, 25–26
kingdom, 58, 66, 116, 151, 174

liberation theology, 48, 117
Lutheranism, 40–43, 45, 121

martyrdom, 39, 154–56, 157–58
Mennonites, 44–45
mission, 46, 101–12, 132–35, 156–57
Monophysites, 16, 39
Mormonism, 53–54

nationalism, 73–74, 85–86, 99, 101; in the church: 81, 97, 127, 134–35
nations: as Gentiles, 94–95; Church as, 59, 61, 65, 71–86, 90–113, 170; divine purpose for, 90–93; mission to, 101–12, 132–59; multiplication of, 71, 80, 90, 100, 112; sociology of, 72–74, 99–101, 134–35, 151–52; vs. Israel, 94–95, 99, 125–32, 153

Oriental Orthodox: 39–40

papacy, 16–17, 19, 31, 37–38, 163
Pentecostalism, 3, 48–49
persecution: 40, 44–45, 157–58
phenomenology, 139–40
pluralism, 49, 104, 128
pneumatology, 35–36, 44, 48–49, 78
predestination, 42, 43, 82–84, 137
Presbyterianism, 44, 46
priesthood: 22, 35, 36, 38; of all believers, 41, 43, 47
primitivism, 50, 151
prosperity gospel: 48
Protestant: ecclesiology, 23, 25–26, 40–49, 124, 150; exegesis, 5–6, 98; liberal, 46–47; vs. Eastern Orthodox, 33, 37, 150; vs. Roman Catholic, 14, 15–20, 26, 46, 54, 124. *See also individual denominations*
Puritans, 44, 45, 50, 115

Subject Index

Reformation, 38, 43, 104, 130, 147, 155
Reformed church, 43–44, 130
Roman Catholic: ecclesiology, 25, 37–39, 117; exegesis, 5–6, 38; vs. Eastern Orthodox, 37–39; vs. Protestant, 14, 15–20, 26, 46, 54, 124

Salvation Army, 4
supercessionism, 98, 112

theodicy, 123–24
tongues, 102–4, 106
totus Christus, 13–14, 122, 149, 150
Tractarianism, 18
tradition, 38, 41–42, 150–52
translation, 103–6, 158–60, 163

World Council of Churches, 107, 118, 119, 121, 169

Author Index

Afanasiev, Nicholas, 35–36
Anderson, Benedict, 99
Athanagoras I, 31–32, 36
Augustine, 13, 25, 78, 84, 115, 137, 161

Barth, Karl, 84, 129–30, 150
Bellarmine, Robert, 15, 115
Bérulle, Pierre de, 164
Bonhoeffer, Dietrich, 79–80, 84, 173
Bourignon, Antoinette, 4
Breuilly, John, 73–74
Bulgakov, Sergius, 32, 35–36

Calvin, John, 43–45, 47
Congar, Yves, 15–16, 25
Crummell, Alexander, 85–87, 111
Crutzen, Paul, 2
Cyprian, 16, 39

Dix, Dom Gregory, 7–8, 173
Dulles, Avery, 21, 23–27, 33, 118
Durham, James, 5

Eisen, Robert, 94, 96
Eyl, Jennifer, 92

Field, Richard, 17
Forsyth, P. T., 78–79
Frege, Gottlob, 60–61

Gibbon, Edward, 132
Gilbert, Margaret, 75–77, 78

Girard, René, 137
Goldman, Alvin, 75
Guder, Darrell, 156

Haight, Roger, 29, 72
Harnack, Adolf, 132
Hauerwas, Stanley, 117
Hus, John, 16

Irenaeus, 16

Jáki, Stanislas, 14
Jocz, Jakob, 128–30, 132, 140
John Paul II, 26, 154
Joris, David, 4

Khomiakov, Aleksie, 33
Kimbrough, S. T., Jr., 32n6
Kolakowski, Leszek, 4

Lindbeck, George, 98, 122, 124
Loisy, Alfred, 58
Luther, Martin, 40–43, 45, 47, 155

Martyr, Justin, 127
Mathetes, 47
Maximus the Confessor, 150
McNeill, John T., 46
Mendelssohn, Moses, 94
Minear, Paul, 22
Moltmann, Jürgen, 122

Author Index

Newbigin, Lesslie, 116, 131
Niebuhr, H. Richard, 135
Neale, John Mason, 18
Norbert, Elias, 149

Origen, 150

Partridge, George, 73
Philaret, 30–32
Pius XII, 25, 78

Rahner, Karl, 25
Ratzinger, Joseph, 117–18
Renan, Ernest, 98, 99, 104
Reventlow, Henning Graf, 4
Robinson, H. Wheeler, 70–71

Sanneh, Lamin, 103–4, 106, 134

Scheffler, Johann, 18
Serle, Ambrose, 22–23, 24
Silesius, Angelus. *See* Scheffler, Johann
Stannard, David, 133
Stoermer, Eugene, 2

Tertullian, 156
Torquemata, Juan de, 16–17
Tyndale, William, 62–63, 64, 65, 69, 83

Vansittart, William, 18

Watson, Cynthia, 169–70
Wiesel, Elie, 131, 132
Willimon, William, 116–17
Wycliffe, John, 16, 84

Zizioulas, John, 122

Scripture Index

Genesis	71, 100, 136–37, 164
1	71
1:22	80
1:26–28	71
1:28	80
4	82
6	100
8:17	80
9:7	80
10:5	100
10:20	100
11:6	100
11:8–9	100
12:2	59
16:10	80
17:2	80
17:4–6	59
20:11	110
33:10–11	140
33:11	136
39:8–9	110

Exodus	
19:6	59, 109
33:17	172

Leviticus	
19:2	109

Deuteronomy	59, 82–83, 92, 111
4:10	92
6:1–9	150
7:6–8	83
8:2	150
17:14	134
18:9	134
29:24–25	153
29:25	111
30:15	110
32:5	152
32:7	151
32:8	111
32:10	150
32:43	59

Judges	
5:19	138
20	153

1 Kings	
11:29–33	153

Nehemiah	
9	153

Scripture Index

Psalms

26:8	69
45:16	71
72	112n11
79:4	153
79:8–13	153
88:18	153
130	95
137:5–6	55
147	87

Song of Songs 5–6

1:7	6
5:7	50
8:6	6

Isaiah 94, 126

2:2–3	94
5:1	171
5:13	148
6:3	164
6:9–10	126
10:12–15	138
34	137
49–53	154
49:3	111
49:6	95, 111
53:5	153
54:1–5	71
62:2	172

Jeremiah 156

5:21	148
7:25–26	151
31:18–20	153
50:4–7	138

Lamentations 140

Ezekiel

12:2	126
20:32	134
25:6–7	138

Daniel 102

Hosea

4:6	148

Joel 125

Amos 96, 110

2:1–5	96
6:1	134
9:7–10	97

Obadiah 136, 137, 138

10–15	135–36

Zephaniah

2:8	138

Zechariah 27

13:6	27, 51

Malachi 137

Matthew 13, 93, 102

1:1–17	81
1:1	146
3:9	145
5:14	148
5:48	109
12:41	151
16:18	13
23:15	95
24:12	159
27:26	153
28:16–20	93
28:19–20	110

Scripture Index

Mark

4:12	126
8:18	126
10:43–45	108
10:45	172
10:35–39	157
14:50	153

Luke

1	149
1:38	173
2:22–52	151
3:23–38	81
6:40	172
9:41	152
9:46	153
13:28	151
13:31	152
15:17–18	153
20:37–38	151
21:3–4	8
22:24	153
22:27	108
24:7	153
24:25	102
24:27	102
24:32	102
24:44–48	102, 149
24:46–49	93

John

1:14	69
2:21	69
3:17	109
4:34	155
5:36	155
5:45–47	151
8:56–58	151
10:3	172
10:16	82
11:52	82
12:24	156
13:31–32	154
14:12	155
16:4–33	147
17:4	155
19:30	155
20:21	157
20:22	157
21:18	154
21:19	152

Acts

	59
1:6	174
2	125, 130
2:41	146
2:44	120
15:28	78
16:33	146
28:25–28	126

Romans

	91, 137
1:1–5	91
1:13–15	91
1:28	153
6:3–6	147
8:15	145
8:17	145
8:23	82
8:29–30	83
8:29	82, 172
8:33	83
9–11	74, 128
9:4	145
9:5	146
9:6	129
9:8	129
9:11	83
9:13	137
9:25–26	59
10:12	102
10:13–15	102
11:7–8	126
11:21	96, 127
11:28	83, 151
12:5	69
12:10	152
15:8–12	92
15:10	59
16:25	126

Scripture Index

1 Corinthians

	107
1:14	146
3:9–23	171
10:4	171
11:23–30	108
11:23	150
12:27	69, 182
13:4–7	108
13:9–12	109
14:7	103
14:33	151
15:1	150
15:20	82
15:22	74, 80
15:23	173
15:24	173
15:45	80, 81, 174
15:47	81

2 Corinthians

	108
5:21	156
11:23–30	108

Galatians

2:20	172
3:13	156
3:23	146
3:28	92
3:29	145
4:29	129

Ephesians

	91
1	84
1:4–5	32
1:4	84
1:5	84
1:11	84
1:22	84
1:23	84
2:1–3	110
2:14–18	127
2:15	81
3:6	91
3:9	91
3:15	81
5	54–55
5:23	172
5:25–26	172
5:28–30	172
6:1–9	146

Philippians

2:5–11	164
2:10–11	131
2:30	154
4:3	172

Colossians

1:10–13	110
1:15–19	150
1:16	81
1:18–24	154
1:18	14, 69
3:11	92

1 Timothy

2:6	154

2 Timothy

2:8	146

Hebrews

2:10	82
2:13	82
9:14	155
12:5–6	153

James

1:18	82

1 Peter

2:9	109

2 Peter

1:4	172
1:10	83

1 John

1:1–2	126
2:12–14	150
3:2	173
4:10	171
4:19	171

Revelation

	164
1:17	82
2–3	153
2:17	172
4:8	164
7	130
7:4	59
7:9–12	163
7:9	112
12	173
16:16	138
21	71
21:12	59
21:27	172
22:16	146

www.ingramcontent.com/pod-product-compliance
Lightning Source LLC
Chambersburg PA
CBHW031431150426
43191CB00006B/470